DEAD
RIGHT

DEAD RIGHT

DAVID FRUM

A New Republic Book
BasicBooks
A Division of HarperCollins*Publishers*

Designed by Cassandra Pappas

Library of Congress Cataloging-in-Publication Data
Frum, David, 1960–
    Dead right / David Frum.
        p. cm.
    "A New Republic Book."
    Includes bibliographical references and index.
    ISBN 0-465-09820-7 (cloth)
    ISBN 0-465-09825-8 (paper)
    1. Conservatism—United States. 2. United States—Politics and gov-
ernment—1945–1989. 3. United States—Politics and government—
1989–   I. Title.
JC573.2.U6F78 1994
320.5'2'0973—dc20   94–7477
                                                                  CIP

95 96 97 98 ◆/RRD 9 8 7 6 5 4 3 2 1

To the memory of my mother

Contents

Preface to the Paperback Edition

A cynical cartoonist once depicted a bratty boy urging his younger brother to look for Christmas presents in the basement. "But last time I did that, you locked me in the cellar for three hours!" the little brother protests. The older boy suavely replies: "This time I won't."

I kept thinking of that exchange in the aftermath of the Republican congressional victory in 1994. Make no mistake: I cheered the results of that election as lustily as any Young Republican with a file folder full of resumes to mail. But conservatives tempted to suppose that the Republican breakthrough in Congress portends a dramatic reduction in the pretensions of the federal government need to keep their eyes on the cellar-door latch as they rush downstairs.

The danger is not that history will repeat itself, that the mistakes and disappointments of the Reagan years will be replicated by the new Republican Congress. The medieval historian Robert Lopez used to tell his graduate students: "History never repeats itself. It only seems to, to those who don't know the details." The danger instead is that conservatives and Republicans will make new mistakes and encounter new disappointments so long as they continue to succumb to the great temptation of the Reagan years: to attempt to use government for conservative purposes rather than to push it back within its proper limits.

The message of *Dead Right,* in one paragraph, is this: the conservative movement was born in revolt against the size, cost, and arrogance of the modern state. Over the past two decades, as part of the price for its emergence as America's dominant ideology, conservatism has quietly walked away from that founding principle. Instead, all too many conservatives have developed a startling tolerance for the use of government power to reform society along traditionalist lines. Unfortunately for conservatives, using government in this way is a doomed project. Modern government, like a twisted knife, necessarily cuts to the left.

How much of the book's argument remains standing in the wake of the stunning Republican triumph of November 8, 1994? Virtually all of it.

The Contract with America that the Republicans campaigned on in 1994 promised to streamline and rationalize the federal government, not shrink it. In fact, the Contract actually pledged to repeal President Clinton's single largest spending cut, the clawback of Social Security payments to higher-income pensioners. And this was astute. It wasn't Medicare or an overzealous Occupational Safety and Health Agency that galvanized Republican voters. It was anger against illegal immigration and disgust with welfare. It was dislike for a president who held steadfast to his promise to end the ban on gays in the military, while breaking his word on a middle-class tax cut. It was resentment of state-enforced racial preferences and a steadily rising level of contempt for a government that seemed actively hostile to religion and morality. In other words, and as predicted in chapters 5 and 6, the Republicans ran and triumphed less as a libertarian party than as a moralist and nationalist party.

That's why the most dramatic Republican surge was recorded among white male voters earning between $15,000 and $30,000 a year and, to a slightly lesser extent, their wives. These voters felt that the values they treasured, the culture they had grown up in, and their own economic prospects were under attack. They felt that their government ignored them, and that it supported and protected people—from the lewd surgeon general, to the condom-distributing teachers at the local school, to the self-righteous artists subsidized by the National Endowment for the Arts—who despised them.

During and after the election, Democratic politicians and liberal-minded commentators expressed great irritation with the voters' mutiny against liberal cultural values. They complained that the voters were caught up in mindless negativism, that they were—as Peter Jennings put it in an editorial on ABC radio—indulging in the political equivalent of a preschooler's temper tantrum. Even if true (and it wasn't), this complaint was beside the point. Democracy is based on the insight that the foot knows best where the shoe pinches. The people are entitled to be bothered by whatever bothers them.

On the other hand, democracy does not require us to believe that the foot knows how to cobble shoes. It's the responsibility of political elites to hearken to popular grievances, to devise principled and constitutional remedies, and to persuade the voters to adopt them. *Dead Right* is concerned above all with the responsibilities of conservative political elites. Conservatives noticed long ago that the public responds to conservative themes, but not to conservative policies. A wonderful example is the (sadly, probably apocryphal) story told among journalists of the old lady who opposed the Clinton health plan because she didn't want the government interfering with her Medicare. What could be more tempting to conservatives than to stick to the themes and forget the policies? Conservatives are going to be mightily tempted over the next few years to campaign on a program of middle-class tax cuts, welfare reform, curbs on immigration, and the abolition of affirmative action while maintaining a discreet silence about Social Security, Medicare, farm programs, student loans, and the other colossal middle-class benefits. This moralist, nationalist, and statist conservatism could prove a big winner: indeed, activist pro-business government, enforcement of moral standards, and the imposition of an American identity on more or less reluctant groups have been the winning formula in American politics for close to 200 years.

But conservatives know, or should, that the problems they care most about are intimately related to big government. Big government has to be paid for, and its immense costs have relentlessly forced taxes on the middle class upward. Big government instills in middle-class pensioners and hospital patients and farmers and college students the same greedy sense of entitlement that conservatives deplore in the poor. Big government, by relieving families of responsibilities for child and elder care that they once discharged for themselves, weakens family bonds. In other words, conservatives might have been expected to seize on the widespread perception of cultural decline not merely as an opportunity to win elections, but as an invitation to teach conservative doctrine in its entirety. Even in 1994, though, Republicans shied away from the unpopular task of telling the voters the full truth about the conservative critique of government.

The full truth doesn't include closing the fire department. Conservatives aren't anarchists. They don't want to abolish police, parks, or public libraries. Nor do they regard the right to do precisely as one pleases as the supreme political good. Chapter 7 explains why it's wrong to accuse conservatives of inconsistency for refusing to equate sexual permissiveness with economic and political liberty. What conservatives do believe, or should, is that the cultural conservatism that most Americans seem to want can be achieved only by means of the economic conservatism they still rather mistrust. Cultural conservatism is like happiness: you can win it only indirectly, as the by-product of seeking something else.

The eager acceptance of that last claim among conservatives since the initial publication of *Dead Right* has been immensely encouraging. Still, it must be confessed that the book's subordination of cultural conservatism to economic conservatism irked many critics on the right. Those critics complained that *Dead Right* laid too much stress upon the morally

and culturally corrosive effects of big government. Cultural corruption has many causes, they said, and it is simpleminded to
blame government alone. That's right enough, so far as it goes.
The trouble is, the other causes those critics cited—from the
decline of religious faith to TV—extend well beyond anyone's
ability to control, and certainly beyond anyone's ability to control by means of political action. By all means, conservatives
outraged by cultural trends they deplore should write articles or
preach sermons against them. But that's not politics. Politics is a
debate about what the state should and shouldn't do. And conservatives involved in the practice of politics or who write about
politics need to recognize that there's not much the state can do
to stop networks from broadcasting comedies in which children
smart-mouth teachers. What you can do through politics is
shrink the power of the federal octopus so that local schools that
want to expel smart-mouthed students don't get dragged into
federal district court on due-process charges. The chicken-and-
egg question—whether it's culture that influences politics or politics that forms culture—raises many fascinating intellectual
questions. For conservatives, though, the only plausible hope of
reforming the culture is by eliminating state-created and state-
funded incentives to misconduct.

Must conservatives who want to practice consistency therefore hare off in doomed pursuit of some laissez-faire utopia that
never was? Happily, they needn't. The results of 1994 suggest
that voters have come to accept at least two conservative ideas:
that modern government is hugely wasteful, and that at least
some of its programs corrode important values among vulnerable people. As a result, a majority of the congressional electorate seems to believe that government could do significantly
less than it now does without inflicting harm on anyone. More
than that, a majority of the electorate now seems to believe that
eliminating many of government's functions might even help
others, by removing programs that lure them into or keep them
in destructive ways of life.

Sooner or later, the voters would notice that real budget

cutting means taking real money away from real people who have come to expect it. It's possible that that would bring the budget cutting to a screeching halt. On the other hand, politics is a dynamic business, and acting on one opportunity often brings others into being. Franklin Delano Roosevelt—the architect of the modern American state—had intended only to slap a few patches onto the American economy. But as each repair exposed another defect, he was forced to hammer and saw and plaster until the entire structure had been renovated beyond recognition. And, impelled by the logic of the situation, the public went along with him until, in the end and without ever consciously intending it, it found itself living in a brand-new political home.

Obviously the discontent Americans feel today can in no way be compared to the misery of the 1930s. But the dynamic qualities of politics have not changed. A serious welfare reform has to raise questions about middle-class welfare. Widespread acceptance of the premise that government largess has shattered the stability of the black family must, as I argue in chapter 8, lead to an inquiry into the causes of the crumbling of the divorce-wracked white family. And as we start to withdraw the lures and snares that have helped tempt people into the conduct that has led so many Americans to despair of the moral health of their society, we will find ourselves—just as Roosevelt did—building, willy-nilly, a new kind of state for the next century.

What would such a state look like? Here's my vision.

Government should protect people only from risks they cannot easily protect themselves against: unemployment, disability, natural disasters, and catastrophic illnesses. Social welfare programs should not protect nonindigent people against the predictable results of their own actions or the inevitable cycles of life: the costs of retirement and college, the regular fluctuations of farm and factory prices, the miseries caused by idleness and addiction. Obviously, any changes in the pension system and Medicare would have to be phased in slowly. Rep. Chris Cox, who sits on Sen. Bob Kerrey's entitlements reform commission, has speculated that one way to do that would be to halve the Social Security tax on workers under forty, and let them pay the money into IRAs instead. But the sums at stake are so colossal that even relatively modest reforms would yield breathtaking results. The Social Security Administration says it does not keep track of the dollar value of the benefits it pays to middle- and high-income households. It can say, though, that in 1994, the U.S. put a total of some $300 billion into the households of pensioners, about one-fifth of whom enjoy incomes of $30,000 or more.

Sickness is almost as predictable as old age, but the second largest domestic program, Medicare, spent some $140 billion in 1994 to protect the nonindigent elderly against routine medical problems. At the same time, Medicare fails to protect the elderly against the catastrophic medical expenses for which government help is most needed and most justifiable. Medicare's elaborate system of deductibles and co-payments was supposed to induce some awareness of costs and some sense of responsibility in its beneficiaries, but nearly 80 percent of the elderly now purchase private insurance to cover this "gap" or else receive it free, courtesy of Medicaid. Four-fifths of older Americans therefore have sloughed virtually all the costs of health care off their own shoulders—in the process raising their medical expenses, according to one careful estimate, by about 18 percent. At the same time, the existence of Medicare makes impossible the best and most obvious solution to the health care problem: that people should buy (either through their employers or on their own) a single health insurance policy when they enter the workforce, which would charge them the same annual premium from their early twenties until death, just as a life insurance policy does. Instead, and because of Medicare, workers and their employers insure themselves only up to retirement age, leaving the bills beyond that point to be paid by the taxpayer.

Pensions and Medicare together amount to a $440 billion annual expenditure. But even the relatively small programs that would get the ax under a predictability test are large enough by non-Washington standards: nearly $13 billion for student loans, a little more than $10 billion for agricultural supply management programs, $11 billion for low-income housing and energy assistance. To be sure, a welfare state that protected people only against unforeseeable disasters would not be small. And it would probably continue to take responsibility for an irreducible minimum of antipoverty programs as well: food stamps, supplemental Social Security, childhood immunization, and school lunches. Even so, a predictability test holds out the hope of a one-third reduction in the cost of the federal government's domestic programs as the current generation of retirees passes from the scene.

In the past, culturally minded Republicans have rebelled whenever economic conservatives spoke too enthusiastically about practicing a little liposuction on the body politic. They believed that Nixon and Reagan had created a New Majority out there, made up of "conservatives of the heart," as Patrick Buchanan called them. This New Majority was patriotic and religious, but it still hearkened after the protection of the social welfare system built by Franklin Roosevelt and Harry Truman. For goodness' sake, they reasoned, why alienate them with radical economics? Stick to invectives against artists who dip crucifixes in urine.

Cutting government benefits that protect people against predictable risks is, however, one economic program that cultural conservatives ought to be able to support. The central preoccupation of cultural conservatives is the eclipse of one type of American personality—self-reliant, self-controlled, hardworking, and patriotic—and its apparent replacement by another—dependent, hedonistic, narcissistic, and whiny. In the past, there has always yawned a chasm between the magnitude of the problem that cultural conservatives observed and the radicalism of the solutions they were prepared to contemplate. Getting rid of the National Endowment for the Arts won't take MTV off the air.

If cultural conservatives would recognize that the tough old American character they mourn was a rational response to the toughness of American life, they would find their differences with economic conservatives evaporating. Victorian personalities do not flourish in a world of Great Society welfare programs. Cultural conservatives now recognize that AFDC and other antipoverty programs have stifled self-reliance among the poor. They concede that government-mandated racial preferences have exacerbated intergroup animosity. They should be able to perceive that the Federal Housing Authority and student loans and Social Security bear at least some of the responsibility for corroding the character of the middle class. And they should be teaching the electorate to perceive it too.

A textbook example of how this ought to be done: in the last Congress, Sen. Phil Gramm (R.-Tex.) introduced legislation to delete $126 billion from the nutrition, housing, and health budgets and to use the money to finance a doubling of the per-child tax exemption, from its then-level of $2,350 to $4,700. Gramm's message was simple but powerful: Republicans do not want to change the amount spent on feeding, housing, and caring for children; they want to change the identity of the spender. The proposal didn't pass, nor was it seriously meant to. It was meant to teach, and the lesson should be repeated.

Another example: Medicaid, the medical care program for the poor that ranks as the third biggest program in the federal budget, is actually operated by the states. Medicaid expenditures have been growing at a nightmarish rate, up from less than $17 billion in 1981 to nearly $100 billion in 1994. One state, New York, bears much of the blame: with 7 percent of the U.S. population and 9 percent of Medicaid patients, New York consumes 18 percent of federal Medicaid dollars. Republicans should propose eliminating federal Medicaid grants to the twenty-five states with above-average incomes in exchange for more generous federal tax credit for state and local tax payments. Let out-of-control local spending be those localities' problem—and let voters nationwide understand where the blame should fall.

One reason for the intractability of Social Security spending is that a depressing number of American pensioners sincerely believe they are merely receiving back what they paid into the system's trust funds. Before constructing a more rational, and individualistic, pension plan, Americans will have to be disabused of this illusion—by, for example, including with each Social Security check a statement of the amount paid in contributions during the beneficiary's working life versus the total amount paid thus far in benefits.

Attention to overspending was often derided in the early 1980s as "root-canal Republicanism"—a mindless determination to inflict economic pain. Whether or not that label was deserved in the past is a debatable proposition. What ought to be clear now, however, is that it is no longer politically or morally feasible to deliver the broad middle-class tax cuts that virtually all Republicans favor without also excising large portions of the functions of government. The public reaction against the Clinton health plan offers realistic hope that the voters can be made to understand that. More to the point, the public reaction against the Clinton crime bill and its lavish social spending offers realistic hope that the voters have also come to understand the connection between overgovernment and America's social failures: violence on the streets, welfare dependency, illegitimacy, and family breakup.

And if Republicans will not take on overgovernment, at this uniquely favorable opportunity, they need to ask themselves what their party stands for instead. Twice in two years, American voters have shattered seemingly indestructible political dynasties: first, the three-term succession of Republican presidencies, and now the Democratic dynasty on Capitol Hill. If that does not signal smoldering discontent among voters with America's existing political arrangements, it's hard to know what more the public will have to do—march on Washington with sharpened pitchforks and burning hayricks? After the disillusionment and disappointment of the Bush administration and the later Reagan years, the voters have been indulgent enough to extend Republicans a second chance. But humility is called for: the GOP's hold on America's affections does not look much less precarious than the Democratic Party's. It's hard to measure exactly what the voters want from their new Republican legislators—perhaps they themselves don't fully know. But the opportunity is there for conservatives to enact a good dose of their remedy for the social ills that alarm Americans, in the hope of setting in motion a dynamic that will lead to substantial political reform in a conservative direction. When should they start? What better time could there be than right now?

—January 1995

Acknowledgments

This book is saturated with the ideas and expressions of my wife, Danielle. I understand now what a vastly greater writer meant when he said that his wife's "exalted sense of truth and right was my strongest incitement, and whose approbation was my chief reward."

I owe special thanks to my father too. My happiest moments with this project were spent at work in the gazebo at the back of his garden. Every page of this book benefited from his uneuphemistic criticism, his wisdom, and his unstinting generosity.

Erich Eichman, Peter Brimelow, Gerald Rosberg, Austen Furse, and Peter and Yvonne Worthington read early versions of the book, and helped me enormously with their advice and encouragement. Conversations with William F. Buckley, James Grant, and Rep. Newt Gingrich at the very beginning of the project and with George F. Will and Norman Podhoretz at the end helped me to understand some of the more puzzling aspects of my story.

My colleagues at *Forbes* magazine and my editor, Stewart Pinkerton, in particular, exhibited superhuman tolerance for my distracted mental state. My former colleagues at the *Wall Street Journal* editorial page, especially Tim Ferguson, taught me more about conservatism and conservatives than I could ever have learned on my own. The *American Spectator* printed the article that inspired this book, and took a lot of abuse for it. I'm grateful to R. Emmett Tyrrell, Wladyslaw Pleszczynski, and Christopher Caldwell.

Peter Edidin's editorial attention has been uncompromising. He always paid me the compliment of believing I wanted to hear the worst. My agent, Mildred Marmur, taught me everything I know about the 90 percent of the book business that ain't literature.

My mother, Barbara Frum, died just as I was to have begun work on this book. It, like so much else, has suffered beyond description by her absence.

DEAD
RIGHT

CHAPTER 1

Athwart History

The material temptations of politics are greatly overrated. Even at the very pinnacle, what do they amount to? A limousine? A few tens of thousands a year in speaking fees? Nobody ever got rich from the honest perquisites of the profession, and even the crooks and chiselers have generally contented themselves with surprisingly small bags of swag. But the moral temptations, those are a different matter entirely. They are as huge and glittering as the material temptations are small and tawdry. To walk to a podium, to look into the eyes of a crowd of thousands, to feel the room grow quiet as it waits for you to speak— can there be a stronger temptation than the desire to please the crowd, to say only what it wants to hear and nothing it does not? This book is the story of how a great political movement succumbed to just that temptation and of the consequences of that succumbing.

Since its formation in the early 1950s, the intellectual movement known as American conservatism has stood for two overarching principles: anticommunism abroad and radical reduction in the size, cost, and bossiness of the federal government at home. Anticommunism has lost most of its zest, for the time being anyway. The bossiness of government might have seemed to be an issue with staying power, but conservatives have tired of it all the same. The country's leading conservative politicians and intellectuals may attack this or that ridiculous feature of overweening government, they may propose this or that more or less libertarian alternative to President Clinton's plan to reorganize the American medical system, but radical criticism of the very idea that Washington should extract and redistribute one-quarter of the nation's wealth has simply petered out. The single-parent family; tumbling educational standards; immigration; crime; ethnic balkanization—the conservative magazines and conservative conversation bubble with ferment over these. About morality and nationality, conservatives have a lot to say. But their fervor for eliminating the progressive income tax and the redistribution of wealth via Washington has cooled, when it has not disappeared altogether.

This would not be so disturbing if American conservatism, as it has often been urged to do, had evolved into a European-style Toryism that accepted colossal government as an appropriate element of modern life. It has done no such thing. Cynicism about and disdain for government among conservatives has, if anything, intensified in the late 1980s and early 1990s. Listen to Rush Limbaugh or read the editorial columns in the *Wall Street Journal* and you will hear politicians described in language that we once applied only to the most hardened criminals. For all the muttering about this or that revelation of government waste and abuse, however, conservatives plainly do not feel the same zeal for minimal government they once did. The man who has to be considered the leading conservative contender for president, Jack Kemp, describes himself as a "bleeding heart conservative" opposed to "root canal" economics. His most formidable rivals are a passel of Republican governors in Michigan, Wisconsin, South Carolina, Massachusetts, and California who aspire to modernize government, not hack away at it. In Congress, the Republicans stamp and holler to preserve Social Security—that ancient conservative bugbear—inviolate. In the press, think tanks, and academia, you can feel conservative attention wandering away from overgovernment to the newer and zestier topics of race and sex, following the same exciting path that the Left trod away from the social welfare politics of the 1960s to the identity politics of today.

Conservatives have lost their zeal for advocating minimal government not because they have decided that big government is desirable, but because they have wearily concluded that trying to reduce it is hopeless, and that even the task of preventing its further growth will probably exceed their strength. However heady the 1980s may have looked to everyone else, they were for conservatives a testing and disillusioning time. Conservatives owned the executive branch for eight years and had great influence over it for four more; they dominated the Senate for six years; and by the end of the decade they exercised near complete control over the federal judiciary. And yet, every time they reached to undo the work of Franklin Roosevelt, Lyndon Johnson, and Richard Nixon—the work they had damned for nearly half a century—they felt the public's wary eyes upon them. They didn't dare, and they realized that they didn't dare. Their moment came and flickered. And as the power of the conservative movement slowly ebbed after 1986, and then roared away in 1992, the conservatives who had lived through that attack of faintheartedness shamefacedly felt that they had better hurry up and find something else to talk about. And so they have.

The new topics could well enhance conservatism's appeal. Social conservatism is potentially more popular than economic conservatism. But severed from economic conservatism, social conservatism too easily degenerates into mere posturing. The force driving the social trends that offend conservatives, from family breakup to unassimilated immigration, is the welfare function of modern government. Attempting to solve these social problems while government continues to exacerbate them is like coping with a sewer main explosion by bolting all the manhole covers to the pavement. Overweening government may not be the sole cause of America's maladies. But without overweening government, none would rage as fiercely as it now does. The nearly $1 trillion the federal government spends each year on social services and income maintenance—and the additional hundreds of billions spent by the states—is a colossal lure tempting citizens to reckless behavior. Remove those alluring heaps of money, and the risks of personal misconduct would again deter almost everyone, as they did before 1933 and even 1965. The great, overwhelming fact of a capitalist economy is risk. Everyone is at constant risk of the loss of his job, or of the destruction of his business by a competitor, or of the crash of his investment portfolio. Risk makes people circumspect. It disciplines them and teaches them self-control. Without a safety net, people won't try to vault across the big top. Social Security, student loans, and other government programs make it far less catastrophic than it used to be for middle-class people to dissolve their families. Without welfare and food stamps, poor people would cling harder to working-class respectability than they do now. Big government does for the 98 percent of society that is not rich what her millions did for the late Barbara Hutton—it enables them to engage in destructive behavior without immediately suffering the consequences.

It was awareness of the social consequences of social services, not mere Gradgrind-like zeal for economic efficiency, that initially convinced conservatives to resist the expansion of the welfare functions of government. From its beginning, the American conservative movement has devoted itself to one supreme mission: to warn the country that it had embarked on the wrong path. The first step on the path was taken very long ago. "Like Macbeth, Western man made an evil decision, which has become the efficient and final cause of other evil decisions,"[1] wrote Richard Weaver in 1948, in a book whose title gave the conservative movement one of its most enduring slogans, *Ideas Have Consequences*. Weaver thought the evil decision was taken in the fourteenth century, which has struck most conservatives since then as a little excessive. Still, they basically agree with him as to what the evil decision was. It was a decision in favor of moral arrogance, in favor of the radical reconstruction of the world along lines suggested by whatever reformist or revolutionary ideology happened to hold power at the moment. Moral arrogance inspired the French and Russian revolutions. The same moral arrogance, conservatives believed, lay at the very core of post–New Deal liberalism and of everything else that conservatives thought themselves to be defying when, in William F. Buckley's memorable metaphor, they took their stand athwart history to shout "Stop!"

Nonconservatives may roll their eyes at conservatives' fondness for sweeping moral assertions. Conservative rhetoric can sound a little overbroad, if not positively bats, to nonconservative ears. Conservatives, however, see the things they dislike in the contemporary world—abortion, the slippage of educational standards, foreign policy weakness, federal aid to handicapped schoolchildren—as all connected, as expressions of a single creed, a creed of which liberalism is just one manifestation. "It is not new," Whittaker Chambers observed of this creed in another seminal conservative book, *Witness*. "It is, in fact, man's second oldest faith. Its promise was whispered in the first days of the Creation under the Tree of the Knowledge of Good and Evil: 'Ye shall be as gods.'"[2]

When Chambers wrote that sentence, history, as Buckley had said, seemed to be roaring in the wrong direction with the power of a locomotive. Chambers gloomily concluded that by breaking with communism he had crossed from the winning to the losing side. Certainly none of those who founded *National Review* in 1955 could have realistically hoped at that time ever to win a national election. They had learned from the writers who most influenced them—Albert J. Nock, José Ortega y Gasset, Irving Babbitt—that in a world of mass production and mass culture, only a tiny "remnant" of civilized men, in Nock's words, could be relied upon to preserve the old virtues. It was that remnant's mission to explain to anyone who would listen how the modern world had gone wrong, and to hope for a burst of luck before it was too late.

And then something remarkable happened: the burst of luck arrived. Sometime in the mid-1960s, liberalism went mad.

In 1962, the conservative writer James Burnham had solemnly defined liberalism as the ideology of Western suicide. At the time he coined that maxim, he sounded hysterical. Liberalism was then still the ideology of Lend-Lease and the arsenal of democracy, of the great universities that had given refuge to European scholars fleeing Hitler, of the New Deal social consensus, of the men who designed the atom bomb. Ten years later, Burnham's one-time hysteria had become prophetic. And—even better luck for conservatives—liberalism's nervous breakdown in the late 1960s and early 1970s coincided with (or ushered in, depending on how you look at it) the most frightening period of social and economic instability since the Great Depression. Humiliating military defeat in Vietnam; two oil shocks; double-digit inflation; unlegislated tax increases as inflation drove taxpayers into higher tax brackets; bussing and racial quotas; the upheaval in sexual mores; college campus insurrections—all in barely a decade—destroyed liberalism's credibility as a philosophy of government. By 1983, the number of Americans willing to describe themselves to pollsters as "liberal" had fallen to a postwar low of 23 percent, barely more than half the number of those calling themselves "conservative." Conservatives, surrounded and outnumbered since the Crash of '29, felt as miraculously relieved as the inhabitants of the besieged city of Jerusalem on the morning that they woke up to find that Sennacherib's besieging army had melted away.

In retrospect, we can see that what happened in the late 1970s was not so much a victory for conservative ideas as a collapse of liberalism. That's not, however, how it seemed to people on the Right at the time. Washington is a supercharged city, and every little political blip seems to those who live through it to announce the arrival of an epochal moment, to be a tectonic shift. The election of Ronald Reagan in 1980 promised to transform everything. In 1981, Burton Yale Pines, a *Time* magazine correspondent who was soon to go to work for the rapidly expanding Heritage Foundation, published a book called *Back to Basics*, which described how a heterogeneous mass of political forces were restoring America's old moral virtues, its impatience with government control of the economy, and its intellectual and aesthetic standards. For a few years afterward, representatives of those polyglot forces would converge at the Heritage Foundation, first in its cramped Capitol Hill townhouse, and then in its glittering new headquarters near Union Station. Baptist antipornography crusaders in drip-dry shirts would nibble soggy Washington canapes beside alumni of City College, and sip Coca-Cola tolerantly as goldbugs from the U.S. Chamber of Commerce knocked back the chardonnay. Conservatives in those days believed that the country had undergone, or was about to undergo, a "realignment," a fundamental change in the political landscape, analogous to 1800 or 1932. They believed that the newly conservatized Republican Party would gain seats in the 1982 off-year congressional elections, the first time the president's party had done such a thing since 1934. They believed that the country had entered upon a period of moral regeneration. Under Reagan's leadership, America would stand up to Communists and Third World thugs, fix the domestic economy by relieving it of the burden of overgovernment, and repair the damage done to the social fabric by fifty years of secular liberalism. After decades of rejection and even vilification by both the nation's elites and the voting public, conservatives felt themselves in 1980 and 1981 to have been awarded a mandate at long last. It was a sweet experience but, in the end, a distorting one.

Viewers of the cable talk shows that proliferated in the 1980s have seen this scene a hundred times: two pundits will be haranguing each other about some political point, and one will try to clinch his case by announcing triumphantly, "The American people don't agree with you!" Strictly speaking, this shouldn't be much of an argument—it begs the reply, "Well, then, the American people are wrong." But it's always *felt* to be deadly. In a democratic culture, feeling yourself at one with a crowd of people is a joy as intense as receiving the king's soiled handkerchief was at Versailles. Having tasted that joy in the early years of the

Reagan presidency, conservatives have become addicted to it. Their message has adapted accordingly.

Conservatism has always been in danger of devolving from a philosophy of limited government to an ideology of middle-class self-interest. This is why David Stockman issued his famous caution that the Reagan administration must attack weak claims, not weak claimants, and why he became so bitterly disillusioned when, five years into the administration, strong claimants with weak claims were battening on the public fisc as lustily as ever. The early 1990s are in some ways an even more conservative era than the 1980s were. Slow economic growth has squeezed government budgets, especially state and local budgets. Far more than in the 1980s, governors and mayors face voters who profess to prefer budget cuts to tax increases. But those same voters continue to expect lavishly equipped suburban high schools, subsidized tuition at state colleges, toll-free highways, and environmental improvement at others' expense. What could be more tempting to a politician than to teach voters to blame taxes and regulations not on the require-ments of the middle class but on the inordinate demands of the poor? What could be more reckless than to attack bloated edu-cation, highway, and farm budgets, which largely benefit the middle class? Trouble is, the refusal to take that apparently reckless course dooms all other conservative hopes to futility. If you cannot say "no" to middle-class constituents, you cannot lighten the crushing load of government upon society. And it is that burden, in turn, that makes the social problems that con-servatives fret about so intractable.

Frustrated on economic issues and apprehensive about social issues, post-Bush conservatives look back on the accom-plishments of the early Reagan years the way seventh-century Romans must have looked at their aqueducts: to think that we once built all this!

Jack Kemp embraced an economic theory that at the time had no academic backing to speak of, no popular support—

no known popular support anyway—and with one or two elected officials and the *Wall Street Journal* editorial page and Jude [Wanniski's] book [*The Way the World Works*] and six Hill staffers transformed the character, at least temporarily, of the Republican Party. [Supply-side economics] became the governing doctrine of the Republican Party in '80 and the governing doctrine of the nation in '81.

That's the reverent observation of Bill Kristol, former chief of staff to Dan Quayle, who runs his own think tank, the Project for the Republican Future.[3] The memories of past victories both inspire and oppress the conservatives of the early 1990s, inducing them to abandon the vast antique structure of conservative philosophy to search for a mid-1990s equivalent of Kemp-Roth, a single lever to propel conservatives back into popularity and their opponents out. But because the budgetary difficulties left behind by Ronald Reagan make it very difficult to find such a lever in the central government's economic policies, conservatives have found themselves either frantically experimenting with side issues, such as curbing civil lawsuits, or switching their attention from economics to social reform, to the problems posed by the underclass, declining educational standards, influence-peddling and corruption in the American political system, Third World immigration, and the disintegration of the traditional family.

This is understandable enough. Conservatives still feel as they did in the 1930s and 1950s about the social tendencies of contemporary America. They still fear that the beliefs, habits, and institutions that made America both great and good are dissolving. If anything, their dismay is stronger today than ever before. During the Cold War, conservatives could externalize the danger they perceived to American civilization. After 1989, the external menace vanished, but the danger to American civilization remained. Indeed, the post-1989 revelation of how poor and backward the Soviet Union had all along been brought home to conservatives how very damaged Western society must be if so pitiful an adversary could have intimidated us for so long. That's why so few on the Right had much appetite for V-J Day–style victory celebrations after the fall of the Berlin Wall. "There is no 'after the Cold War' for me," wrote Irving Kristol, father of Bill, in 1993:

> So far from having ended, my cold war has increased in intensity, as sector after sector of American life has been ruthlessly corrupted by the liberal ethos. It is an ethos that aims simultaneously at political and social collectivism on the one hand, and moral anarchy on the other. . . . We have, I do believe, reached a critical turning point in the history of the American democracy. Now that the other "Cold War" is over, the real cold war has begun. We are far less prepared for this cold war, far more vulnerable to our enemy, than was the case with our victorious war against a global Communist threat.[4]

While conservatives continue to adhere to their traditional analysis of what is wrong with American society, in the 1980s they threw away their traditional policy for resisting the corrosive liberal ethos—fierce reductions in the scope and scale of government, especially the federal government in Washington. Critics of conservatism have delighted in pointing out, as Daniel Bell did in *The Cultural Contradictions of Capitalism*, that the consumerism liberated by the market economy corrodes the traditional virtues of piety, family loyalty, and self-control every bit as much as liberal social reforms do. They ask, with some force, whether sex education in the public schools is really worse than Madonna on the airwaves. Some writers, like the Canadian philosopher George Grant, have actually argued that socialism, by its very inability to produce consumer goods and sustain large-scale enterprise, should be more congenial to conservatives than capitalism. But if capitalism creates new opportunities to misbehave, it is welfarism that makes the exercise of those opportunities safe, or at least safer than ever before.

Conservatives know that, and the most audacious of them—like Charles Murray—advocate the outright elimination of social programs linked to family breakup, such as welfare, food stamps, and rent supplements for unwed mothers. But conservatives have also learned that most Americans like big government. The major domestic spending programs—Social Security, Medicare, aid to farmers and to veterans—are all hugely popular, and especially popular, ironically, with the Republican Party's core constituencies. For a brief and wonderful moment, supply-side economics held out the hope of limiting government in a way that offended nobody. Alas, that part of the supply-side vision was quickly falsified by events. The tax cuts of 1981 did indeed boost federal revenues. But they did not boost them anywhere near enough to keep up with the commitments Social Security and Medicare had made to the old, the disabled, and the sick. By the mid-1980s, it was obvious either (1) that taxes must rise, (2) that federal generosity must be scaled back, or (3) that the United States must borrow on a scale never before seen in human history and wait to learn how long the international bond market would finance the binge. The first option was anathema to conservatives. Because of the giddy experience of 1981, and conservatives' yearning to retain the popularity they enjoyed in those happy days, so was the second. That left only the third.

While this third option protected conservatives from political danger in the short run, it inflicted a terrible disaster on them in the long run: it left them speechless. If minimal government was off-limits—and it was—conservatives found that they did not have anything else of very much weight to say. Hence the triviality and faddishness of so much of conservative political and intellectual life since the mid-1980s. To fill the void, new types of conservatism have arisen since the mid-1980s: conservatisms that agree with much or most of traditional conservatism's appraisal of what's wrong with American society but that are casting about for some new solution to society's ills. These new conservative sects can be divided into three broad groups—optimists, moralists, and nationalists—each led by a prominent political figure: Jack Kemp, William Bennett, and Patrick Buchanan. The new sects differ about many things, but all agree that the time has come to quit fretting about the power of the central government and to begin using it.

In one sense, this could be good news for America: it could portend greater social consensus, with virtually everyone agreeing about the proper functions of government, even if the parties quibble over details. That's how academic political scientists and earnest liberals have always wanted politics to work. The leading political book of 1992, E. J. Dionne's *Why Americans Hate Politics*, argued that Americans would be a lot likelier to vote if politicians quit arguing about abortion and flag burning and filled their speeches instead with meaty details of the latest highway bill or the fine-tuning of the earned-income tax credit. I suspect, however, that the abatement of the fifty-year struggle over the size and role of the federal government will make politics a lot nastier. If everyone agrees about big government, the only way to mobilize and excite voters is precisely to emphasize the wide and growing gulf between Americans of differing backgrounds, races, and moral convictions. And if so, the future holds not an endless succession of solemn policy debates, but more of the furor ignited by the issue of gays in the military—more of the kind of politics that Midge Decter had in mind when she contended that Reagan's electoral victories were due "not so much to a wish for radical new policies as to an open declaration of war over the culture. And a culture war, as the liberals understood far better than did their conservative opponents, is a war to the death. For a culture war is not a battle over policy, though policy in many cases gives it expression; it is rather a battle about matters of the spirit."[5]

Early in 1993, Hillary Rodham Clinton delivered a much-ridiculed speech in which she used the phrase "the politics of meaning." The speech was jumped upon—hard—by the press, culminating in a surprisingly brutal article in the *New York Times Magazine*. Much of the contempt was provoked by journalists' awareness that the phrase originated with Michael Lerner, editor of *Tikkun* magazine and one of the country's most tireless self-promoters. It's a rare newspaper that does not throw away a dozen letters a year from Lerner inviting reporters to come interview him—exactly the sort of thing that causes editors and reporters to inwardly swear never to mention the man's name in print. Despite its origin, the phrase is a good one, not as a description of the Clinton administration's policies—which still conform to the old welfare state tactic of seizing as much of your opponents' wealth as you can and delivering it to your allies and clients—but as a description of the Right's. For most conservatives, shrinking government has always been a political *means* rather than an end in itself. The end was the preservation of the American heritage, and beyond that, the heritage of the classical and Judeo-Christian (or Christian *tout court*) West. If that heritage could be preserved without fighting an ugly and probably doomed battle to shrink government, most conservatives would drop the size-of-government issue with hardly a pang.

And drop it they did. Late in the 1980s, somebody (apparently Fred Barnes of the *New Republic*) coined the wicked phrase "big government conservatives." Well, we're all big government conservatives now. Confronting the Clinton health plan, the biggest expansion in the role of government in everyday life since affirmative action and the costliest since Social Security, the leading congressional Republicans have fallen mute and helpless. Senate minority leader Bob Dole expressed his willingness to work with the president. Conservatives have long since adjusted themselves to defalcations from duty by Bob Dole. But the number-two Republican in the House of Representatives, the fiery Newt Gingrich, has also accepted some sort of universal health care as inevitable. "I know there's a debate over this by my good friends who say we should be against everything," Gingrich said in a December 1993 speech. "That's nuts." Jack Kemp has contemplated taking a dive too: "You can't get a license to drive a car without auto insurance.

So why not the same with health care?" he mused to a newspaper reporter.[6]

It's a cowardly thought. Conservatives are fighting harder against, say, gays in the military than against the Clinton health plan because they think that the fight against gays in the military will be easier; because they know that on the one issue the crowd on the other side of the microphones will be with them, and fear that on the other, the crowd will not.

It is, of all people, the pugnacious Pat Buchanan who has pressed most vociferously for taking this easy but ultimately doomed course. Reflecting on his 1992 presidential campaign in his articles and speeches, Buchanan talks about "conservatives of the heart": secretaries and steelworkers of deep beliefs and simple patriotism. Buchanan's sense of where these conservatives of the heart might be located was generally defective— he suffered a nasty reception when his campaign bus ventured into Flint, Michigan, on the mistaken theory that a congregation of them might be found in the birthplace of the sit-down strike. But his conviction that conservatism's traditional skinflint doctrines must be modified or jettisoned in order to win these good Americans over has swiftly become nearly canonical doctrine. What will conservatives talk about instead? And with what consequences? Those are the questions this book will try to answer.

CHAPTER 2

Houston: "Wall-to-Wall Ugly"

From the news reports, you'd think the Republicans had hired Leni Riefenstahl to stage-manage their 1992 convention. "The whole week was double-ply, wall-to-wall ugly," *Newsweek* complained.[1] The party platform was, reported the *Boston Globe,* "loaded with puritanical, punitive language that not only forbade abortions, but attacked public television, gun control, homosexual rights, birth control clinics and the distribution of clean needles for drug users."[2] According to *Time,* the "darkly apocalyptic" words of primary challenger Patrick Buchanan on the third night of the convention "all but raised the specter of race war."[3]

Comments like this drive Republicans nearly crazy. Was it so very nice when Bob Hattoy charged on the second night of the Democratic convention that "AIDS doesn't discriminate, but George Bush's White House does.... If George Bush wins, we're all at risk in America. It's that serious. It's that terrible." When Jesse Jackson called King Herod "the Quayle of his day"? Hard things get said in politics, occasionally even by Republicans, and Democrats and the press should learn not to whimper about them. Still, if the purpose of a convention in modern media politics is to put a party's most attractive face before a mass television audience, then the Houston convention self-evidently flopped. Houston is now indelibly engraved in America's political memory as a disaster on the order of the Democrats' Chicago convention in 1968 or the Republicans' San Francisco convention of 1964.

What had gone wrong? Republicans blamed a hostile media; but the media were equally hostile in 1980, 1984, and 1988. Most of the convention's critics, on the other hand, put the blame on a right-wing coup that had seized control of the Republican Party in the name of "family values." Thus Charles Kuralt of CBS reported with alarm that "the only excited, demonstrative delegates any of us could find were the ones from the religious right . . . far more interested in imposing ideological purity on this party than they are in winning the election."[4] But it is simply childish to imagine that Houston was stage-managed by crazed Baptists. One hesitates to disabuse anyone of romantic illusions about American democracy, but political conventions—especially those staged by the incumbent party—are controlled by the national campaign organization, which is to say, by the man they are about to nominate. The delegates' floor at Houston could have been thronged with religious maniacs, bloated Rotarians, or pacifist vegetarians, and it would not have influenced the content of the convention one whit. Who would speak at Houston, in what order, and what those speeches would be permitted to say—these decisions came, not from Pat Robertson's Virginia Beach headquarters, but from the topmost heights of Bushdom, from almost pathological moderates like campaign chairman Bob Teeter, convention boss Craig Fuller, and Republican National Committee chairman Richard Bond. The writing of the platform is not exactly an exercise in participatory democracy either. There was no coup at Houston. The convention reflected the Bush men's own conception of smart politics.

The conjunction of the phrases "Bush men" and "smart

politics" now clashes incongruously upon the ear. In the articles and books published since the election, the Bush-Quayle reelection team has been ridiculed as about the dumbest collection of clowns ever to wreck a national campaign. Fair enough— although we should all be careful of the tendency of people who write about campaign organizations for a living to insist that it is campaign organizations that determine the outcome of elections. But look at the dilemma the Bush reelection team had been called upon to resolve. Their boss had fecklessly alienated his party's core supporters at exactly the same time that a surprisingly prolonged recession was antagonizing the nonideological voters who swing American elections. At Houston, the Bush men felt themselves obliged to achieve two equal and opposite purposes: to galvanize the party's Right and appeal to the country's mushy middle. Galvanizing the Right on behalf of George Bush was never going to be an easy job. Conservatives had long distrusted him, even before the broken tax pledge of 1990. Now they had begun openly to wonder whether it might not be healthier for the movement if Bush lost: "Do us a world of good, get out of office, think things through, recharge our batteries, let the Democrats worry about the deficit." The task of whipping up the conservative party's base in 1992 would have stumped even a Lee Atwater. For people with scant intuitive or visceral connection to the Right, it was near impossible.

Instead, like tourists in Paris, they compensated for their lack of a conservative vocabulary and grammar by absurdly and exaggeratedly mimicking the accents and gestures of the people to whom they were trying to communicate. So the convention managers invited Dr. D. James Kennedy of the Coral Ridge Presbyterian Church to deliver a hellfire-and-damnation invocation on Monday evening. "We have turned our back upon Thy laws by every imaginable immorality, perversion, vice, and crime; and even now a hideous plague stalks our land. . . . Oh Lord, we know that there are those who are atheists and secularists here in our midst that would lead us down . . . [the] godless trail to destruction."[5] Pat Robertson was summoned to the

podium to warn that "when Bill Clinton talks about traditional
family values, I don't believe he's talking about either families
or values. He's talking about a radical plan to destroy the traditional family and transfer many of its functions to the federal
government."[6] Patrick Buchanan won a coveted prime-time
television spot to declare, "There is a religious war going on in
this country. It is a cultural war as critical to the kind of nation
we shall be as the Cold War itself—for this war is for the soul
of America. And in that struggle for the soul of America, Clinton and Clinton are on the other side; and George Bush is on
our side."[7] And of course, Ronald Reagan reminded loyal conservatives everywhere whose party they would be letting down
if they didn't stick by Bush.

At the very same time, and with what must have seemed to
them great cleverness, the organizers of the 1992 Republican
convention put together a convention whose content was so
moderate as to pull in every mush-minded voter from Brook-
line, Massachusetts, to Marin County, California. Speaker after
speaker blasted the Democratic nominee, Governor Bill Clinton, from the *left*, for spending and regulating *too little*. Chairman Bond personally attacked Clinton for underpaying his
state's public school teachers.[8] The Republican attorney general
of California charged that Clinton did not splash enough money
upon drug treatment.[9] One of President Bush's environmental
advisers smugly quoted Clinton's admission that on occasion he
had been obliged to sacrifice Arkansas's environment for business's sake.[10] The chairman of the National Black Republican
Council was shocked, *shocked*, to report that "Arkansas is one
of the only two states without a Civil Rights Law, and one of
only nine states without a law banning housing discrimination."[11] Admiral James Watkins, secretary of energy, angrily
itemized the Clinton ticket's unwillingess to subsidize alternative
fuel boondoggles.[12] President Bush, on the other hand, was
praised for spreading the wealth with a lavish hand. He'd
brought "unprecedented federal assistance to local transit programs," crowed the mayor of York, Pennsylvania.[13] "Allow me

to remind you that President Bush enthusiastically signed the Americans with Disabilities Act," said blind athlete Craig Mac-Farlane.[14] "The Administration has proposed $4 billion in homeless assistance, an amount cut back by the Democrat-controlled Congress," the platform observed proudly.[15] Secretary Watkins boasted that President Bush had put the government's research labs "in partnership with United States industries" to develop "the next generation [of] super computers."[16] If the middle pages of the platform called for moral scrutiny of those who contract AIDS, the daughter of a big contributor was given ten minutes of prime television time to tell the nation that the president had shown only "affection" and no "judgment" toward her HIV-infection.[17] In her screechy nominating speech, Secretary Lynn Martin praised the president's Clean Air Act. Senator Dole in his introduction of the president boasted of the 1991 Civil Rights Act. And the president was repeatedly lauded for doubling the funding of Head Start.

Nor, on inspection, does the supposedly harsh and punitive 1992 platform live up to the press's terrifying descriptions of it. The platform's antiabortion plank was repeated virtually verbatim from 1980, 1984, and 1988. The party's position on the legal status of homosexuality—no recognition of same-sex marriage, no inclusion of sexual orientation in civil rights statutes, but also no discrimination against victims of AIDS—hardly crosses over the border into kookland. The platform did not attack birth control clinics but "programs in *public schools* that provide birth control or abortion services or referrals."[18] (Italics added.) Perhaps distributing contraceptives to legal minors without the knowledge or consent of their parents is indeed a good way to reduce the teen pregnancy rate, but you don't have to be Pat Robertson to wonder if perhaps it isn't. In any case, a reading of the convention proceedings and the platform together leaves the strong impression that the platform was not meant to be taken very seriously. "Promoting opportunity, we reject efforts to replace equal rights with quotas or other preferential treatment," the platform said,[19] but every committee convened at the convention was required to be half composed of women and the speaking roster was filled with the names of nobodies selected only because of their sex or race: the mayor of Jefferson City, Missouri; the mayor of Diamond Bar, California; a former special assistant to the president for national security affairs; the minority leader of the lower house of the Maryland legislature; a Florida state committeeman; the associate director of the office of national drug policy.

As for the notorious "family values" preached at Houston, the slogan had been so badly mauled by the Democrats and the press in advance of the convention that Republicans themselves had lost their enthusiasm for it. Instead, Barbara Bush was despatched on the second-to-last night of the convention to vacuum all content from the phrase: "When we speak of families, we mean extended families. We mean the neighbors, even the community itself. We've met heroic single mothers and fathers who have told us how hard it is to raise children when you're doing it all alone. We've talked to grandparents who thought their child-raising days were over, but are now raising their grandchildren because their children can't. . . . We have met so many different families, and yet they really aren't so very different." "We've taught our children to respect single parents and their challenges," said a nervous Dan Quayle in his acceptance speech.

So what voters heard at Houston was a Republican insistence that something be done to strengthen the family, combined with a striking absence of ideas about what that something should be. Would unmarried mothers be denied welfare? Would divorce for parents of minor children be restricted? Would the Federal Communications Commission get smut off television? Would taxes on male heads of households be cut to help their wives to leave the workforce? Good God, no. The Houston Republicans wanted to be seen as more moral than Bill Clinton's Democrats, but only slightly more moral, comfortably moral, not frighteningly moral, not *judgmental*. Except for Buchanan, Robertson, and Dr. Kennedy, the Houston orators blended moralism and vacuity. Unfortunately, precisely because the convention was so vacant, hostile auditors could choose to hear anything they cared to. If "family values" meant nothing by the time the Republican convention programmers had finished editing everyone's speeches, then there was equally nothing to stop the oversensitive or the malicious from claiming that the phrase in fact meant, "Let's hate homosexuals and unmarried black mothers." Cheap rhetoric, like cheap merchandise, can be disconcertingly fragile and unreturnable.

If anything, the Houston convention testified not to the ascendency of the Right, but to the rebirth of moderate Republicanism. The relationship between the conservative movement and the Republican Party has never been a satisfactory one for either side. The Republican Party antedates the conservative movement by a hundred years, and will probably still be collecting votes long after today's ideological conservatism has faded as deep into the American memory as the Mugwumps have done. The party has institutional interests and imperatives of its own. From the catastrophe of 1936—an election that primitive polls misled the Republicans into believing they might win—until 1980, the Republican Party has twitched with the anxiety that afflicts the weaker party in a two-party democracy: the anxiety of knowing that in a fair two-way fight, it is done for. The only hope for survival, let alone victory, for the weaker party is to hug the middle of the spectrum as hard as it can, hoping that the stronger party's overconfidence will lead it to indulge its more extreme members and alienate swing voters. Thus, in 1872, the shattered Democratic Party nominated Horace Greeley—a protectionist, abolitionist New Yorker whose newspaper had strenuously supported the Civil War—in hopes that they might scoop up Republican votes offended by the blatant boodling of the Grant administration; thus in 1948, Thomas Dewey declared himself strenuously in favor of Social Security, a higher minimum wage, and foreign aid, in the hope that President Truman's excessive reliance on the radical CIO unions and his backing of civil rights laws would repel business-

minded Democrats and white Southerners. As late as 1976, the
Republican Party was dominated by jittery moderates: so much
so that a delegation of conservatives led by *National Review*
publisher Bill Rusher pleaded with Ronald Reagan, after his
narrow defeat that year at the Kansas City convention, to split
from the GOP and form a conservative third party.

Reagan of course brushed Rusher off. And, as it turned
out, he was right: moderate Republicanism was no longer able
to deny him the party's nomination. Moderate Republicanism—
or, to give it its old name, liberal Republicanism—was a by-
product of the Democratic Party's one-time dependency on
white Southern and Northern Catholic votes. In the 1940s and
1950s, distaste for the Democrats' ethnic political machines and
their racist Southern wing kept liberals like Leverett Saltonstall,
Frank Sargent, and Jacob Javits in the Republican Party. We
forget now, but it is worth remembering, that the state of Connecticut's ban on birth control devices—the law that led to
Griswold v. Connecticut, the 1965 Supreme Court decision that
created the constitutional right of sexual privacy, and then by
logical extension to *Roe v. Wade*—survived into the twentieth
century on the strength of *Democratic* voting power. Protestant
Connecticut Republicans from the Greenwich panhandle and
the countryside repeatedly tried to get rid of the ridiculous
thing, only to be thwarted again and again by Catholic Democrats from the state's cities. The last try occurred in 1957. A
bill to legalize contraception for married women rocketed
through the Republican lower house, 158 to 71. The Democratic Senate overturned the lower house by voice vote. Of the
fourteen senators known to have voted in favor of birth control,
thirteen were Republican Protestants. Of the seventeen known
to have voted against, fourteen were Catholic Democrats.[20]
Mrs. Griswold herself, the chairwoman of the Connecticut
chapter of Planned Parenthood who maneuvered the New
Haven police into arresting her and thus testing the law, came
from an old Republican family and was a friend of Connecticut
Senator Prescott Bush, father of the future president and him-

self a strong advocate of population control. The emancipated upper-class Protestant women of the Republican Party put support for an Equal Rights Amendment in the party platform as early as 1944; it would take the ethnic and Catholic Democratic Party twenty years longer to endorse the ERA.

But the post-1972 Democratic Party was a far easier home for secular liberals. Purged of its racism and moral traditionalism, it absorbed much of the strength of liberal Republicanism, winning GOP converts like the present senior senator from Michigan, Donald Riegle. Then the Republican electoral catastrophe of 1974—which cost the Republicans virtually every congressional seat in which there was any sprinkling of liberal voters—finished off what remained of the party's moderates. Like the Spanish conquistadors who occupied lands emptied ahead of them by European diseases, the conservatives who took over the Republican Party in the late 1970s were occupying recently vacated ground. Even so, as the party swung rightward in the 1980s—to the point where most of its present "moderates," such as Senator Robert Dole, would twenty years ago have seemed more than conservative enough, even to *National Review*—the old moderate Republicanism revived too. A successful party attracts unideological opportunists, and the Republican Party of the 1980s was a very successful party. Perhaps even more important, the Republican Party is the party of rich people, and opposition to abortion has never sat very easily upon upper-crust Republicans; neither have ideological politics generally. Upper-crust people are business-minded, and business normally wants from government not philosophical consistency, but special favors. George Bush was the natural candidate of these Republicans, and his issues—like the capital gains tax cut—were their sort of issues. Robert Bartley, editor of the *Wall Street Journal*, complained that the Bush administration was the most aristocratic since John Adams's. It was not until primary season that it occurred to Bush's organization that they might after all need the orange-juice-drinking, polyester-wearing, church-going type of Republican too. Hence the firing of John

Frohnmayer—director of the National Endowment for the Arts during the Mapplethorpe photograph imbroglio—after the New Hampshire primary; hence the Buchanan speech in prime time at Houston.

Awareness of the latent power of upper-class Republicans has long irked movement conservatives. In style, at least, ideological conservatives feel a lot more comfortable with the populist, traditionalist, hawkish Democratic Party of the 1940s than with the white-shoe traditions of the GOP. "I don't think Pat Buchanan likes Republicans very much," muses George Will in conversation,[21] and indeed it is hard to imagine a preincarnated Buchanan casting a happy ballot for Governor Dewey or Wendell Willkie. (It is hard to imagine Norman Podhoretz, Peggy Noonan, or Rush Limbaugh doing it either.) Pat Buchanan's 1992 campaign took him one February evening to a Republican fund-raising supper in York, Maine, the site of a television station that broadcast into the northern reaches of neighboring New Hampshire. Unlike the more rough-hewn New Hampshire party, Maine Republicans look like Central Casting Republicans: the men in blazers and loafers, the women sleekly dressed and coiffed. It was Buchanan's worst evening of the week—his audience could hardly be bothered to listen to him, and he was equally offhand with them. Conservatives have always seen the Republican Party as a prize to be won, a problem to be solved, certainly not as an institution to which they owed loyalty for its own sake. The Party has felt equally dubious about them. Thus, for all the broadcast babble about the archconservatism of the Houston convention, ideological conservatives felt little sense of responsibility for what happened there. This was a convention meant to manipulate them, as it was meant to manipulate a half-dozen other voting cohorts identified by the president's centrist strategists as adding up to an electoral majority.

Twelve years before, a Republican Party over which ideological conservatives exercised far more control had selected Detroit—the headquarters of the United Autoworkers, the blackest big city in the nation—as the place in which it would nominate Ronald Reagan. It was a daring choice, as daring as siting a Democratic convention in Salt Lake City or Orlando. Reagan ventured to Detroit because he hoped to win—because he believed he deserved to win—the votes of blacks and union members who had never voted Republican before. He was going to cut their taxes, rejuvenate their economy, and stand up to their enemies in Moscow and Tehran. He exuded confidence that all Americans shared common interests, that all possessed wholesome values, and that the policies he advocated would benefit everyone. In 1992, by unhappy contrast, the Republicans had been forced back into their southwestern redoubt. Their speeches were defensive. "My opponent," Bush said in his acceptance speech, "says America is a nation in decline. Of our America he says we are somewhere on the list beneath Germany, heading south toward Sri Lanka. Well, don't let anyone tell you that America is second-rate, especially somebody running for president."[22] "You can't be one kind of man and another kind of president," said Lynn Martin,[23] ignoring eight years of arguments by Republicans that one could be quite an, ahem, "disengaged" man and still be a great president. In 1980, Republicans argued that you should judge a president by his ideas and accomplishments; now they beseeched the nation to judge Bush by the likeability of his personality, as if their candidate were running for student council president.

The Republican strategy was as defensive as their candidate's words. The country was suffering a strange sort of recession in 1992, one that struck especially hard against Republican constituencies. Home prices were tumbling, big corporations were laying off middle managers, aerospace engineers were waiting by the mailbox for their unemployment checks, and retirees' income from their certificates of deposit had been cut in half. Homeowners, middle managers, defense workers, and retirees—it sounds like a description of a Ross Perot rally. Indeed, in the end Perot would draw his support almost entirely from former Republicans. Perot got 19 percent of the vote in

1992. Bill Clinton won the election, even though he drew three percentage points less of the popular vote than Michael Dukakis had in 1988, because George Bush's share of the vote dropped by sixteen percentage points. Clinton became president because Republicans, some of them lifelong loyalists, deserted a too-complacent president for a paranoid billionaire who told them that all was not well, that the country was in danger of being eclipsed by Germany and Japan and of being submerged by cheap Mexican labor.

As their coalition broke up before their eyes, as so many former Republicans suffered extreme economic distress, often for the first time in their lives, the old Reagan faith that what was good for one was good for all sounded more and more unconvincing. Conservatives were ready for a tougher message, one more critical of their country and of their compatriots. The cheery "morning in America" themes of Reagan's 1984 reelection campaign struck them as far less accurate an account of their country and their culture than Patrick Buchanan's blunt picture of the suppression of the Los Angeles riot in his convention speech. "The troops came up the street with M-16s at the ready, and the mob threatened and cursed; but the mob retreated because it had met the one thing that could stop it— force, rooted in justice, backed by moral courage. . . . And as those boys took back the streets of Los Angeles, block by block, we must take back our cities and take back our culture and take back our country."[24] This is the language of people who feel threatened, and threatened by something far bigger than mere economic adversity. It is the sort of language that came naturally in 1992 to Perot too, although in his speeches the threat emanated not from a black mob but from foreign economic competitors and illegal immigrants. It is the sort of language that America will be hearing much more of in the next decade—not always from conservatives, either. Indeed, America heard a great deal of it in the debate over the North American Free Trade Agreement. Animating the extraordinarily broad opposition to the agreement was a dramatic collapse in American self-confidence—and a startling new fear of foreigners, even foreigners who had once been the butt of "mañana" jokes. Bush is not ordinarily thought of as a perceptive man, but one of his campaign documents, at least, captured the national mood very well: "We are a nation at peace. But being at peace with others and being at peace with ourselves are different things."[25]

Much has been said about the damage the collapse of communism has inflicted on the fragile cohesion of the coalition that elected Ronald Reagan in 1981, and almost all of it is off-key. Obviously the Democrats' weak-mindedness toward the Soviet Union and communist insurgencies in the Third World helped to alienate the always-hawkish voters of the white South. But it is simply wrong to imagine that any but a handful of the journalists, intellectuals, policy-makers, and politicians who formed the conservative intellectual movement of the 1970s and 1980s were bound to that movement by anticommunism alone. Exceptions there undoubtedly were: former U.N. ambassador Jeane Kirkpatrick comes to mind. For the most part, though, it was not the momentous victory over communism that disrupted conservative unity, but the infinitely more trivial victory over Michael Dukakis. "Nothing in life is quite so exhilarating," Winston Churchill wrote in his memoir of the Boer War, "than to be shot at without result." And nothing in politics is quite so seductive as winning an election with a godawful candidate. Few conservatives had felt much enthusiasm for the George Bush candidacy in 1988, but when he won, they drew an intoxicating lesson from his victory: Republicans had carried five of the past six presidential elections, the last of them with a man almost all conservatives regarded as unfit for the job. That string of victories proved to them that the Right must be the natural party of government. I remember hearing doubts in early 1989 about whether we would ever again see a Democratic president in our lifetimes. "It should be remembered," wrote conservative-leaning political analyst Michael Barone in his widely (and justly) acclaimed book *Our Country,* "that Bush gained his lead just as voters were focusing hard for the first time on the choice before them, and that in American politics, where both parties start out with about 40% of the electorate in almost any presidential contest, the 53%–46% win by Bush in 1988 will probably look no more accidental or contingent in the long run of history than does Franklin Roosevelt's 53%–46% defeat of Thomas Dewey in 1944."[26]

If Barone was correct, then conservatives faced both an unexpected opportunity and a challenging ideological problem. The opportunity: given a long enough lease of power, conservatives could hope to achieve a social transformation of their own, just as liberals had in the 1930s, 1940s, 1950s, and 1960s. The challenge: while the conservative coalition of 1981 agreed wholeheartedly that the federal government should stop doing what it had been doing up until then, it did not agree at all about the policies that government should pursue instead. So long as conservatives thought of themselves as essentially an opposition party, this lack of consensus upon a positive program was a remote enough problem. But once they had accustomed themselves to power, conservative disunity would matter. This was especially true because the program that had united conservatives in the first place—shrinking the welfare functions of the federal government—had proven so impossible to execute. Ronald Reagan owed his 1980 presidential victory to what seemed at the time to have been an inspired political stroke borrowed from a visionary young congressman named Jack Kemp. There would be no more threats to throw widows out into the snow, no more Taft- and Goldwater-style calls for self-reliance, cheese-paring, and pay-as-you-go. No more flinty frugality. Rather than fight and lose the battle over the welfare state for the hundredth time, Reagan would change the subject from spending to taxes. Later, after the tax cuts had worked their magic, there would be plenty of time to start chopping at the excesses of big government. Reagan's domestic policy was, then, essentially a gamble—a gamble that with the proper tactics he could bring the federal government under control, without mobilizing against him the pro-spending constituencies that had triumphed over presidents Nixon, Ford, and Carter.

The gamble did not pay off—and the failure was due to conservatives' own fecklessness. While federal revenues shot upward in the booming 1980s (including revenues from the personal income tax, just as Arthur Laffer had predicted), federal spending swelled even faster. Conservatives would later airily pin the blame for the spending binge on a hostile Democratic Congress. But a quick flip through the pages of the budget documents of the decade shows that the fastest-growing spending was on Republican constituencies: pensioners, farmers, and veterans. The result—Ronald Reagan's two administrations piled up more debt, in inflation-adjusted dollars, than Roosevelt and Truman had incurred to win World War II. In just four years, George Bush accumulated three times more debt (again adjusting for inflation) than Woodrow Wilson had taken on to fight World War I.

Conceivably, the failure of the Reagan gambit might have persuaded conservatives—in government and out—to redouble their zeal for scaling back the functions of the state. They could have said, as Newt Gingrich said in a contemplative mood on one of his early morning walks, "We failed, but that doesn't mean our failure was inevitable."[27] That is not, however, what happened. The preponderance of the Right—including Gingrich himself—accepted the view expressed by *New Republic* editor Fred Barnes in 1989: anything Reagan had left undone could not be done. It was time now to accept Irving Kristol's decades-old claim that "the welfare state is with us, for better or worse, and . . . conservatives should try to make it better rather than worse."[28] The eminent political scientist James Q. Wilson warned his fellow-conservatives that "telling people who want clean air, a safe environment, fewer drug dealers, a decent retirement, and protection against catastrophic medical bills that the government ought not to do these things is wishful or suicidal politics,"[29] and by and large they heeded him. In the spring of 1992, *Policy Review* sent a questionnaire to twenty moderate-to-conservative senators. What would you do, the magazine asked, to cut $25 billion from the budget? The real news was not that only five bothered to answer, or that only one of the five, Colorado Republican Hank Brown, had any useful suggestions to offer. The real news was that *Policy Review*, the official organ of the Heritage Foundation, the intellectual arsenal of Reaganism, thought that $25 billion—or rather less than 2 percent of federal expenditure—was as ambitious a spending target as it could realistically set. Whatever they might say in their after-dinner speeches or in their op-ed pieces, conservatives had effectively thrown in the towel on government spending. As Heritage itself despairingly wondered, in the briefing book it compiled for the new Bush administration in 1989, "If Ronald Reagan and his 'Reaganauts' could only slow down the growth of government spending, not reverse it or eliminate wasteful programs, what hope is there for any other conservative president?"[30]

Understandably, then, conservatives were greatly tempted simply to stop thinking about shrinking government and to find a new and less frustrating message—one that played to the great political strength that conservatives felt themselves to have after the defeat of Dukakis. That new message was found in a phrase they borrowed from the Marxist Left: the culture. "We cannot raise the white flag in the culture war," wrote Patrick Buchanan in defense of his controversial speech to the Republican convention in Houston, "for that is a war about who we are. Nor can conservatives become conscientious objectors—because culture shapes politics, culture is the Ho Chi Minh trail to power. Surrender this province, and we lose America."[31] Conversely, by holding this province, conservatives could hold America. George Wallace's startling popularity in 1968 convinced conservative psephologists that the "real majority" (in the phrase of two conservative Democrats, Ben Wattenberg and Richard Scammell) was economically moderate and culturally conservative. The Chicago pipefitter who had served in Korea;

the Jackson, Mississippi, housewife who attended prayer service every Saturday night; the hardware store owner in Tampa with six children—these were the famous "Reagan Democrats." They were the strength and power of the Republican Party of the 1980s, and none of them was interested in hearing that tuition was about to rise at the state university.

As the 1980s progressed—and family breakdown, drug abuse, ethnic balkanization, the politicization of the arts and the universities, and urban decay all accelerated—more and more conservative intellectuals decided that reordering conservative politics to appeal to these new constituents made more than merely tactical sense. Ronald Reagan and Barry Goldwater's laissez-faire view of government had presupposed the essential moral and cultural health of American society. Reagan's successors, on the other hand, saw a society decay. As compared to the emergence of a dependent underclass, the budget of the Export-Import bank hardly seemed to matter very much. A great historian of the classical world, Sir Moses Finley, noted how in the later Roman Empire the old civic ideology of the ruling elite faded away, "reflecting (and contributing to) a cumulative depression in the status of the lower classes."[32] Perhaps something similar is underway in America too. As families disintegrate, as the poor become ever more dependent, as new immigration weakens the country's cultural links to Europe, American conservatism seems to be adapting by jettisoning its Reaganite optimism and individualism. A very secular anxiety—a fear that something had gone deeply wrong with the soul of the country, something that tasty Reaganite medicine could not cure—was the true inner meaning of Houston.

CHAPTER 3

The Failure of the Reagan Gambit

"You do it with mirrors." That was Congressman John Anderson's mocking explanation of how candidate Ronald Reagan could keep his promise to rebuild the country's defenses, cut taxes, and balance the budget simultaneously. The congressman was wrong. If federal spending had risen no faster than inflation between 1979 and 1989, the United States could have spent every dollar it did on defense and enjoyed all the Reagan tax cuts—and would have still run a federal budget surplus big enough to pay either for the repeal of the corporate income tax or a one-third cut in everyone's Social Security payroll taxes.[1]

But while it was theoretically possible for Reagan to do what he set out to do, it was never going to be easy. If you want to control the rise in the cost of Social Security, for example, you cannot simply enact a law saying that the program's cost will rise no more than x percent a year—unless you're prepared to tell Mr. Jones, when he becomes eligible for a pension, that the money has run out and he cannot have one. To save money on Social Security, you must fight the brutal political conflict necessary to change the rules that govern the program, either by raising the retirement age or by cutting the amount that retirees collect. The Reagan administration was never prepared to suffer the consequences of doing such a thing, especially not after the battering it took in 1981, when David Stockman incautiously proposed stabilizing the system's shaky finances by phasing out benefits for those who left work before age sixty-five.

There was no arithmetic reason that the Reagan program could not have succeeded. Reagan's budgets were wrecked by the inability and unwillingness of the most conservative administration since Coolidge's to resist the rise of social welfare spending.

Defenders of the Reagan administration learned over the decade to shrug off the titanic debts this failure racked up: nobody had ever proven the connection between deficits and high interest rates, they said; the deficits were the fault of the Federal Reserve for squeezing the economy too tight in 1981; compared to Italy or Canada, the United States was hardly borrowing much at all; anyway, it was all Congress's fault—just give the president the line-item veto and stand back.

How in the world had conservatives come to this embarrassing excuse-making? It was their own cleverness that was to blame. Back in the good old days when conservatives contented themselves with 39 percent of the vote, Barry Goldwater had brought cheering audiences to their feet with thunderous promises to carve up government's bloated carcass:

> I have little interest in streamlining government or in making it more efficient, for I mean to reduce its size. I do not undertake to promote welfare, for I propose to extend freedom. My aim is not to pass laws, but to repeal them. It is not to inaugurate new programs, but to cancel old ones that do violence to the Constitution, or that have failed in their purpose, or that impose on the people an unwarranted financial burden. I will not attempt to discover whether legislation is "needed" before I have first determined whether it

is constitutionally permissible. And if I should later be attacked for neglecting my constituents' "interests," I shall reply that I was informed that their main interest is liberty and in that cause I am doing the very best I can.[2]

Ronald Reagan gained the presidency in 1980 because he did not talk like that, and the Republican Party kept power for twelve years because it did not govern like that. Reagan promised in 1980 that no needy person would lose any benefits under his administration. Whatever budget savings he needed would come from squeezing out "waste, fraud, and abuse." When President Carter accused him in their October 1980 television debate of planning to make Medicare less generous, Reagan flattened him with his famous "there you go again" rebuttal.

Throughout his long previous political career, Reagan had always taken the orthodox Goldwaterite line that government spending was the primary culprit and that taxes were only a derivative problem. In the late 1970s, though, Reagan adopted the emollient vision of Congressman Kemp. Kemp pooh-poohed the old Republican obsession with spending. It was tax rates that mattered, he said—and in his ebullient moments, nothing but tax rates. "Instead of high tax rates with low production, government can raise the same amount of revenue through low tax rates that will apply to the high production base that will result from lessening taxes and increasing incentives. . . . Instead of widespread fears about the deficits of the Social Security system, there will be solvency, with funds for the expansion of public and private retirement benefits."[3] Lower taxes; more benefits—you had to wonder why nobody else had ever thought of that. The New Dealers used to describe their government as Hamiltonian means to Jeffersonian ends. Supply-side economics might be thought of as adapting Franklin Roosevelt's means to Goldwater's ends. For two generations, conservatives had chosen as their champions harsh, dour men like Herbert Hoover, Robert Taft, and Barry Goldwater, men who never believed in sugarcoating the pill. Kemp insisted that it was time to stop prescribing pain. It was time for Republicans to appear—not to appear, to be—a generous, open-handed party, a party of hope and opportunity. Barry Goldwater had actually opposed the Kennedy tax cut of 1963: "If we reduce taxes before firm, principled decisions are made about expenditures, we will court deficit spending and the inflationary effects that will inevitably follow." Reagan and Kemp turned Goldwater on his head. Spending cuts were no longer to be seen as a precondition for tax cuts; they had become the antithesis of tax cuts, the one thing that could destroy the political consensus that made the tax cuts possible.

In the short run, that was smart politics and not-too-bad public policy. The supply-side tax cuts of 1981 were predicated on two correct observations: first, because inflation had pushed so many middle-class Americans into tax brackets once reserved for plutocrats, the average family had suffered through a decade of unlegislated tax increases by 1980. A family of four at the median income—a crummy $9,867 in 1970—was paying 20 percent more income tax in 1980 than it had in 1970, even though the median income had, for the first time since the Depression, actually fallen over the decade. (Adjusting for inflation of course.)

The second correct observation was that highly progressive income taxes truly are economically perverse. Government does not raise much revenue from a 70 percent tax bracket (the top rate in 1980), not at least in a country where an obliging Congress stands ready to drill holes through the tax code for generous contributors. A high top rate exists only in order to reconcile the ordinary taxpayer to losing one-third or more of his income in taxes—on the theory that if he can be gulled into thinking that the rich pay even more, he won't mind being soaked himself. Conservatives had opposed the progressive income tax for generations. What was news in the Reagan campaign—what was news about the conservatism of 1980—was that opposition to high tax rates was joined to the espousal of lavish social welfare spending.

To a party sick of defending itself against accusations of hard-heartedness, Jack Kemp's happy economics was as welcome as the invention of the tank must have been to the British infantry in 1917. Instead of sprinting through the mud toward the enemy's machine guns, how'd you like to sit dry and snug inside a bulletproof moving box? But by 1990, it was clear that without savage spending cuts, the Reagan tax cuts (or as much of them as remained after a decade of stealthy tax increases) could not be preserved. The Reagan gambit had failed.

With both parties tacitly agreed that no major spending program should shrink, and with only the Republicans determined that taxes not rise, it was already predictable, even in the earliest years of the Reagan mandate, that when the time came to deal with the deficit, the deficit would be dealt with on Democratic terms. Indeed, the Reagan-Bush deficits would have been even bigger, and the job of pooh-poohing them even more difficult, if conservative antitax diehards had not quietly acquiesced in a series of stealthy tax increases in 1981 and 1989.

The most militant supply-siders reconciled themselves to the tax hikes of the 1980s by denying that government's gross tax take mattered very much, so long as tax rates were kept low. Paul Craig Roberts, a *Wall Street Journal* columnist who served as assistant secretary of the Treasury in the first years of the Reagan administration, argued that it was essential to distinguish between "lower average tax rates, which do not improve incentives, and lower marginal rates, which do."[4] "The concept of marginality," wrote Jude Wanniski in his 1977 treatise, *The Way the World Works*, "is crucial to an understanding of economic behavior." Wanniski cited the example of West Germany, which cut its tax rates from their 1948 top rate of 95 percent to 53 percent a decade later. "To the Keynesian," a fighting word in Wanniski's lexicon, "who sees no difference between tax rates and tax revenues, nothing has changed in Germany. The government was getting 35 percent of national income sixty years ago and is still getting 35 percent of national income. The difference, of course, is that with the correct rates, Germany's national income has risen tenfold."[5]

Up to a point, Wanniski was of course right. In the seven years between the end of the Vietnam War and the onset of the 1980 slump, the federal government collected 18.7 percent of gross national product. During the seven fat years from 1983 to 1989, the top marginal rate fell to 28 percent—and the federal government still collected 18.6 percent of gross national product in revenue. Along the way, GNP grew by one-third. But the higher revenues thrown off by low marginal rates, handsome as they were, were not handsome enough to pay for the spending that the Reagan administration refused to challenge. And so—at first surreptitiously, later more blatantly—tax rates reversed their descent. Nowhere was the reversal more onerous than in the arcane realm of payroll taxes.

In order to maintain the fiction that Social Security is an insurance rather than a welfare scheme, its creators financed it with a separate payroll tax, originally 1 percent. To keep the rickety contraption from bankruptcy, the payroll tax has had to be raised and raised again: by an average of three percentage points per decade for each of the past four decades. In 1977, Congress approved yet another series of Social Security tax increases. At the behest of President Reagan's 1983 Social Security commission, Congress brought forward the dates on which the 1977 taxes were to take effect. Endlessly rising Social Security taxes nullified the 1981 Kemp-Roth tax cut for most taxpayers. Include Social Security, and a family at the median income actually saw its marginal income tax rate rise between 1980 and 1984.[6] Of course, their taxes would have been even higher without the 1981 cut—but they probably did not stop to figure that out.

Given the immensity of the nation's debt, even the most hard-boiled supply-siders had to recognize after 1986 that there could be no further large reductions in taxes. From then on, conservatives would have to exert all their power simply to prevent the Reagan tax cuts from eroding. This one budgetary fact accounts for much of the paralysis and fatigue that gripped the conservative movement after the mid-1980s. Indeed, because the Republicans had crippled themselves by their refusal to take action on federal spending, Democrats had won the argument over taxes even before Bill Clinton moved into the White House. By Inauguration Day, 1993, the average effective federal tax rate—a rate that includes not only income taxes, but also excise taxes, payroll taxes, and the portion of corporate taxation passed on to consumers—had already risen to within one-tenth of a percentage point of where it had been on Inauguration Day, 1981.[7]

Confronted with this sad story, Reaganite budgetmeisters have a ready answer: it was all the fault of the backsliding Bushies who betrayed the cause with the tax-laden 1990 budget deal. But in fact, more than half the tax cut was lost between 1985 and 1989. If it's not honest to blame the loss of the tax cut on George Bush, it's even worse to blame the chronic overspending that made the tax cut unsustainable on a profligate liberal Democratic Congress. Of course liberals and Democrats are profligate. That's why God makes conservatives and Republicans—to stop Democrats from spending the nation into bankruptcy. But, through the 1980s, the conservatives failed to do their job. Despite the caterwauling about Reagan's supposedly savage budget cuts in 1981, not one major spending program was abolished during the Reagan presidency. Only one spending program of any size was done away with, and even that—the worthless Comprehensive Employment and Training Act—was instantly replaced by another program, the Jobs Partnership Training Act, meant to achieve almost exactly the same end.[8]

Was the Reagan administration downcast by this meager record? Not a bit. Ronald Reagan, says Martin Anderson, the future president's chief economic adviser during 1976 and 1980 campaigns,

> was not calling for reductions in federal spending, or even for just holding the line. All he wanted to do was stop it

from growing so fast. Repeatedly, during the campaign, in the transition, and then at White House meetings, Reagan would look around him and say, "Federal spending is going up like this" (raising his arm straight from the shoulder at a 45-degree angle). "We have to bring it down to here" (lowering his arm to about a 30-degree angle).[9]

The only question that remained was, where was "down here"? If "down here" had meant the rate of inflation, then everything would have been fine—better than fine. But it didn't. Federal spending rose by an average of 2.75 percent a year after inflation during the Reagan administration. Federal revenues rose by only 2.4 percent after inflation. In a trillion-dollar government, a one-third of one percentage point difference adds up— to a total deficit, over the Reagan years, of $1,492 billion. That's a colossal number, an incomprehensibly huge number, but it can be understood as the sum of innumerable small acts of conservative timidity.

One of the heresies that sprouted after the Protestant Reformation was "perfectionism," the doctrine that once a soul was saved it became incapable of sin. Perfectionism sprouted again among the Reaganites. If you belonged to the movement, you were one of us, and everything you did was sinless, no matter how sinful it might appear to the unsaved. Take, for instance, the story of Edwin Meese, Yale man turned California populist, who came East in 1980 to occupy the grandly named office of counselor to the president. In the division of labor that established the troika that ran the White House during Reagan's first term, Meese claimed the most important job. While Michael Deaver occupied himself with public relations and the media, and James Baker, the chief of staff, scheduled the president's appointments, Meese would superintend the administration's entire domestic policy. Conservatives were delighted. They mistrusted Deaver and Baker and, for that matter, most of the Reagan cabinet, but Meese had loyally served Reagan since the mid-1960s. He wore the Adam Smith neckties that proclaimed one a true believer. His door was open to conservative activists such as Richard Viguerie and Paul Weyrich; he hired staffers recommended to him by the Heritage Foundation and other conservative groups; he accepted conservative awards and spoke at conservative functions. It was Meese, said *National Review*'s Washington columnist, who kept Reagan "true to his real, orthodox self."[10]

It's curious, then, that of all Reagan's senior advisers, it was Meese who most consistently took a powder on issues of government spending and regulation.

When the California orange growers cartel, Sunkist, came under attack from agriculture secretary John Block, Meese bounced to its defense. Since the Depression, California fruit producers have been governed by an amazing regime of controls upon the number of oranges (or almonds or peaches) that each farmer may grow. If the antitrust laws mean anything, they should mean that Sunkist is illegal. But the growers always had one voice chiming in on their behalf at the White House: Meese. Meese's largesse fell on the cities as well as the countryside. The most widely and deservedly ridiculed of the government extravaganzas of the 1970s was the Urban Development Action Grant program, a federal subsidy for real estate development in distressed downtowns. Critics of the program wondered why Washington should pay for luxury hotels in Los Angeles, but not Meese, who protected it from David Stockman's pencil five years in a row. Meese talked Reagan into "voluntary export restraints" on Japanese automobiles, and in February 1981, it was Meese who seized on a stray comment of David Stockton's and announced to the *New York Times* on his own initiative that Social Security, Medicare, veterans' benefits, Head Start, Supplemental Security Income for the poor, and ghetto summer jobs programs would be exempt from Reagan's budget cuts.[11]

Meese seems genuinely to have persuaded himself that the programs cherished by his friends and constituents were legitimate functions of government. This act of self-deception was made possible, in large part, by his own extraordinary mental slovenliness. William Niskanen, one of the economists who served on Reagan's council of economic advisers, recalls, with irritation, how Meese

> would often be speaking to some 4-H group at a time an important issue was being resolved. Memos would pile up in his in-basket for months without being answered. His concept of management was to revise organizational charts, issue executive orders, and arrange for presidential pep talks. . . . After Meese was nominated as attorney general, a former Meese aide argued that he should not be replaced [as counselor to the president]: "Ed Meese's office ought to be put to some other more worthwhile use, such as the National Museum of Lost Memos or Abandoned Briefcases."[12]

But Meese's self-deception was encouraged too by the mental atmosphere of the Reagan years. Conservatives who had breathed animosity against overbearing government out of office, found themselves, once elected, making extraordinarily rapid and happy peace with the beast.

That is how the Department of Education escaped unscathed from the Reagan ax. President Carter had elevated the old education bureau within the Department of Health, Education, and Welfare to a separate department of the cabinet in 1980, as a direct payoff to the public-school teachers who cast so many votes in Democratic primaries. Candidate Reagan had pledged himself to abolish the new department, as well as Carter's other cabinet creation, the Department of Energy. At the very beginning of the Reagan administration, the president's chief headhunter, Pendleton James, told Terrell Bell, the newly appointed education secretary, of "the great distinction that would be mine [Bell's] if I could, some day early in the Reagan administration, walk into the Oval Office and hand the president the keys to the Department of Education and say: 'Well, we've shut the abominable thing down. Here's one useless government agency out of the way.'"[13]

Instead the department survived and prospered. Its budget bloated up from $14.7 billion in 1981 to $21.5 billion in 1989. What went wrong? At the time, much of the blame was heaped on Bell, a self-righteous educrat who made no secret of his desire to keep the department alive. ("Those who accused me of being part of the educational establishment were right," he concedes in a memoir published under the pompous subtitle, "The story of the struggle between the conscience of an educator and the ideologues who had chosen him to abolish the Department of Education.")[14] But Bell did not act alone. When he made his pro forma attempt to abolish the department in 1981, he discovered that Howard Baker, the first Republican Senate majority leader since 1954, actively opposed abolition. That would not have surprised the Reaganites very much, since Baker symbolized almost everything they disliked about their own party—he was a man of Washington, a pragmatist, a good loser. But Senator Roth, of Kemp-Roth, also backed the department. So too did Trent Lott of Mississippi, who with Newt Gingrich of Georgia led the young conservative fire-eaters in the House of Representatives. Even before Bell departed in January 1985, Education had become known as a place where deserving conservative activists without much else to recommend them could collect their reward. The Office of Civil Rights within the department won special recognition as a training ground for young black conservatives. That's where Clarence Thomas got his start, as did Michael Williams, an assistant secretary, who in an act of gallant futility tried to eliminate race-specific university scholarships in the early months of the Bush administration.

Acknowledging that the Education department was here to stay, the administration replaced Bell with one of the most dynamic conservatives of the Reagan-Bush era, William Bennett. Bennett's speeches denouncing bureaucracy, moral relativism, and educational faddishness, electrified conservatives. He pleaded for school choice and strict national math and reading standards. He lit up the drab and dreary second Reagan term. And all the while Bennett was serving this juicy red meat, his department continued in busy disregard of him to perform the tasks for which conservatives anathematized it: enforcing bilingual education, telling local schools how to teach their pupils, drawing up busing schemes, and forgiving college students for defaulting on their federal loans. Of the 47 percent rise in federal education spending between 1981 and 1989, three-quarters occurred under William Bennett.

Although the Department of Justice housed the hated trust-busters and the officious meddlers of the civil rights division, conservatives came to an entente with it as well. Reagan's first attorney general, the seemingly sleepy William French Smith, presided over one of the great unqualified successes of the administration, the reconstruction of antitrust law on market-oriented principles. But Smith, who had been Ronald Reagan's own personal lawyer before 1980, was also the administration's proudest budget-buster. Needless to say, as Smith wrote in his posthumously published memoirs, he was "in sympathy with the goal of reducing government spending." However, "law enforcement and the DOJ were different from other agencies of the government. . . . The function of the Department of Justice is much more akin to that of the Department of Defense than to other agencies. . . . The Department of Justice, in our opinion, was truly involved in domestic defense." The rest of the administration, Smith reported happily, came to see things his way. "During my time there, DOJ's budget for law enforcement doubled, going from $2.1 billion in 1981 to $3.7 billion in 1985, which represented the greatest percentage increase of any department or agency—including the Department of Defense."[15] Throw in the non–law enforcement parts of the department's budget, and by the time Smith returned to his law practice in California, the Department of Justice was costing the taxpayers 50 percent more than it had in 1981. After four years under Smith's successor, Edwin Meese, the department was spending exactly twice as much as it had in 1981.

The National Aeronautic and Space Administration also unexpectedly turned out to be vital to national security. William F. Buckley noticed in the 1960s that the greater the distance between the place where revenue is raised and the place in which it is spent, the better liberals like it: they prefer county to municipal taxes, state taxes to county taxes, federal taxes to state taxes, and (if it could only be!) United Nations taxes to federal taxes. In an equivalent quirk of psychology, the farther from the earth's surface that government money is spent, the better conservatives like it. The space agency's pharaonically costly and pointless programs—the space shuttle, the manned space station, its yearned-for manned voyage to Mars—found their staunchest defenders on the Republican Right. Newt Gingrich explained to the 1984 Conservative Political Action Committee meeting "why liberals oppose a strong American presence in space." (Answer: because they hate America.) Reagan himself, and later Vice President Quayle and Chief of Staff John Sununu, would succumb to the heroics of space flight. Even in the austere year of 1981, NASA beat an 11 percent raise for the agency out of David Stockman. By 1986, the NASA budget had jumped 75 percent. On George Bush's inauguration day, NASA was spending twice as much as it had been on Ronald Reagan's. As of Bill Clinton's, its budget had hopped up another 33 percent.

Budget hawks are always muttering about cutting off the farmers. Yet farmers are the staunchest Republican voters this side of Park Avenue. And so room was found within the framework of conservatism for another grand exception. More than half of all farm debt is now held not by flinty bankers but by the warmhearted folks of the federal farm credit system—who forgave almost $9 billion in farm debt just six months before the 1988 election. (Bush ran strongly in the farm belt that year.) Shortly before leaving office, President Reagan signed legislation to enlarge the farm credit system further still, creating the Federal Agricultural Mortgage Corporation, authorized to guarantee loans of up to 80 percent of the value of a farm, up to a maximum of $2.5 million per farm. In 1981, as farmers suffered the pain of low crop prices and high interest rates on all the money they had borrowed in the giddy inflationary late 1970s, conservative Republican and Democratic legislatures salved their hurt with a new farm assistance program. The scheme tripled their federal aid, from $9.8 billion in 1981 to $29.6 billion in 1986. (To put that gift in perspective: the extra $20 billion the farmers got in 1986 was nearly three times the entire federal contribution to Aid to Families with Dependent Children that year.)

Almost as sacred to conservatives as the farmer is the small businessman. Since its creation by President Eisenhower, the Small Business Administration has exemplified almost everything that's wrong with the modern state. Its creditworthy borrowers could obtain financing from banks; its noncreditworthy borrowers should not be obtaining financing at all. It maintains its existence by granting preferential access to credit to borrowers with political connections, or who come from politically powerful regions, or who belong to favored minority groups. And yet, faced with a proposal to shut the wasteful thing down, the man Reagan had appointed to run it personally lobbied Congress to keep the SBA in business—and went unreprimanded by the White House. True, the agency did not survive unscathed. Its $2 billion budget in 1980 was battered to $510 million in 1984 and $85 million in 1989. Survive, however, it did. In the final year of the Bush administration, it managed to extract $975 million from the Treasury.

Dearest of all Republican constituencies is the veterans. In the 1980s, the great cohort of World War II veterans reached their sixties—the age at which people begin to make heavy use of medical care. This enormous crowd of people (the enlistment of the U.S. armed forces peaked at nearly 13 million uniformed servicemen and women in 1945) started to show up at the Veterans' Administration hospitals at exactly the same moment that a great medical technology cost inflation set in. In 1980, the VA spent $21 billion. In 1989, the agency—now a fully fledged cabinet department—spent $30 billion; in 1992, the year the eighteen-year-olds of 1945 turned 65, $34 billion. Harry Walters, Reagan's first head of the VA, cheerfully recalls that all he had to do to kill any Stockmanesque hint of skimping on these sums was to suggest with a smile that they take the matter up with the president. Everyone knew what the president would say.[16]

The argument that the Reagan gambit argue might have worked if only George Bush had not lost his nerve in 1990 and signed his wicked budget agreement—that indeed the gambit *had* worked until George Bush betrayed it—rests, more or less, on the fact that federal spending as a share of GNP slid from 24.4 percent in 1983 to 22.1 percent in 1989, before zooming back up to 25 percent in President Bush's last year in office.*

Doesn't that show, the diehards ask, that the country was growing its way out of the deficit even without radical surgery on popular government programs? But there is another way to look at the budget, and it suggests truths less comfortable to conservatives. In reality, federal spending rose explosively during the golden age of Reagan. Between 1983 and 1989, federal spending jumped from $808 billion to $1,144 billion (in constant 1990 dollars). The spending-GNP ratio sank because gross national product was then zipping upward even faster than federal expenditure. But booms do not last forever, and government spending programs do.

Admittedly, the Bush administration was slacker on spending than the Reagan administration. But the spending-GNP ratio depicts Bush in an unfairly harsh light for one other reason. It was not until 1988 that the bill for the savings and loan debacle began to arrive: $10 billion that year, $22 billion the next, $58 billion in fiscal 1990, $66 billion in 1991, and $80 billion in 1992. George Bush did not cause this disaster, but, once

*These are fiscal years.

the disaster occurred, Bush had no option but to pay its cost. And the Reagan budget record looks even less parsimonious if you consider only the domestic budget. After 1985, the defense budget actually shrank, opening room for more domestic spending without bumping the overall spending totals.

In other words, the Reagan administration managed to reduce the federal government's grab at GNP only so long as Congress overrode its wishes on defense spending, the bill for the savings and loan debacle could be postponed, and the economy boomed. Not a sustainable set of conditions. Without them, the Reagan administrations look nearly as spendthrift as Bush's administration. "There turned out," notes former Reagan economic adviser William Niskanen,

> to be relatively few consistent fiscal conservatives in the administration or in either party in Congress. Many of the smaller programs that constitute the American welfare state were created under Republican presidents and continue to be defended by Republicans in Congress. All too often, the conservatives in both parties were more protective of programs that served their own states and favored constituencies than of their commitment to a responsible fiscal policy.[17]

Foremost among those inconsistent fiscal conservatives was the president himself. In his memoirs, Reagan quotes from his personal diary for 1982: "The press is trying to paint me as now trying to undo the New Deal. I remind them that I voted for FDR four times. I'm trying to undo the 'Great Society.' It was LBJ's war on poverty that led us to our present mess."[18] Even if we take seriously Reagan's claim that he wanted to undo the Great Society, protecting the New Deal meant protecting the farm programs, the veterans' programs, the vast apparatus of government-guaranteed credit, and the biggest, costliest single federal expenditure of them all: Social Security. But of course Reagan's claim about the Great Society cannot be taken seriously. The spending program that above all others

busted the Reagan administration's budgets was the most daring of all Great Society schemes—Medicare. Medicare absorbs
most of the medical costs of the nonindigent elderly. The federal authorities set the basic rules that govern the program: beneficiaries must be over sixty-five; certain procedures are covered, others are not; and so on. Beyond that, the expense of the
program is limited only by the appetites of the old for medical
treatment and the ingenuity of doctors and hospitals in invent-
ing treatments.

In its first year of operation, 1966, Medicare cost $64 mil-
lion, rather less than the federal government spent on student
exchange programs that year. Critics at the time feared that
Medicare might cost as much as $10 billion by the end of the
century. If only the critics had been right. Like a virus, the program's $6 billion cost in 1970 doubled to $13 billion in 1975
and doubled again to $32 billion in 1980. The virus could not
metastasize at this pace forever without killing its host. But
what to do? Medicare could—option one—have been abolished
outright. Campaigning for Barry Goldwater, Ronald Reagan
had denounced the still unenacted program as socialized medicine. As president himself, how could he live with such a mark
of infamy upon his administration?

Easily, it turned out. So—option two—the program could
have been radically reformed to create incentives for doctors
and hospitals to save money. Discussions of Medicare too often
take for granted the premise that advances in medical technology must cost more money. But in every other field of life,
technological advance saves money. The computer I'm writing
on is smart enough, its advertisements say, to fly a jet. It cost
less, after inflation, than the IBM Selectric I coveted as an
undergraduate. I can fly to London from New York for less
money in real terms than it would have cost to take the Twentieth Century Limited to Chicago two generations ago. It's not
technology that raises costs, or not technology alone; it's technology plus the absence of price competition. But sad to say,
installing incentives to induce a government-financed industry

to cut costs while improving service is neither intellectually nor politically easy. The Reagan administration preferred to think about other things.

That leaves two final options: either do nothing at all or else impose administrative caps upon the program's costs—by, for example, raising the age of eligibility, reducing the number of procedures covered, or shrinking the portion of the cost of medical care met by government. This last option had the disadvantage of being bitterly unpopular. Ronald Reagan specifically abjured it in the 1984 campaign, pledging never to ask Medicare patients to pay a larger portion of their medical bills.

In the end the Reagan administration settled upon a judicious mixture of options three and four: onto a basic policy of doing nothing, it superimposed a complex system of price controls in 1983, which set caps on payments to hospitals for 468 different groups of illnesses. The mixture did not work very well, not from the taxpayer's point of view anyway: the cost of the Medicare program rose by an average of nearly 12 percent a year between 1980 and 1993, by which time it was gulping down more than 11 percent of all federal revenues. It was Medicare more than any other program that unbalanced the budget and corroded support for the Reagan tax cuts. Worse, the vast flood of Medicare money drove up the cost of all medical procedures, consuming employer profits that might otherwise have raised cash wages and tempting employers to tighten the generosity of the benefits they offered. Fear for the safety of wages and health benefits, in turn, fueled the voter anxiety that booted George Bush out of the Oval Office. If Reagan had understood a little more clearly the full implications of conservatism's can't-get-something-for-nothing wisdom, Bush might still be pitching horseshoes on the White House lawn.

But the consequences of the fantastic cost of unlimited free medical care were at first easy to ignore. For a short time, Ronald Reagan's government delivered an amazing thing to the American voting public: post–Great Society government at pre–Great Society prices. In 1983, the federal government took

proportionally less in taxes out of the private economy than it
had at any time since 1966, without any substantial reduction
in the scope of federal benefits. That's an intoxicating mix,
especially when combined with a booming economy. The few
remaining hardliners who urged spending cuts onto the administration looked grouchy and irrelevant. When confronted with
a plan to trim the Social Security program in September 1981,
Jack Kemp spoke for the new view. "What happened to the
party of growth and opportunity? At the first sign of trouble,
we're being stampeded into the slash and cut medicine that
kept us in the minority for decades. This is just more root canal
politics. I won't apologize for the deficit for a minute, but we
can't be panicked by it either."[19] Kemp was echoed by some of
the best brains in conservative journalism. "Social Security,"
wrote the most prominent of the young "Third Generation"
conservatives, Dinesh D'Souza, "however inefficient, is not a
handout but an earned benefit; it would be cruel, not to say
politically unpopular, for government to renege on its promise
to the elderly."[20] "A conservative doctrine of the welfare state,"
George Will agreed, "is required if conservatives are even to be
included in the contemporary political conversation."[21]

Conservatives did have a doctrine of the welfare state: the
doctrine was that the welfare state should be allowed to hurtle
forward whenever the political cost of halting it was likely to be
inconvenient in the shortest of short runs. A cruel joke of the
1980s went: it's not that Ronald Reagan lacks principles, it's
just that he does not understand the ones he has. The two
greatest fiscal catastrophes of the Reagan era both took place
because the joke was not completely false; because a conservative administration set out the crystal and china for the world's
costliest pair of free lunches: Medicare and deposit insurance.
And, in an almost annoyingly neat outburst of poetic justice, it
was the indigestion from these high-fat meals that brought
twelve years of Republican rule to their end. Just as Medicare's
costs depressed personal incomes, the failure of the savings and
loans constricted the nation's money supply and deflated the

economy. The ensuing recession was the most protracted of the postwar era. And the 1992 election occurred nearly thirty months into it.

The savings and loan industry was already a ticking time bomb when the Republicans took power in 1980. Even by the sunny accounting methods preferred by the savings and loans, 30 percent of all thrifts were losing money in the second half of 1980; the total profits of the industry as a whole had slumped by 75 percent from their level two years before.[22] Savings and loans were preinflationary institutions that had survived into an inflationary world. They borrowed money at the market's fluxuating interest rates and lent it at fixed rates as ten-, fifteen-, and thirty-year mortgages. When the prevailing interest rate shot up to 14 percent and more, a savings and loan with its money lent out for the next two decades at 7 percent flopped in pain like a fish on hot sand. So in 1980, the thrifts' friends in Congress again set out to save them, as they had so often done since the mid-1960s, when the industry first fell victim to unstable money. This time Congress raised the maximum size of a federally insured deposit to $100,000 from $40,000, with no limits on the number of accounts a depositor could have. Now the thrifts could borrow much larger sums of money. But since the greater the amount of their 14 percent borrowings, the greater the loss on their 7 percent lendings, this solution could only be a partial one.

Afterward, as titanic estimates of the carnage rolled in— $100 billion, $200 billion, $500 billion—Republican partisans fingered the Democratic Congress as the culprit. And there were plenty of Democratic culprits. Democratic congressmen lolled on savings and loan yachts, ate at savings and loan banquets, dallied with savings and loan whores. Democratic congressmen, led by Speaker Jim Wright, who came from Texas where the conduct of the savings and loans had been particularly egregious, refused to vote the money that the deposit insurance system needed to shut insolvent thrifts down, postponing the thrifts' demise and permitting them more time in which to run up even more colossal debts. Democratic congressmen enacted the Competitive Equality Banking Act of 1987, which ordered bank regulators to exercise "forbearance" in dealing with busted savings and loans in depressed areas of the country, such as, for example, Speaker Wright's Texas.

But that's not the whole story. Yes, of course the congressional Democrats deserve obloquy for prolonging the savings and loan spree and raising the cost of the final bailout from the $100 billion that would have been incurred as late as 1985—by which time the magnitude of the savings and loan collapse was clear to anyone who cared to know—to whatever the final reckoning will prove to be. What else would one expect of them? But it is as true, and as shameful, that the Reagan administration handed out the credit cards that made the spree possible— and did so in flagrant violation of its own professed principles. It was no Democratic congressman who signed the Garn–St. Germain Act of 1982 that sent the thrifts off to the heads-I-win-tails-the-taxpayer-loses casino. "I think we've hit a home run today," Reagan said as he handed over the presidential pen, and in a sense he was right. This particular ball would fly farther and faster than anyone could have conceived. Garn–St. Germain repealed the restrictions that confined the savings and loans to residential mortgage lending. Now they were free to try their luck at every three-card monte stand in town. In April 1982, Richard Pratt, the Reaganite chief thrift regulator, eliminated the rule requiring thrifts to divide their ownership among at least 400 shareholders. From now on, a savings and loan owned by just one man could borrow unlimited amounts of money in $100,000 tranches backed by the full faith and credit of the government of the United States. The following year, regulators dropped the amount of personal capital that a savings and loan owner must have at risk in the thrift from 4 percent of the money out on loan to 3 percent. (It had been 5 percent until 1980.) But because all these figures were calculated as five-year averages, a rapidly growing thrift could remain in business with radically less capital. And if even that obligation was too stringent, Garn–St. Germain enabled thrifts to issue "net worth certificates"—scout's honor promises that they could lay hands on some money if they really needed to—and use them instead of cash in counting their capital.

Now suppose a savings and loan used all these concessions, and did business with as little as half a million in capital. And suppose that, despite all its government had done for it, one of the thrift's loans failed anyway, wiping out that half a million. Goodbye savings and loan, right? Certainly not: thrift accounting rules permitted it to take as long as ten years to recognize the loss on its balance sheet. Until then, it could stay in business, borrowing money at the taxpayer's risk, lending it to whomever it liked, with no capital of its own whatsoever, or even with a negative net worth of hundreds of millions of dollars.

Thanks to techniques like these, the number of thrifts deemed insolvent by Washington dipped from an uncomfortable seventy-one in 1982 to a bearable forty-eight in 1983. The number, however, that were solvent according to the regulators but insolvent according to generally accepted accounting principles rose and rose and rose: 166 in 1982, 245 in 1983, and 374 in 1984.[23]

In 1980, the ideologically consistent Reaganite answer to the problem of failing thrifts was utterly straightforward: close them. Deposit insurance, like Medicare, like any invitation to spend or borrow money at somebody else's expense, is an invitation to recklessness. But about the last thing that an administration accused of Herbert Hooverism needed in the midst of a grueling recession was a coast-to-coast string of bank failures. The strict logic of free enterprise welcomed these failures, but the strict logic of free enterprise clashed, as it so often does, with a tacit but far more powerful conservative axiom: respect for the independent businessman as the salt of the earth. Republicans saw the savings and loan owners as honest bankers plunged into trouble through no fault of their own by a government that had irresponsibly generated inflation. Just as Reagan was persuaded in 1981 that the big three automakers deserved protection from Japanese imports because federal mileage and safety regulations had made them uncompetitive (although the Japanese were subject to the same regulations), so conservatives convinced themselves that the savings and loan operators deserved relief.

The relief effort, as we all know, failed. By the late summer of 1990, some 600 thrifts had shut down, and fewer than half of the 2,500 that survived could be considered healthy. Over-building, much of it financed by thrifts, had by then shattered real estate markets throughout the country. It's not inconceivable that the recession then beginning was in some way made worse by the income tax increase George Bush agreed to in October. But it was the excessive delay in snuffing out the thrifts and all the inevitably ensuing consequences of the day that caused and prolonged the economic troubles of the early 1990s.

The Reagan administration consented to the savings and loan disaster for many reasons, but at the bottom of them all was one damning weakness: it could not abide the consequences of applying its free-market principles to residential mortgage lending. Even if the Reagan administration had some-how summoned up the courage to tell the savings and loan operators of 1981 that, sorry, they were out of business; even if they could have told the old folks of Sun City that from now it was their responsibility to investigate the soundness of the banks in which they deposited their money, not the federal government's; even then, the administration would have quailed before the task of telling the great home-owning middle class that mortgages from now on would be written by unsubsidized lenders.

Everywhere that middle-class home ownership clashed with free market orthodoxy in the Reagan years, home ownership won. Since the war, the federal government had intervened in the mortgage market to help favored borrowers get housing credit. That's how Levittown got built. Still, as late as 1970, the mortgage market was overwhelmingly a private one. Only 7.7 percent of private residential mortgages were protected by any federal support in 1970, and fewer than 3 percent enjoyed an unconditional federal guarantee, that is, a promise that the federal government would pay the mortgage if the homeowner could not. Then came party time. Between 1970 and 1980, the federal role in private residential mortgage finance doubled: now 18.8 percent of residential mortages were supported by the federal government; 11.4 percent with an unconditional guarantee. And between 1980 and 1989, the federal role doubled again. When Ronald Reagan moved into his California retirement house—appropriately enough, one paid for by other people—38.2 percent of all American home mortgages were federally backed. The mortgage risk of almost 40 percent of American home buyers had been effectively nationalized.[24]

So, indeed, had much of the rest of the risk in the American economy. In order to disguise the cost of government, the Reagan and Bush administrations had converted many programs of direct assistance—such as grants to college students—to government-guaranteed loans. By the end of the Reagan years, the U.S. government would have directly lent $250 billion to private borrowers, and guaranteed another $450 billion in borrowing. With $700 billion in "assets," Uncle Sam's bank was larger than Citibank, the Bank of America, the General Motors Acceptance Corporation, the Chase Manhattan Bank, Chemical Bank, and NationsBank combined. The term "assets" belongs in quotation marks, because—despite the slap-happy lending standards of banks and savings and loans in the 1980s—federal credits were three times more likely to be defaulted upon than private-sector obligations.

By the end of the 1980s, denial was no longer possible. As wasteful as the federal government undoubtedly is, there is no feasible way to lighten its burden other than by yanking goodies away from the voters. Reagan's escape route was blocked. As Conservatives absorbed the failure of the Reagan gambit, their interest in the whole tedious budget business visibly waned.

Permanent reductions in taxes required endless, dogged resistance to the acrimonious demands of insatiable interest groups—not only unappealing groups, like welfare mothers, but attractive, patriotic, Republican groups, like veterans, farmers, and the elderly. Who wanted to say "no" all the time? Who wanted to alienate the Reagan Democrats? Who wanted to concede leadership of the conservative movement to nerds with calculators? Especially when the country was gripped by a far graver crisis, and one that engaged conservatives' passions far more intensely than the budget now did: the crisis of "the culture."

One late-nineteenth-century morning, an old joke goes, two Viennese Jews meet at the rack of bamboo newspaper holders in their neighborhood cafe. Goldstein reaches for the leading liberal daily; Rosenzweig takes a scurrilous anti-Semitic tabloid.

"Good God, Herr Rosenzweig," says Goldstein, "what are you picking up that garbage for?"

"I'll tell you," Rosenzweig answers. "In your paper, I read about old Jewish men murdered in Romania, about Jewish women raped by Cossacks in Russia, about Captain Dreyfus unjustly accused in France. In this one, I read that Jews control the banks and stock exchanges, that we hoard sacks of gold in our cellars, that every government on earth trembles at our orders. I prefer good news."

It became something of a commonplace, in the more touchy-feely precincts of liberalism, to complain during the 1980s about something called the "culture of Reaganism." Apparently America had been seized by a paroxysm of greed, materialism, and religious fanaticism. You could read about it in *Dissent,* the *Village Voice,* and *Tikkun,* in the *Nation* (on its sloppier days), and in the suddenly abundant academic journals of a curious new field called cultural studies. It was never very clear what exactly the phrase was supposed to mean, but conservatives derived a secret pleasure from reading these jeremiads. The gratification was, however, sadly brief. Sooner or later, the conservative put down his copy of *Tikkun,* or stepped out of the theater from whose stage some actor had been hectoring him, and then his cultural powerlessness smacked him in the face.

What are you talking about? conservatives would think. You fellows still run all of high culture: the museums, the theaters, the publishing houses. You set the tone of most mass entertainment: television drama, sitcoms, and talk shows; pop music; and Hollywood. You predominate in the news media and the mainline churches. The education of the young, from the day they first flick on "Sesame Street" until the day they leave law school, is your uncontested domain. You set the tone of national life; you determine what sort of satire is funny and what is offensive; you control taste, fashion, and etiquette. Despite all our election victories, the country is still rushing into a permissive, multicultural future. We had the presidency for twelve years—but you still form the nation's culture.

As frequently as they would use the word "culture," it was never entirely clear what conservatives meant by it. Some, like Hilton Kramer and Samuel Lipman of *The New Criterion,* seemed to use the term "culture" to mean "cultcha"—arts and letters, the sciences, intellectual life generally. Even Pat Buchanan was moved to promise, in one of his campaign speeches, "We cannot stop with simply defunding agencies. We must also seek out and support poets, writers, painters, sculptors and architects who are truly great and deserving of patronage. In the coming Golden Age of America, we must not only dump over the cult of Mapplethorpe, we must replace him with an American Michelangelo."[25]

Others, like Midge Decter and Bill Bennett, used the word morality too—and in particular, the attitude of the mass media, the entertainment industry, and the nation's religious, political, and intellectual leaders toward morality. Others still, like the editors of *Chronicles* magazine, which subtitles itself a "magazine of American culture," adopted the term in almost an anthropological sense, to mean the civilization created on this continent by European immigrants—a civilization now in danger from its non-European elements. But whatever they might individually mean by the word "culture," conservatives of all stripes infused it with desperate meaning.

Some might object that there is something more than a little ludicrous about the American conservative movement presenting itself as a defender of artistic excellence. Few intellectual movements have ever displayed so much philistinism so proudly. Jack Kemp numbers the *Wizard of Oz* among the supreme artistic achievements of the American people—an opinion that would command a depressing number of assents on the Right. Early in 1993, *Chronicles* magazine devoted an issue to a celebration of the sort of visual art that it thought conservatives ought to be supporting: softly pornographic female figures, tempest-tossed seas, and vapid still lifes; in other words, kitsch—maybe an improvement over the Frederic Remington bronzes that Ronald Reagan fancied, but kitsch all the same.

But then, perhaps a little dose of philistinism was a useful innoculation against the perversities of high culture in the 1980s: the huge, crudely executed canvases sprawling with figures of Central American soldiers and martyred old bag ladies; the Whitney exhibition that passed out buttons reading "I can't imagine wanting to be white" in place of admission tickets; the thin little novels bearing gold stars from the profs at the Iowa writing school. Politics in a work of art is like a pistol shot in the middle of a symphony, Stendhal had said; to conservative art critics, the art of the 1980s was a free-fire zone. The plight of the academy was even more dismal. There is "a remarkable unity of purpose" to the hotsy-totsy theories prevalent on campus, observed *New Criterion* editor Roger Kimball in his book *Tenured Radicals*: "nothing less than the destruction of the values, methods, and goals of traditional humanistic study."[26] The ideologies conservatives blamed for the destruction of the universities and the arts were the same ideologies responsible for the corrosion of the moral life of the larger society. From José

Serrano's NEA-subsidized photographs of crucifixes submerged in urine it was but a step to Madonna simulating sex with a black Jesus on cable television; it was an even shorter step from Madonna to ACT-UP's disruptions of Roman Catholic masses and desecrations of the Host. The collapse of standards in high culture, conservatives felt, proceeded in neat tandem with the degradation of ordinary life.

If there had been any one thing that had distinguished the conservatism of the 1970s from earlier versions of the philosophy, it was a new faith in the goodness of ordinary people. Heavily influenced by the gloomier Roman Catholic theologians, the older generation of conservative thinkers questioned whether the ordinary man was quite all that he was cracked up to be. The happy conservatism of the 1970s felt no such doubts. Were public morals and decency in decline? Don't blame the people; blame the IRS. "A thousand people can grow up to produce opera, Broadway musicals, or a *Wizard of Oz*. A few generations later, with government in the way, a thousand people are born to create; but of the fraction who survive the system, many end up making porno."[27] This cheerful thought, as unconvincing as it would have seemed to the dominant conservative school of the 1950s and early 1960s, which stressed the need for the firm smack of authority, has an ideologically impeccable pedigree of its own, traceable to a conservative theorist named Frank Meyer. Meyer argued that in a traditionalist society, libertarian means achieve conservative ends. Since the American people were God-fearing, patriotic, and morally responsible, if left alone they would form a society in which any conservative could be comfortable. It was government that was responsible for any antitraditional tendencies in American life. But over the 1980s, as every social indicator important to conservatives pointed further and further into the danger zone, an awful doubt began to spread among them: what if the American people were ceasing to be as God-fearing, patriotic, and morally responsible as they used to be? What if government were not the only—nor even the worst—subversive force?

The more loudly and forcefully conservatives made that point, the more they found themselves doubting the Meyer thesis that curbing government was the best way to promote virtue among the people. It was evident that after twelve years of fruitless attempts to curb government, the American people were less virtuous than ever. Maybe the Meyer thesis was wrong; maybe curbing government was just too difficult. Either way, it seemed that the best course was to promote virtue a little more directly.

In the late 1970s, there was no more radical proponent of the Meyer thesis than George Gilder. Cut tax rates, Gilder argued in his hugely influential 1981 book, *Wealth and Poverty*, and morality will revivify. High taxes

> penalize the family that depends on a single earner who is fully and resourcefully dedicated to his career. Two half-hearted participants in the labor force can do better than one who is competing aggressively for the relatively few jobs in the upper echelons. . . . What has been happening is a drive, conscious or not, to flush the wife out of the untaxed household economy and into the arms of the IRS. . . .
>
> As families break down under the pressures of taxes and welfare, moral constraints tend to dissolve, mobility and anonymity increase, economic transactions become less traceable, and the temptations grow for concealed and undocumented income.[28]

Ten years later the tax code was no longer so steeply progressive, and welfare was less generous than at any time since the mid-1960s. Yet America in 1990 was producing more illegitimate babies and broken families, ingesting more drugs, suffering more crime, reveling in more obscenity, and trusting less in its institutions than in 1981. Every household connected to cable television received the twenty-four-hour at-home lubricity of MTV: pulsating sexual beats, gyrating near-naked bodies, and gleefully Dionysiac lyrics. "Rock music has one appeal only, a barbaric appeal to sexual desire—not love, not eros, but sexual desire undeveloped and untutored," Allan Bloom complained in his famous tirade against rock in *The Closing of the American Mind.*

> Picture a thirteen-year-old boy sitting in the living room of his family home doing his math assignment while wearing his Walkman headphones or watching MTV. He enjoys the liberties hard won over centuries by the alliance of philosophic genius and political heroism, consecrated by the blood of martyrs; he is provided with comfort and leisure by the most productive economy ever known to mankind; science has penetrated the secrets of nature in order to provide him with the marvelous, lifelike electronic sound and image reproduction he is enjoying. And in what does progress culminate? A prepubescent child whose body throbs with orgasmic rhythms; whose feelings are made articulate in hymns to the joys of onanism or the killing of parents; whose ambition is to win fame and wealth in imitating the drag-queen who makes the music.[29]

Not that the other channels are much of an improvement over MTV. "L.A. Law" broadcast television's first homosexual kiss. Graphic heterosexual sex, a rarity even in the movies two decades ago, can be seen on the networks every night. Diligent researchers at the American Family Association in Tupelo, Mississippi, counted 743 prime-time sex scenes on the three big networks during sweeps week in spring 1992. Eighty-seven percent of the sexual encounters, the group complained, occurred outside of marriage.[30] Twenty years earlier, Irving Kristol had wondered, "How can a bourgeois society survive in a cultural ambiance that derides every traditional bourgeois virtue and celebrates promiscuity, homosexuality, drugs, political terrorism—anything, in short, that is in bourgeois eyes perverse?"[31] Since then, the ambiance has grown in every measurable way worse.

For most of American history, an aesthetic and sexual

avant-garde had huddled fearfully against the edge of the continent on Manhattan Island, straining to flee over the Atlantic whenever the franc fell low enough. In the 1980s and early 1990s, the avant-garde got its revenge. The scourge of AIDS gave school boards across the country an excuse to promote teenage sexuality by distributing condoms and startlingly graphic sexual advice. Philistines who objected often found themselves on the wrong side of the civil rights laws. In 1981, Wisconsin became the first state in the nation to enact penalties against employers and landlords for refusing to contract with homosexuals. Massachusetts followed in 1989 and Hawaii in 1991. Another dozen states adopted protections for homosexuals employed in the public sector over the decade. In 1989, a New York court recognized homosexual lovers as family for purposes of the city's rent control statutes. New York, Los Angeles, Washington, D.C., and a dozen other cities have offered the homosexual lovers of their civil servants all the benefits of a wife or husband. Altogether, more than a hundred cities and counties have extended the protection of their laws to homosexuality.

To conservatives, the new acceptability of homosexuality was at worst defiance of the law of God, at the very least a symptom of society's waning comprehension of the distinction between the sexes. They were unhappily aware of the concessions their own presidents had made to sexual modernism. George Bush was the first president to order women into combat, in the 1989 invasion of Panama, but the steady redefinition of combat roles as noncombat roles that made Bush's action possible occurred quietly over the course of the Reagan defense buildup. It was during the Reagan administration too that the Equal Employment Opportunity Commission, under the leadership of Clarence Thomas, initiated its first investigations of sexual harassment, which a 1986 Supreme Court majority defined to include inappropriate comments or attitudes.

If it was sexual distinctions—and above all the sexual division of labor—that held the traditional family together, the erosion of those distinctions ought to precipitate family breakdown. So it did. Through the 1980s, conservatives watched horrified as the country hurtled toward a future of family instability more extreme than anything human beings have known since the age of famines and plagues. True, the divorce rate peaked in 1981 and has fallen slightly since then. But that's not quite the achievement it seems. American states radically liberalized their divorce laws in the 1970s. The rise in the divorce rate over that decade was driven by the bust up of marriages that dated back as far as the 1930s. There was, in other words, a big backlog of fragile marriages.[32] The slight dip in the divorce rate does not mean that this year's marriages are more stable than those of a decade ago, but merely that the backlog has been cleared.

Which is why the number of lives touched by divorce continues to grow. In 1960, there were forty-two currently divorced American women—that is, women who had divorced and not yet remarried—for every 1,000 married women living with their husbands. By 1980, the proportion of divorcees in the population had tripled, to 120. Despite the dip in the divorce rate, in 1990 there were 172 currently divorced women for every 1,000 married women. (The proportion of currently divorced men in the population is substantially lower, reflecting men's greater ability to remarry.)

As they witnessed the disintegration of marriages all around them, young men and women understandably hesitated to marry themselves. In the rapid sequence of happy images in the "Morning in America" campaign ad, a young bride threw her arms around her mother's neck. It may have been morning in America, but it sure was not wedding season: the 1988 crop of brides had delayed marriage longer than any cohort of women since 1940. In 1970, only 10 percent of the twenty-five- to twenty-nine-year-old women in America were still unmarried. Ten years later, 20 percent of these late-twentysomething women were, and by 1991, more than one-third of women in their late twenties had not married. Man shortage or no man shortage, in just two decades the number of husbandless women pushing thirty had tripled. The trend was the same for women in their early thirties: only 6 percent of them had never married in 1970, and still only 9 percent in 1980, but nearly 19 percent in 1991.

Some of the women delaying marriage were living with a man outside of marriage—an arrangement once scandalous, now nearly universal. A 1988 federal survey found that nearly 58 million American women had lived with a man out of marriage at one time or another. Many of them found that the consequence of postponing marriage was a life alone. Only slightly more than half of these cohabitations led ultimately to marriage. In 1970, there were 670,000 women between the ages of twenty-five and forty-four living alone. Twenty years later, there were more than 3 million. No wonder Nickelodeon broadcasts two episodes of the "Mary Tyler Moore Show" every night.

As the institution of marriage crumbled, so did America's once-stern condemnation of procreation outside marriage. Nearly one in five American children was born illegitimately in 1980; more than one in four by 1990. The problem is notoriously worst among blacks, but white illegitimacy spread in the Reagan and Bush years too: 17.7 percent of white children were illegitimate in 1990, up from 11 percent in 1980. Liberals often suggest that illegitimacy is the result of low self-esteem and lack of access to birth control. Conservatives see it as the logical consequence of society's abandonment of its ancient insistence upon female chastity. When asked at a Heritage symposium what should be done about single mothers, Midge Decter replied, "If we are talking about thirteen and fourteen year olds, the answer is to stop sleeping around. . . . What is needed is not a new government program, but a new ethos— one in which these little girls will be encouraged to keep their knees together until they grow up and find husbands."[33]

Conservatives nodded their heads when Charles Murray warned, in an October 1993 *Wall Street Journal* article, that fatherlessness was America's prime social problem. Fatherlessness, said Murray, had brought into existence a *Lord of the Flies* society of ungovernable young men, first in the black ghettoes, but very soon—as white illegitimacy rates rose—in lower-class white areas as well. Add children of the divorced to the illegitimate, and a total of one-quarter of all American children lived with only one parent by 1990. If they felt in an especially gloomy mood, conservatives could factor into their *Lord of the Flies* scenario not just the fatherless, but also latchkey children and children raised in impersonal institutions. More than half of all married women whose youngest child was less than twelve months old worked in 1991. A vast new childcare industry was summoned into being in the 1980s. By decade's end, 30 percent of children under five spent their days in the care of non-relatives.[34]

To pro-life conservatives, the ghastliest proof of the unabated decay of American morality in the Reagan 1980s was the administration's diffidence in the face of what seemed to pro-lifers a crime so horrible that they had to wonder when and how divine retribution would crash down upon the land: the killing by abortion of nearly 2 million children a year. True, Ronald Reagan had, as president, published an essay denouncing abortion, and appointed one justice, Antonin Scalia, who agreed that *Roe v. Wade* was wrongly decided. Otherwise, though, Reagan accomplished relatively little for the anti-abortion cause. Two of Reagan's three appointees, Sandra Day O'Connor and Anthony M. Kennedy, and one of Bush's, David Souter, voted to uphold the essential principle of *Roe*—that abortion is a constitutional right—in what will likely prove to be the Court's last reproductive rights case for many years, *Planned Parenthood v. Casey*. When that same allegedly conservative Court was asked in the 1991 case of *Lee v. Weisman* whether it was permissible to invite a clergyman to deliver an invocation mentioning God at a high school graduation ceremony, it replied no, by a five-to-four vote.[35]

Americans, Patrick Buchanan wrote in his 1988 autobiography, "no longer share the same religious faith, the same code of morality, the same public philosophy. . . . Our politics partake of the savagery of religious wars because, at bottom, they are religious wars."[36] And in 1992, religious conservatives believed their side was still losing.

It would be absurd to suggest that anything that the Reagan administration consciously did—other perhaps than goose the job market and thus entice women to work outside the home— was responsible for the family's troubles in the 1980s. But conservatives were queasily aware that the Reagan administration had done little to help either. The American family's essential problem is that it is the one involuntary association—other than the state itself—that survives in American life. You can quit your church, change your ethnic name, and chuck your job, but there's nothing you can do about your relatives. The spirit of the family is at odds with the individualism that prevails throughout American society. The family has survived, even so, because individuals need their families to protect them in childhood, provide for them in old age, nurse them in sickness, and tide them over in hard times. Houston's family values orators were attempting to warn the country that state services can render those family economic functions redundant. How big a catastrophe this is depends on how self-reliant you are. The educated and the capable, particularly educated and capable men, can prosper despite the family's decrepitude. The strong can live alone, but the weak cannot. "It may be true," opined the editors of the *Wall Street Journal*,

> that most of the people in Hollywood who did cocaine survived it, but many of the weaker members of the community hit the wall. And most of the teenage girls in the Midwest who learn about the nuances of sex from magazines published by thirtysomething women in New York will more or less survive, but some continue to end up as prostitutes on Eighth Avenue. Everyone today seems to know someone who couldn't handle the turns and went over the side of the mountain.

These weaker or more vulnerable people, who in different ways must try to live along life's margins, are among the reasons that a society erects rules. They're guardrails.[37]

Nobody hit the wall harder than poor urban blacks. Just as the collapse of intellectual and aesthetic standards in the universities and the art world exacerbated the decline of moral standards in the general public, so declining public morality weakened the cohesion of American society, by creating and enlarging a poor black underclass that stood apart from, and threatened, middle-class society.

Who was to blame? Bill Bennett might manfully insist that the corruption originated in the uppermost stratum of American life: "Over the last twenty years or so, the traditional values of the American people have come under steady fire, with the heavy artillery supplied by intellectuals."[38] Other, grimmer conservatives thought the danger came from below: from the ghettoes and from immigrants. Samuel Francis, the political columnist for *Chronicles*, observed with horror that

the historic core of American civilization is under attack. Quotas, affirmative action, race norming, civil rights legislation, multiculturalism in schools and universities, welfare, busing, and unrestricted immigration from Third World countries are all symbols of that attack and of the racial, cultural, and political dispossession they promise to inflict upon the white post-bourgeois middle class.[39]

Certainly the greater visibility of an apparently burgeoning black underclass preoccupied conservatives more than ever at the end of the 1980s. In the 1960s, black adolescent girls who made the two mistakes of dropping out of high school and giving birth out of wedlock had a 22 percent chance of ending up on welfare by age twenty-five. In the early 1980s, black girls who made those same two mistakes had a 48 percent chance of a life on welfare.[40]

Happily, one of those two mistakes did become less common among blacks in the 1980s: the number of blacks dropping out of high school fell substantially between 1970 and 1990, although at the price of steadily less-demanding curricula. But the other underclass mistake, illegitimacy, gobbled up all the gains from rising black educational attainment. Four out of five children in inner-city areas like the Bedford-Stuyvesant district of New York were born to unmarried women. Marriage withered even among middle-class blacks: more than one-quarter of black women aged thirty to thirty-nine never marry at all.[41] It was this family breakdown, conservatives insisted, that accounted for the calamities of the black poor in the 1980s. Conservative demographer Nicholas Eberstadt found that it was marriage or nonmarriage—not race, not class, not age, and not the presence or absence of prenatal programs—that best predicted a woman's chance of giving birth to a healthy child. An unmarried white college graduate was less likely to bear a healthy child than a married black high school dropout. Nonmarriage accounts for black America's heartbreaking infant mortality. While white America's infant mortality rate is improved on by only three countries in the world—Japan, Sweden, and Switzerland—the black infant mortality rate, which is more than twice as high, lags behind Bulgaria's. Among blacks in Washington, D.C., the infant mortality rate trails that of Panama, Yugoslavia, and the ex–Soviet Union—despite city-funded door-to-door prenatal health services.

Family breakdown explained, too, the rise in the crime rate among the black poor. Statisticians had expected crime rates for the country as a whole to fall as the population aged in the 1980s, and so they did between 1980 and 1985. That expectation reckoned with crack, a cheap smokable cocaine that seduced thousands of fatherless teenagers. Crime financed the crack user's addiction. The new wave of criminality hit not just the cities, but the nearer suburbs in which the black lower middle class had settled, such as Prince Georges County in Maryland and White Plains, New York. The nation suffered 28 percent more robberies, 23 percent more murders, and 45 percent more assaults in 1990 than it had in 1985. Half of all murder victims were black. Five hundred people, nearly all of them poor black men, were murdered in Washington, D.C., in 1990—as many homicides as in all of New England, a region with a population twenty-two times greater than the District's. Sometimes the violence turned inward: suicides among children under fourteen doubled during the 1980s.

America had once been "the best poor man's country in the world"—the country in which it was easiest to begin with nothing and rise to modest comfort and, given talent and drive, wealth. Suddenly the country appeared to be filled with poor people who had lost the will to seize opportunities: deranged old men pushing shopping carts filled with tin cans, haggard women shrieking curses on the streets of Kalorama and the Upper East Side. Few conservatives were impressed by the late Mitch Snyder's patently bogus claim that there were 3 million homeless people in the United States. Something between the Census Bureau's count of 250,000 and the Urban Institute's estimate of 600,000 seemed right. But nobody could deny that seven or eight years before there had seemed to be virtually none and that now there were lots. Nobody could deny either that America's inner cities had become more terrifying than ever, vast bleak expanses of concrete and broken glass, where drug dealers fire automatic pistols almost randomly, where young women of thirty-five have already become grandmothers, and where the people seem ignorant, violent, addicted, diseased, unemployable, and hopeless.

Many of the older neoconservatives had grown up in the very neighborhoods that now rank at the bottom of America's list of slums. Norman Podhoretz and Irving Kristol were both raised in poor areas of Brooklyn. For people like them, the plight of the black urban poor was especially poignant—and exasperating. "'Why can't they be as we were?'" Irving Kristol explained, is not just "the fogy's lament. . . . In truth it is a legitimate question—if it is meant seriously as a question, and not merely as a reproach."[42] Brownsville's Jews had seized the educational and career opportunities America extended to them; why didn't Brownsville's blacks? What was going wrong with America's escalator of ethnic mobility?And why can't we do something about it?

Even liberals conceded that America's integrity as a polity suffered because of the misconduct of violent and promiscuous poor people. "New York can spend all the money it wants . . . rebuilding Times Square," wrote *New Republic* contributor Mickey Kaus. "But if tourists continue to be murdered by roving 'wolfpacks,' Times Square will never be a place where most ordinary New Yorkers go unless they have to, and even then they'll hurry through looking over their shoulder and avoiding all possible human contact."[43]

Unlike Kaus, however, conservatives suspected that elements of the black elite were every bit as dangerous to American norms as the violent underclass. In the spring of 1987, a group of demonstrators led by Jesse Jackson assembled on the lawn of Stanford University to chant "Hey, hey, ho, ho, Western culture's got to go." They were referring to Stanford University's undergraduate curricular requirements, but the slogan lodged uneasily in conservative consciousnesses. This was what the whole cultural controversy was about, wasn't it? The Columbus quincentennial, multicultural curricula, the plaque at Little Big Horn—all these endless arguments reduce to whether or not the United States should remain primarily a society located in the Western cultural tradition. Western guilt and self-hatred are not new phenomena: they undergird the eighteenth-century noble savage myth and Gauguin's paintings. But in the Reagan 1980s, hostile critics of Western civilization achieved an unprecedented power and prominence—not just soapboxes on ghetto streetcorners, but museum curatorships, school trusteeships, university vice presidencies. New "Afrocentric" curricula popped up in American classrooms. The first appears to have emerged in Portland, Oregon, designed by Georgia State Professor Asa Hilliard. Washington, D.C., quickly followed, as did

Detroit and New York City. Just as little Vietnamese children began their history lesson with *"Nos ancêtres, les gallois"* during French colonial times, today little Vietnamese children in New York learn about "our ancestors who built Zimbabwe" and draw maps of Africa.

It was bad enough that black leaders wanted their people to be hived off in educational ghettoes, there to be taught that the ancient Egyptians invented the telephone. Worse, the rest of society was expected to wallow in self-hatred and self-abasement. The Stanford protesters succeeded in eliminating the Western culture requirement. Instead, all students must study a non-Western culture, and professors must give "substantial attention" to issues of race and, as it is now demurely if incorrectly called, "gender." Mount Holyoke and Dartmouth require courses in non-Western, but not in Western, civilization to graduate. Wisconsin demands an ethnic studies course but has no Western civilization or American history requirement. The effect of bombarding young people—and older people too—with constant sneering references to "whitemalepatriarchy" was to demoralize them. As the Cold War group the Committee for the Free World warned in its final December 1990 newsletter, "Even the citizens of a sturdy democracy cannot resist forever the erosions of a culture that continually disconfirms their beliefs, their principles, their very daily lives. A demoralized society cannot mount a defense of itself, in the end not even in that bedrock definition of defense as the military means necessary to hold off an enemy bent on your destruction."[44]

Nor was it the underclass that challenged the conservative ideal that life's rewards ought to be distributed at least roughly according to achievement. America's goodies are now divided up like loot from a sacked city, distributed by politicians in proportion to race, ethnicity, and sex. By an intellectual process not dissimilar to that which transformed slavery from a necessary evil in the minds of eighteenth-century Southerners to a positive good by the nineteenth century, the "affirmative action" of the 1970s—acknowledged by its practitioners to be an unfortunate deviation from the merit principle—evolved into the "diversity" of the 1980s. Since most federal, public-sector affirmative action is a product of executive orders, Ronald Reagan at any moment in his presidency could have abolished the noxious thing with a few signatures. He never dared. And when the Supreme Court finally delivered the abolition of local government and private-sector affirmative action to George Bush, neatly gift wrapped in the 1988 *Birmingham Firefighters* decision, he could not rush to the return counter fast enough. Then, the 1989 decision *Ward's Cove v. Atonio* told civil rights plaintiffs that they could no longer win job discrimination cases by invoking statistical evidence of minority underrepresentation. They would have to prove instead that they themselves had suffered discrimination personally. Taken together, *Birmingham Firefighters* and *Ward's Cove* created a new rule of law: civil rights plaintiffs must prove actual wrongdoing before they could collect, and the standard of proof for white and black plaintiffs would be equal. These were the cases overturned, and more, by the Civil Rights Act of 1991, with the votes of 38 Republican senators and 128 Republican representatives, and the signature of a Republican president who had pledged never to sign a "quota bill."

It was an expensive surrender. Peter Brimelow and Leslie Spencer of *Forbes* magazine estimated in 1993 that the direct, indirect, and opportunity costs of affirmative action denied the U.S. economy 4 percentage points of potential gross national product every year.

Nowhere has the quota culture enraged conservatives more than at the universities. Whatever their opposite numbers may say about them, conservative intellectuals are intellectuals who intensely care—for both disinterested and career reasons—about the moral and ideological climate on campus. It was to the merit system on campus that conservatives from poor backgrounds often owed their first great opportunity in life. Reflective conservatives even began to wonder whether it wasn't to their opponents' hegemony on campus—where principles are tested, and where the young are imbued with the ideas that often last a lifetime—that their disappointments in Washington could be traced. And there was no purpose for which the radicals on campus used their power more mercilessly than the destruction of the old idea of merit. In his lectures, Dinesh D'Souza, author of a 1991 conservative critique of campus racial politics, *Illiberal Education,* tells of asking an admissions officer at Berkeley what the odds of admission would be for a black or Hispanic student with a B-plus average and a combined SAT score of 1200 out of a possible 1600. One hundred percent, the officer replied. And if the student were Asian? About 5 percent. "From the moment students arrive on campus," D'Souza writes, "they know that the rules have somehow been politically rigged, and their fate as individuals depends on whether they belong to the favored group or the unfavored group."[45] Of course, the rule-rigging cannot end at admission, or universities will suffer even more embarrassing minority dropout rates than they now do. D'Souza describes the University of North Carolina's "minority recognition ceremonies," at which black and Hispanic students who maintain a B average are singled out for special praise.

Unfortunately, no matter how strenuously university administrators insisted that the quality of the preferentially admitted students (and faculty) was the same as it had always been, the other students and faculty noticed the difference. To prevent them from commenting on it, universities have had to resort to elaborate techniques of persuasion and repression. Harvard hosts an annual antiracism week. Dartmouth, Brown, Michigan, and Wayne State all support sensitivity seminars. Hence too the notorious campus speech codes. The first seems to have been Michigan's, imposed in 1988. Subsequently struck down as unconstitutional, it banned any remark or gesture that "stigmatizes or victimizes an individual on the basis of race, ethnicity, religion, sex, sexual orientation, creed, national origin, ancestry, age, marital status, handicap, or Vietnam-era veteran status" on all university property, including classrooms. Since then, Brown, Emory, Middlebury, Penn State, Tufts, and the universities of Connecticut, North Carolina, Pennsylvania, and Wisconsin have adopted codes of varying degrees of stringency.[46]

The universities exercised their sensitivity policing powers in the name of a society that was becoming, as university administrators never tired of pointing out, ever more diverse. This was, to a growing number of conservatives, exactly the problem. America had chosen to admit enormous numbers of immigrants from Third World countries, and had then allowed them—or their would-be leaders—to dictate how the country should be rearranged to suit them. Immigration is an issue that divides conservatives, or at least conservative intellectuals. (The conservative rank and file, like just about everybody else in America, is intensely hostile to further immigration.) But all conservatives agree that if immigrants do come, they must assimilate. Instead, conservatives see—as former Reagan administration official Linda Chavez complains—that the new immigrant groups "demand that their groups remain separate, that their native culture and language be preserved intact, and that whatever accommodation takes place be on the part of the receiving society."[47] Such demands have been heard before in the long history of American immigration, but in the 1980s they made themselves unprecedentedly effective. The federal education bureaucracy had seized on some ambiguous language in the Supreme Court's 1974 *Lau v. Nichols* decision as requiring the states to teach students in their native tongue. Between 1975 and 1980, the federal government would negotiate more than 500 bilingual education plans.[48] At the same time, the lower federal courts began to order the printing of bilingual ballots. In 1981 the Supreme Court agreed, amazingly enough, that illegal immigrants must be counted for the apportionment of congressional seats. Nine years earlier, in *Plyler v. Doe,* it had ruled that the states were required to provide free public education to the children of illegal aliens. Illegal aliens won the right to collect unemployment insurance from the Texas courts, and to pay the cheaper tuition rates offered to in-state students in California.[49] Some Hispanic activists made bold to demand that all residents of the United States, not just citizens, be given the right to vote.

Racial animosity, family breakdown, secularization, the decline of the work ethic among the poor, the various pathologies of the underclass, the difficulties of immigrant absorption might simply be the normal problems of life that reformers must grapple with. America had, after all, civilized the murderous Irish gangs of nineteenth-century New York, reduced the skyrocketing divorce rates of the 1920s and 1930s, lived through the race riots of 1863 and 1919, and digested the incomprehensibly alien Italian and Jewish immigrants of the turn of the century. But the country that had done those things had possessed a cultural self-confidence lacking in the 1980s, especially among the very elites who ought to be doing the civilizing and digesting. In conservatives' gloomy assessment, the nerve of the country's intellectual and moral leaders had snapped.

Nothing brought home to conservatives the magnitude of their cultural defeat as much as their own personal vulnerability and marginality. R. Emmett Tyrrell, editor of the *American Spectator*, devoted an entire book, his 1992 *Conservative Crackup*, to a sad overview of how little cultural impact conservative intellectuals were having: in the Depression, Tyrrell contended, "the arts, universities, and the media were beginning to reflect the themes of the Roosevelt Administration. During the Reagan Administration no such cross-pollination of ideas from the White House into the culture took place."[50] While left-wing writers like Sidney Blumenthal deplored the rise of a conservative "counter-establishment," conservatives felt themselves to be both poor and powerless. Conservative intellectuals, almost without exception, function in a nonmarket economy. Relatively few of them earn a living from teaching or journalism. Trust funds are rare: in obedience to the law propounded by *National Review* editor John O'Sullivan that social gravity pulls everything to the left, the grandchildren of millionaires join the Sierra Club and Emily's List. Conservatives subsist on grants and gifts from a handful of not-especially-large foundations: the biggest until recently, the Scaife family's, disburses $13 million per year. The ultraliberal Ford Foundation, by contrast, dispenses $300 million per year. Conservatives gained one handsome pot of money in 1985, the $35-million-a-year Bradley Foundation. At almost exactly the same time, however, the large foundation created by the Pew family (who made their fortune from the Sun Oil Company, Sunoco) redirected its attention away from politics. Although the new money from Bradley more than outweighed the lost Pew money, the switch shifted the weight of funding from one group of conservatives to another. Pew's conservatism had been of a distinctly old-fashioned type: it favored conservative individuals and groups who had been around since the 1950s and early 1960s. Bradley's director, Michael Joyce, on the other hand, was friendlier toward the neoconservatives of New York and Washington. The neoconservatives' relative prosperity enraged their poor relations in the provinces. Among conservatives too, the 1980s were a decade of rapidly rising inequality. Not all conservatives had the talent, luck, and bureaucratic savvy to profit from the Republicans' long grip on the presidency.

The Reagan-Bush era found William Bennett an obscure professor, and left him a former cabinet secretary who could charge $25,000 per lecture. Charles Black was a junior political organizer in 1976, and one of the most successful consultants and lobbyists in Washingon by 1992. Pat Buchanan, an exspeechwriter and fledgling columnist in 1976, could, with a straight face, mount a presidential bid. But others had not fared so well, and they resented it. There would never be enough syndicated columns, lecture tours, and television slots to make media stars of the hundreds of young conservative journalists who started work in the 1980s. There would never be enough grant money for all the would-be institute directors, policy experts, and think tank presidents. Inevitably, these personal considerations colored many conservatives' appraisal of the future of their country. The nation was going to hell. Something must be done. But what? As the Bush administration petered out, that question would divide conservatives into three bitter and mutually contemptuous factions.

CHAPTER 4

Optimists: Wrong but Wromantic

Who says you can't turn back the clock? In November 1993, an elegant heiress named Christine Todd Whitman won election as the first female governor of New Jersey on a platform of Republican golden oldies: a neo–Kemp-Roth 30 percent cut in the state income tax, choice in education, and a promise to reduce state spending by squeezing out waste, fraud, and abuse. For romantic Reaganites, happy days were here again. Liberal commentators like Eleanor Clift of *Newsweek* and Al Hunt of the *Wall Street Journal* had predicted victory for the incumbent, Governor Jim Florio, who noisily congratulated himself for his courage in raising income taxes. Florio's reelection would ring the death knell of supply-side economics. Instead, Whitman won handsomely—carrying, interestingly, 30 percent of the black vote, largely because of her choice-in-education message.

Nobody took more pleasure from the Whitman victory than the man who wants to repeat her campaign on a national scale, Jack Kemp, Mr. Supply-Side. Kemp has waited a long time for his moment. Conservative delegates to the 1980 Detroit convention wore "Reagan/Kemp" lapel buttons; when Reagan named George Bush as his running mate, they pinned on "Kemp '88" buttons instead. Kemp adopted Reagan's themes, even his gestures. And the mimic was in turn mimicked: it was Jack Kemp's tax cut that Reagan made the centerpiece of his domestic policy. It was Kemp's influence too that helped transform the apocalyptic Reagan of 1964—the man who warned that America teetered on the verge of totalitarianism—into the sunlit Emersonian of the 1980s.

Kemp burst upon conservative consciousnesses in the late 1970s. Fast-moving, lithe, handsome, exuberant, endlessly cheerful, he was the most exciting phenomenon to hit the Republican Party since Teddy Roosevelt. A barrel-chested former football star every cilium in whose head was nailed in for keeps, he was certifiably a man of the people. Yet he also determinedly set himself to master the recondite monetary theory of Jacques Rueff. A right-wing Republican who hated communism and despised arms control, but who also cared about black America; a nostalgic for the gold standard who also believed in unionism, immigration, and the defense of Israel—Kemp was an unpredictable man who delighted in stringing together unlikely modifiers for his conservatism and himself. He was a "bleeding-heart conservative," a "progressive conservative," an "AFL-CIO conservative"; he was "Yitzhak Kemp," a "classical liberal of the twenty-first century." He refused to mix his pro-growth capitalist cocktail with the faintest tincture of budget-cutting bitters. This was—it was said by conservatives and nonconservatives alike—conservatism with a human face. "People don't care what you know," Kemp likes to say, "until they know that you care."

Kemp is a hugger, a squeezer, and a kisser. I interviewed him in his offices at "Empower America," his presidential campaign vehicle, in late 1993, and was treated to the full force of his personality. Every few seconds, he would lean over and, for emphasis, lightly slap me on the instep. I thought I had let my foot rest too near his coffee table. But when I moved my foot away—whack! He smacked me on the elbow. Kemp has a gift for seeming to speak directly to you. His eyes don't stray from your face and his thoughts don't wander. He possesses all the arts of the masters of modern political seduction, Jack Kennedy and Ronald Reagan.

So it came as quite a shock to Kemp's many supporters in the press, the Washington think tanks, and the $500-a-plate circuit when their hero was flat-out crushed in the 1988 Republican primary in New Hampshire. He ran a very distant third behind the pantywaist George Bush and the despised tax-raising Bob Dole. Of course, Bush enjoyed all the advantages of incumbency, and minority leader Dole lorded it over the Republicans in the Senate, while Kemp suffered the lowly status of a mere member of the House of Representatives. But that humble lot was Kemp's own fault. Kemp had persistently refused opportunities to run for loftier office. He had declined to challenge Jacob Javits for the New York senatorial nomination in 1980—a challenge successfully mounted by Alfonse D'Amato instead—and had then refused to enter the race to succeed Governor Hugh Carey in 1982. A victory in either contest would have enabled him to face George Bush on something more like equal terms in 1988, but Kemp's nerve faltered, as it would falter again in 1990, when he changed his official residence from New York to Maryland to avert being drafted to run against Mario Cuomo. Defeated in the race for the Republican nomination, Kemp asked President Bush for the job of Secretary of Housing and Urban Development.

HUD had never ranked very high in the Washington status world. It ranked lower than ever after the revelation that the department had been pillaged in the Reagan administration. Kemp, however, perceived at HUD a moral and political opportunity for the guilty 1990s. Alexis de Tocqueville long ago noted "that strange melancholy which often haunts the inhabitants of democratic countries in the midst of their abundance, and the disgust at life which sometimes seizes upon them in the midst of calm and easy circumstances." America was suffering such a mood in 1989. There seemed to be widespread disappointment that the stock market crash of 1987 had not ushered in a new depression. Just as Europeans had grown weary of peace in 1914, Americans at the end of the 1980s were gorged on wealth. Too many people had made too much money too quickly; worse, they had made their money in the new financial services and information economy, in ways that seemed incomprehensible to much of the general public. At the same time, too many others seemed to have sunk into almost un-American poverty and hopelessness, hopelessness apparently only made worse by the tens of billions of dollars the country spent to alleviate it. From HUD, Kemp would offer the country a new political formula, one that responded to the failure of the Reagan gambit: a "conservative war on poverty"—compassionate, but not liberal; generous, but firmly tethered to traditional moral values. By accepting poverty as a problem worthy of concern, he attempted to immunize conservative ideology against the charge of heartlessness; a far more powerful charge in a country feeling overstuffed, as America did in 1989, than in the fearful America of 1980. By calling for a *conservative* war on poverty, Kemp acknowledged the failure of the redistributive antipoverty policies of the 1960s, reassuring his listeners that a concern with poverty was not simply a plot to shift money from working people to idle people. Kemp's language subtly paid tribute to the essential moral health of all of the rest of society. The problem was not sexual depravity, or ignorance, or anything at all that might implicate the upper 87 percent of Americans—no aspersions were being cast upon them.

No aspersions were being cast upon the bottom 13 percent either. Kemp condemns proposals to abolish welfare outright as "punitive." He claims to believe that the right incentives will entice almost all the poor out of their poverty. F. Scott Fitzgerald is famously supposed to have said, "The very rich are different from you and me." To which Ernest Hemingway equally famously replied, "Yes, they have more money." In the 1990s, conservatives engaged in a similar internal debate about the very poor, and Kemp took Hemingway's side. In their values,

according to Kemp, the very poor were no different from you
and me. What made them different were the incentives and disincentives faced by people born into poverty. Alter those incentives and disincentives and millions of formerly poor people
would stream into the middle class. As Kemp explained in a
1990 lecture, "An Inquiry Concerning the Causes of Poverty in
the United States," in self-congratulatory homage to Adam
Smith's masterwork:

> America . . . is separated or divided into two economies.
> One economy—our mainstream economy—is democratic
> capitalist, market-oriented, entrepreneurial, and incentivized
> for working families whether in labor or management. This
> mainstream rewards work, investment, saving, and produc-
> tivity. Incentives abound for productive human, economic,
> and social behavior. . . .
>
> But there is another economy—a second economy that
> is similar in respects to the Eastern European or Third
> World "socialist" economy if you will—and it is almost
> totally opposite to the way people are treated in our main-
> stream capitalist economy, and it predominates in pockets of
> poverty throughout urban and rural America. This economy
> has barriers to productive human and social activity and a
> virtual absence of economic incentives and rewards that
> deny entry to Black, Hispanic and other minority men and
> women into the mainstream. . . .
>
> The irony is that the second economy was set up not
> out of malevolence, but out of a desire to help the poor,
> alleviate suffering, and provide a basic social safety net.[1]

Kemp grandiloquently identified himself as the leader of
the "Lincoln wing" of the Republican Party, a slogan apparently meant to suggest that his internal opponents composed
the Jefferson Davis wing. Kemp's disciples preferred the term
"empowerment" conservatives, lifting a phrase from the lexicon of the radicals of the 1960s. Perhaps, though, the conservatism espoused by Kemp and his supporters might best be

called "optimistic conservatism": optimistic because it sees America's social problems as relatively manageable and because its preferred means of managing them assume the basic moral similarity of all Americans. "It's not the values of the poor that are bankrupt," Kemp told the Houston convention, "it's the values of the welfare system that are bankrupt."[2] And Kemp conservatism can be called optimistic for a third reason too: because it prefers to avoid thinking hard about anything unpleasant. The policies Kemp advocates—tenant ownership of public housing, school vouchers, enterprise zones, removal of the ban on welfare to people who possessed assets worth more than a specified amount—presupposed a vision of America's poor as potentially highly competent, hardworking, and even entrepreneurial people. Since that's what the poor had to be like for the policies favored by Kemp & Co. to work, then that was how they must be.

Kemp's ebullience has been curiously undiminished by the disappointments of the 1980s, by the accumulating evidence of American social decay. But the ebullience now has a rather prepackaged look to it, as if the man opposite you long ago ceased to be Jack Kemp and has become instead an adept Jack Kemp imitator. Perhaps it was just the effect of a bad week— Kemp's Empower America organization was substantially funded by financier Theodore Forstmann, and the week I saw Kemp rumors were circulating that Forstmann had stopped his donation.

But then, who needs financiers? Kemp is by far the most popular Republican on the speaking circuit. Forstmann's money may pay the rent on Kemp's by no means lavish half-floor of office space, and the salary of Empower America's titular boss, former congressman Vin Weber. But Kemp more than earns his own way as a speechmaker, and if he should win the party's nomination in 1996, Forstmann will have to curry favor with him. Kemp-style conservatism still dominates the Republican congressional caucus, especially in the House, where representatives Newt Gingrich and Vin Weber convened a Conservative Opportunity Society in the mid-1980s. Weber works now as executive director of Empower America. Kemp-style conservatism still pervades the conservative think tanks with the closest links to Congress, especially the Heritage Foundation, where Stuart Butler's domestic policy shop calls for an acceptance of affirmative action and of a federal role in obtaining health insurance for all. Kemp's activist, optimistic conservatism set the style and agenda of the bright young men and women who thronged the corridors of the old Executive Office Building in the Bush years, desperately attempting to get something, anything, done. Above all, Kemp-style conservatism is powered by the advocacy of Robert Bartley, editor of the *Wall Street Journal,* who probably ranks as the single most powerful man in American journalism since the death of Walter Lippmann.

The core belief of Kemp-style optimists is that America's plush welfare programs, combined with the absence of steady, low-skilled jobs in the immediate vicinity of the urban poor, present poor people with something very much like a high marginal rate of tax if they move from dependency to work. The cut-off of welfare payments to families that owned substantial assets amounts to a high marginal tax on saving. The ready availability of welfare to single mothers, in conjunction with the lack of jobs for the unskilled young men produced by ghetto schools, discourages wedlock. All America need do to move people out of dependency and into work and marriage is reverse the pattern of incentives and disincentives.

But how to do it? Kemp advocates two specific programs: the privatization of public housing and the creation of enterprise zones. Kemp does not just believe in these two ideas: he crusades for them. In testimony before Congress, the new HUD secretary promised that tenant ownership of public housing "is going to save babies, save children, save families and save America."[3] Kemp was inspired by the huge success of the privatization of public housing in Great Britain. More than one-third of the British population lived in housing owned by the state in 1979. Over the next dozen years, 1.5 million of the 6.5

million council houses, as they were called, were sold to their occupants at concessionary prices. The new owners were converted from wards of the state into independent householders— and uncoincidentally from Labour into Conservative voters. Secretary Kemp envisaged a comparable transformation here. In his enthusiasm, however, he overlooked a few big problems. American public housing dwellers are a much harder-core poverty population than were the residents of British public housing before Thatcher. In 1979, one-quarter of British housing was owned by the government, and most of the residents were employed. Only 2 percent of American housing is government-owned and between 70 and 90 percent of its residents subsist on welfare. Americans living in housing projects are therefore going to be far less likely to be able to maintain their new properties, let alone summon up even the nominal purchase price that British council householders were obliged to pay. Nor are they going to be equally eager to do so: because British council housing was populated by working people rather than a welfare population, it was generally in better shape than American public housing is. That meant that $20,000 spent to buy a flat in Wandsworth was a far wiser investment than even a much smaller sum for an apartment in a graffiti covered high-rise on East 138th Street.

Undeterred, Kemp pressed ahead. As a congressman, he had pushed hard for the 1987 sale of the Kenilworth-Parkside project in Washington, D.C., to its residents. Secretary Kemp's Home Ownership for People Everywhere, or HOPE, program would spread the success of Kenilworth-Parkside nationwide— but, along the way, compromises had to be made. To the question, where are we going to put the hard-core poor? Kemp responded by agreeing to build one additional public housing unit for every unit sold. To the question, why would anyone buy these awful places? Kemp and his predecessors had responded by spending vast sums on renovation—at the showcase Kenilworth-Parkside project in Washington, renovation costs hit $130,000 per unit, more than double the cost of build-

ing a public housing unit from scratch. (The project will continue to receive subsidies at least until the mid-1990s.) The
question, how can we be sure that the residents can maintain
their homes? Kemp answered with Operation Bootstrap—
despite its name a Great Society–style agglomeration of social
assistance and counseling connected to Kenilworth-Parkside.
And the question, how do we prevent the beneficiaries of this
$130,000 renovation from instantly selling their homes and
reaping a windfall profit at the expense of the taxpayer? was
met with regulations restricting the rights of the new "owners"
to sell. In most cases, owners would be permitted to sell only
back to the tenant association that ran the project.

"We will not let [Kenilworth-Parkside] fail," deputy assistant HUD secretary David Caprara told reporters from the
National Journal.[4] But by ensuring the project could not fail,
Kemp also guaranteed that it could not succeed—at least not
on conservative terms. What Kemp had done, in his attempt to
extend the market in housing to poor people, was to synthesize
markets as haltingly and unsuccessfully as any Gorbachevian
market socialist. Kemp had reasoned that home owners behave
better than non–home owners and that the conduct of the
non–home-owning poor would therefore improve if they
became owners. But he did not allow for two critical possibili-
ties: perhaps it was good behavior that caused home owning
rather than the other way round; in which case granting home
ownership as a gift would make little difference. And even if the
causality ran the way Kemp thought it did, maybe it wasn't the
mere fact of ownership that changed the behavior of the poor,
but the hard reality of paying a lot of money for an asset and
then being obliged to protect that asset in order to reap a gain
from it. In that case too one had to doubt that owners who have
paid virtually nothing for their asset and who are not permitted
to profit from it will behave like real owners. Nor did Kemp
allow for the demoralizing effects of his project on the poor—
and nonpoor—people who do not live in public housing and
who would very much appreciate the government's swinging by

and doing $130,000 worth of home improvements for them. One effect of HOPE, however, was clear and indisputable: the HUD budget swelled from $19.7 billion in 1989 to $28.1 billion four years later.

Enterprise zones were also a Thatcherite idea, although unlike the privatization of public housing they had not been a success in Britain. The hope had been that by repealing regulations and taxes within a depressed area, policymakers could cause a series of miniature Hong Kongs to come to life within the British Isles. Instead, businesses in the areas immediately adjoining the zones shifted their operations across the boundary line into the zones. Few new businesses were born. Some U.S. states have also experimented with enterprise zones, with even more disappointing results. Why move from downtown Washington to a (hypothetical) Anacostia enterprise zone when you can escape nearly as much of the burden of government by moving to clean, picturesque, and crime-free Loudoun County? Nor does a lightening of the burden of government seem to be sufficient stimulus to incite the people living in Anacostia to rush out and start businesses of their own. The people of Anacostia undoubtedly are overtaxed and overregulated, but they suffer far more grievous problems too: crime, the absence of a commercial culture, the allurements of welfare—all of which remain in place when the ribbon is cut at the entrance to the enterprise zone.

Kemp defends enterprise zones as an idea that has never been properly tested. And perhaps it is true that an enterprise zone is the sort of thing that must be implemented 100 percent correctly before you see any results whatsoever. But without directly criticizing the man who remains the best hope of the Republican Right, more and more conservatives have begun to doubt Kemp's smooth assertions. Unsurprisingly, one of the first to publicize his doubts was George Will, never infatuated with economistic reasoning. "I asked Kemp whether there was really some rate of economic growth—4 percent, or 5 percent, or 6 percent—that would cause women to stop having babies

out of wedlock. He believes there is. I simply don't."⁵ Kemp
has also collected brickbats from conservatives suspicious of
what they take to be his excessively eager overtures to black
voters: he is regularly sneered at by the nationalist writers of
Chronicles magazine, and Pat Buchanan scoffs at his "big rock-
candy mountain" conservatism.

These latter criticisms Kemp easily shakes off. But it is less
easy to dismiss doubts that "incentivizing"—Kemp's term—is
not quite the same thing as marketizing. Too many of the optimists have ceased to understand "the market" as the behavior
that naturally occurs when the state respects contracts and
property rights, and have come instead to see markets as
devices—"mechanisms," as a revealing figure of speech put it—
for eliciting whatever behavior the authorities of the moment
happened to think desirable. One extreme example: with excess
money in his reelection fund, Gingrich paid poor children in his
district a dollar for every book they read over the summer holiday and recorded in a diary. He dubbed this experiment "earn
to learn," and hailed it as an entrepreneurial alternative to the
bureaucratic methods of the public schools. One little girl
somehow managed to read upward of two hundred books over
her summer vacation. A short article by her was printed on the
Wall Street Journal's editorial page. Readers were horrified, and
understandably so. But there was more wrong with earn to
learn than just an outburst of bad taste. "Earn to learn" per-
verted the message of self-reliance that the conservative movement preached. Conservative writers of the 1950s, such as Russell Kirk and Richard Weaver, had resisted market values. Kirk
wanted to preserve the unapologetic elitism of the universities
against mass culture and the countryside against suburbanization; Weaver condemned an aggressive national market economy that threatened to destroy the South's hierarchical way of
life. "Earn to learn" was almost a parody of the acquisitive
spirit that Kirk and Weaver loathed as much as they loathed
communism. Of course Gingrich—an intelligent man—could
see that. When asked about it in a private meeting, Gingrich

defiantly defended the use of monetary incentives in any and all settings, no matter how untraditional. The money economy—so unlovely to Kirk and Weaver—was, in Gingrich's eyes, and those of other optimistic conservatives, unequivocally liberating. Older and younger conservatives disagreed about the social consequences of unconstrained free markets. The older generation saw the market as an atomizing force in society; the newer saw it as a force for harmony and cooperation. Behind this disagreement stood a stunning change in the tone and character of free market economics in a single generation.

Unlike socialism, which has always interested itself exclusively in the distribution of abundance, classical free-market economics was deeply impressed by the fact of scarcity. Nineteenth- and early-twentieth-century political leaders of what were then called liberal views opposed interference in the market for two stern reasons—because intervention would only wreck the economy and impoverish ordinary people even more deeply, and because tampering with contracts and property rights was intrinsically wicked. Then came an intellectual revolution. It is oversimplifying to give all the credit to one man, and even to one article, but it is probably not far wrong. The English economist Ronald Coase (who won the Nobel Prize in 1992) observed that when property rights are strictly demarked, everything—not just goods, but intangibles like risk—can be distributed "optimally." Example: an old-fashioned steam engine is chugging through the countryside blowing sparks. If the sparks land on the nearby fields of hay, they'll catch fire and burn. Suppose that the value of the train traffic is greater than the value of the endangered hay. And suppose that the simplest and best solution to the problem is to stop growing hay within reach of the sparks. Now, everybody can see that the farmers will pull their hay back if the law says that the train company is not obliged to pay them for burning their crop. What Coase contended in his 1961 essay "The Problem of Social Cost" is that with low enough transaction costs exactly the same result will occur even if the law says that the train company is obliged to pay for the hay it burns—because it will be cheaper for the company to buy the land on either side of the tracks and leave it barren than it will be either to stop sparking, to abandon the train route, or to go on paying damages to the farmers.

Academics influenced by Coase have directed most of their energy to working out the implications of his caveat about transaction costs. But the conservative politicians and policy wallahs who absorbed the new classical economics at second- and thirdhand took an entirely different lesson from Coase. To them, the Coase theorem transmuted free-market economics from a dismal science into a utopian vision of a world in which nearly all social problems can be solved voluntarily, without conflict and without bureaucracy. Pick a site for the town dump bureaucratically, and it will take three years of hearings, pro- voke all sorts of improper pressures, and produce endless bit- terness. Set up a Dutch auction instead and award the dump to the lowest bid, and the optimal location is found instantly and without quarreling. Throughout the late 1970s and early 1980s, Coasian concepts surged out of conservative think tanks in the United States and Britain. To politicians and intellectuals in North America and Europe reduced to despair by the explosion of social grievances in the 1960s and early 1970s, whose soci- eties suddenly seemed transformed into ungovernable cockpits of incompatible demands, Coase-inspired policy ideas offered a promise of freedom from politics, of self-balancing social har- mony. And it was because they found this promise of social harmony so seductive that the optimistic conservatives were drawn so deeply into the problems of the black urban poor.

Otherwise, the black urban poor would seem like an odd preoccupation for any brand of conservative. There is not an enormous number of poor people in America, nor an extraordi- narily large population of black people, and neither group votes in large numbers. Sure, yes, conservative intellectuals tend to live in New York or Washington, D.C., where the underclass looks a lot larger and more menacing than in, say, Boise. It is discouraging and enraging to watch the city in which you live be systematically destroyed by people you are forced through the tax system to support. And yes, by living in Washington, conservative thinking has been inevitably tinctured by the culture of government. Nobody ever got an assistant secretaryship by concluding his paper on problem x with the recommendation: do nothing and maybe things will improve on their own. But something else is at work too. The existence of a helpless, hopeless class of people separated from the rest of society by the accidents of birth and skin color appears to give the lie to every sunny tenet of free-market capitalism. So long as the underclass lingers in joblessness and squalor, one social problem will remain that the voters perceive liberals, not conservatives, to have the best answer to. "My feeling," says Kemp, "is that if you have a contest between Scrooge—pure budget-cutting—versus Santa Claus, which is what the Left offers, Scrooge loses. My view is that growth is the only political model that can compete with the Santa Claus of the Left."[6]

Unfortunately, because their goal in fighting poverty was to win moral prestige for themselves—and only secondarily actually to end poverty—optimistic conservatives have habitually shirked the obligation to think through the workability of their empowering policies. Nowhere was this failure worse than in the debate over school choice.

The intellectual ancestry of school vouchers can be traced to John Stuart Mill, who argued in *On Liberty* that government should pay for universal education but ought not directly to provide it. In their modern form, vouchers are yet another of Milton Friedman's brainstorms. Although Barry Goldwater briefly flirted with them, it was the soaring budgets of public schools combined with near-universal unhappiness with their performance that transformed "school choice" into a grand conservative cause. Choice has always appealed to religious conservatives, Protestants and Catholics alike, who have seen it as a means to ease the burden of private-school tuition on their constituents. But choice has only recently emerged as the optimist conservatives' preferred solution to the ever-more

inescapable catastrophe of inner-city education. School administrators and teachers' unions had hijacked the conservatives'
school reform movement of the 1980s, and exploited it to
extract higher pay, less work, and more amenities for themselves—but had signally failed to deliver any improvement in
performance on standardized tests. Advocates of school choice,
such as Brookings Institute researchers John Chubb and Terry
Moe, proposed to force the public schools to reform by
enabling nonaffluent parents to opt out of the public system if
dissatisfied. Armed with a $4,000 certificate, parents would
shop for schools as they shop for anything else, choosing the
one that offered the best combination of convenience, achievement, and congenial values.

Whatever its merits as an educational theory—and despite
Chubb and Moe there is as yet no real evidence that a randomly selected sample of public school students will perform
better in a private school than in a public school—school choice
offers the politicians who back it one huge political asset: its
apparent sidestepping of conflicts over values. The school
reform movement of the early 1980s foundered because teachers, principals, parents, experts, and local communities could
not agree on a definition of "better education." Was a school
that began flunking more kids doing "better"? Was a school
that bought more computers? Should clever students be
"streamed" away from the dunderheads? How, if at all, should
the curriculum be adapted to make black and minority students
feel more comfortable? How, if at all, should the curriculum be
adapted to avoid offending students from religious homes?

In America's first bout of school reform, in the early years
of this century, a cohesive Northeastern Protestant elite
imposed its definition of good education without qualm on the
city schools of the big states. The results, as far as they can be
measured, were superb. In a second bout of post-Sputnik
reform, a not-quite-so cohesive Northeastern secular scientific
elite again imposed its ideas, this time with far less success. In
the 1980s, a less elitist and less cohesive nation was unable to

arrive at any agreed-upon understanding of reform at all. Vouchers seemed a way out. Did some black parents want all-boys schools? No need to wrangle in the statehouse about sexual equality: parents who wanted such a school could send their sons there, those who didn't could pick a coed institution instead. Did other parents want their children to learn that the world was created by the command of God? That was okay too. But with school choice—far more than with tenant ownership or enterprise zones—the optimistic conservatives reached the dead end in their ideology. In the modern regulatory state, there is no escape from disagreement over right and wrong by retreating from the public to the private sphere: the exits are all cut off.

The law is very clear: take even a dime of federal money, and all the federal civil rights laws apply to every part of your school. (The Supreme Court's 1985 *Grove City* decision attempted to limit civil-rights laws' applicability to only those programs that received federal money, but *Grove City* was reversed by Congress's Civil Rights Restoration Act of 1988. Most voucher advocates agree that compliance with the federal civil rights laws should be a condition for receiving state money as well.) It is not clear that a school that accepted vouchers could in fact refuse to admit girls. Or—as the Hasidic schools of New York City do—require boys' school buses to be driven by male drivers. As the federal and state civil rights laws now stand, a school that refuses to accept students who score below a certain mark on a standardized test could fall afoul of those laws, if that test has a disproportionate impact on protected minority groups. The same strictures could well apply to grading practices if they cause too many minority youngsters to fail or drop out. It is too often assumed that vouchers will present no establishment clause problem because the Supreme Court okayed the GI bill (which permitted veterans to spend their tuition money at religious universities) and other forms of direct aid paid to all students including those who attend religious schools. That assumption is a weak one: it is one thing for the

Court to approve, as it did in 1993, the expenditure of state funds so that a deaf boy may bring an interpreter with him to Catholic school, it is quite another for the Court to accept that tens of billions of dollars of public money will be granted to religious schools every year into perpetuity. The fact that Franklin Roosevelt's highly deferential Court permitted the GI bill to subsidize tuition at Notre Dame in the 1940s is not very compelling evidence of what the Clintonized Supreme Court of the future will permit. Voucher advocates intended to bring the virtues of the private schools into the public sphere; there is a much more real risk that they will instead inflict all the vices of the public sphere upon the private. Ordinary Americans seems to recognize this risk better than the conservative intellectuals do, which is perhaps the reason that California's voters resoundingly rejected a voucher initiative in November 1993.

More even than enterprise zones and tenant ownership of public housing, vouchers are the quintessential optimistic conservative policy, because more than any other they attempt to solve a bitter political problem—what shall the schools teach?—by using marketizing techniques to soothe the problem out of existence. As optimists see it, contemporary politics divide far more often over problems of method than of values. In a postelection retrospective in the *New Republic,* former Bush domestic policy adviser James Pinkerton expressed this view starkly. "New Paradigm Republicans and New Paradigm Democrats agree on the same goals—thus the only thing left to argue about is technique."[7] Pinkerton was the man who put the "new paradigm" phrase into Washington parlance in a 1990 speech. The speech won Pinkerton brief but intense fame when budget director Richard Darman ridiculed it in a speech of his own two weeks later, calling it "neo-neoism" and remarking that the phrase reminded him of a song, "Buddy, Can You Paradigm?" Pinkerton was an easy target for Darman: Pinkerton is cloudy and Darman is precise. But, judged by their impact on their target audience, the fuzzy Pinkerton won the exchange.

The new paradigm, as laid down by Pinkerton, was a call

for dropping the argument about what government should do and moving to an argument about how government should do it. In language that a Pinkerton ally, Gingrich, inserted into the 1992 platform, the Republicans' aim should be to "transform the bureaucratic welfare state into a government that is customer-friendly, cost-effective, and improving constantly."[8] Gingrich repeated in his convention speech a complaint he had been making for the past year:

> You can walk into a Wal-Mart store today and have your credit card approved in 2.3 seconds. And yet, it takes the Veterans' Department six weeks to answer your letter. We Republicans see the efficiency of Wal-Mart and UPS; and we want to change the government to be as courteous, efficient, speedy and effective as those companies. The Democrats see those companies, and they want to apply litigation, regulation, and taxation to make sure the companies become more like the government.[9]

Such comments fueled suspicions among other conservatives about what Kemp, Gingrich, and their devotees were really up to. It wasn't welfare the optimists seemed to object to; it was bureaucracy. But did it really make the redistribution of wealth less offensive and destructive if the money were moved by fiber optic cable? Even longtime Kemp and Gingrich acolytes Evans and Novak conceded that Kemp "does not have a clue today how to bring together Christian activists, moderates, country clubbers [with his] supply-siders."[10] There had been something for everyone in Kemp's tax-cutting program of the 1970s. But his urban revival program of the 1990s seemed to Kemp's detractors to be a futile and undignified suck-up to the leadership of the civil rights movement, a group conservatives had almost uniformly opposed for thirty year. Some, like Barry Goldwater and Robert Bork, had opposed the claims of the movement for reasons of abstract principle: because the new civil rights laws of the 1960s infringed too far upon the traditional common law rights of contract, property, and association. Others, like Richard Weaver, personally approved of segregation. This background appalled Kemp.

> The Democrats had a terrible history [on civil rights], and they overcame it. We had a great history, and we turned aside. We should have been there with Dr. King on the streets of Atlanta and Montgomery. We should have been there with John Lewis. We should have been there on the freedom marches and bus rides. We should have been there with Rosa Parks in Montgomery, Alabama, in December of 1955.
>
> . . . I think the whole idea of Kevin Phillips's Southern majority is a disgrace. You want the South, the North, the East, and the West. You want consensus, not coalitions, in my view.[11]

Kempite optimists argued that conservatives must make up for lost time on civil rights. Stuart Butler scolded that conservatives must stop bleeding every time some white fireman was denied a promotion. Two former Reagan Justice Department staffers, Clint Bolick and William H. Mellor, both white, formed a public interest law firm, the Institute for Justice, to protect black interests against restrictive local government regulations. In their first two years of operation, Bolick and Mellor brought court challenges against the Washington, D.C., ban on street shoeshine men and its licensing requirement for hairdressers; against Denver's taxicab licensing system; and against the federal Davis-Bacon Act. In 1986, Gingrich had corralled Republican votes in the House, many of them unhappy ones, for the Martin Luther King, Jr., national holiday. Kemp made himself a frequent guest on black television personality Tony Brown's show—Kemp's influence was a major reason that Brown, with great fanfare, registered as a Republican in 1992—and at meetings of the National Association for the Advancement of Colored People.

Perhaps Pat Buchanan's jibe is right, and this is a "big

rock-candy mountain" sort of conservatism. Certainly Kemp's faith in the power of wealth to harmonize social conflict seems exaggerated if not embarrassingly materialistic. Still, there is something appealing about the man who champions optimism. "It's ironic to me," Kemp scornfully observed during our interview, "that at the collapse of communism there's a collapse of confidence on the Right. They're selling fear and insecurity and a very small-minded view of America. I have a big view of America. . . . Our revolution is now global. It won't be long before the Declaration of Independence is basically the lodestar for everybody from Tiananmen Square to Wenceslaus Square to Soweto, South Africa." The comic history book *1066 and All That* describes the English Civil War as a conflict between the Cavaliers, who were "wrong but wromantic," and the Roundheads, who were "right but repulsive." That's not so fanciful a description of the civil war between Kemp and his conservative enemies. Kemp and the optimists' wrongheadedness, if indeed it is wrongheadedness, about their various pet gimmicks—from enterprise zones to quality circles—is the consequence of excessive faith in the capacity of others. Nothing to be ashamed of in that, and much to be proud of. Kemp never appears to wonder whether the ultimate cause of the troubles of black people might not be black people themselves; he never doubts that there cannot be found an economic solution to every American social problem. For a country that likes to hear about solutions, that's a powerful recommendation in a politician.

Even so, Kemp seems fated to be the James G. Blaine of the twentieth century: the plumed knight of the Republican Party who somehow never quite makes the historical cut. He is the end of something rather than the beginning of something. As his ally Gingrich pursues the House speakership, the Georgian is forgetting empowerment as he forgot space exploration. Heritage's wares will find other customers, and Pinkerton will find other candidates to work for. Even Kemp's friend Bill Bennett is weighing his own independent bid for the presidency.[12] When asked, Kemp, though not an introspective man, will concede the possibility that time has passed him by. "If the conservative movement temporarily moves away from basically Reagan's view—Reagan," he says emphatically, "to, say, the Buchanan view, then I will ride off into the sunset and raise my grandchildren and never be heard from again. But that's what the '94 election will be all about and the '96 election and the '98 election and the millennium election."

CHAPTER 5

Moralists: The Threat from Above

The twentieth-anniversary edition of the *Public Interest* delivered a polite rebuke to Kemp-style optimists: "Over the last two decades, this nation has come face to face with problems that do not seem to respond, or respond enough, to changes in incentives."[1] Lengthen the sentences meted out to criminals, but crime rates do not fall. Allow inflation to silently gulp away the value of welfare payments, but welfare dependency rises. Institute an earned-income tax credit to reward work effort, but black participation in the labor force tumbles. Economics alone could not explicate, or offer answers to, America's social troubles. The result, according to James Q. Wilson, the author of the *Public Interest* rebuke has been "a deepening concern for the development of character in the citizenry"[2] among serious thinkers about public policy. "If we wish to address the problems of family disruption, welfare dependency, crime in the streets, educational inadequacy, or even public finance properly understood, then government, by the mere fact that it defines these states of affairs as problems, acknowledges that human character is, in some degree, defective and that it intends to alter it." The "belief that all that is required is opportunity" to solve America's problem is, not to be excessively polite about it, "mistaken."[3]

Wilson's doubts about the sufficiency of economic opportunity as a social cure-all wielded more and more influence in the Bush years. There had been opportunities galore in the 1980s. Yet when Bill Bennett published an index of leading cultural indicators in the *Wall Street Journal* in early 1993, they showed an America charging at full speed toward barbarism. "Is America on the way down?" *Commentary* editorially asked in 1992, and though it invited the *Wall Street Journal*'s Robert Bartley to argue no, and though too the arguments that Bartley's debating partner, Edward Luttwak, offered for yes were more than a little absurd (for example, the allegedly higher quality of taxi service in Tokyo than New York), the question had been declared open. Wilson collected his essays together in 1991 under the title *On Character;* his 1993 opus, *The Moral Sense,* completed his evolution from number-crunching social scientist to neo-Aristotelian. And as usual, where Wilson led, disciples followed.

Wilson, a past president of the American Political Science Association, is one of the most influential academics in the country. He shares authorship of the "broken window" theory of crime, derived from experiments that show that people really do behave worse when their surroundings are allowed to deteriorate. When the police chief appointed in 1994 by newly elected New York mayor Rudolph Guiliani said that one of his first priorities would be to crack down on the squeegee men who accost motorists at the entrances to Manhattan's tunnels and highways, that was James Q. Wilson you heard speaking. More than anyone else, Wilson is responsible for the resurrection of the cop on the beat, or "community policing" as it is now called. He is a careful writer and speaker, not given to extravagant claims, and for that reason the claims he does make carry immense authority, especially on the political Right.

So while redeveloping the character of the American people, or of any substantial portion of the American people, might seem a daunting project, conservatives were reassured when Wilson reminded them that the task had been done before: by the temperance movement of the nineteenth century and by the public school and other municipal reforms of the Progressive Era. Like today's conservatives, the Progressives of the first two decades of this century confronted violent, disorderly, and impoverished big cities dominated by corrupt political machines that ruled by stoking ethnic animosities. Most urban children failed to get a decent education in those days, public amenities were inadequate when not noisome, and Congress and state governments seemed to have no inkling at all of how to cope. The country was filling up with immigrants who did not speak English, did not understand American customs, and seemed to feel little loyalty to their new country. An urban proletariat of unprecedented size had come into being: impoverished, often foreign-born, prone to political radicalism, violent, apparently unassimilable, and terrifyingly fecund. The very definition of what it meant to be an American was called into question as it had never been before. And yet, those frightening people had indeed been Americanized, thanks to reformers who knew what Americanism meant and did not shy from imposing it in their schools, their public buildings, and their patriotic celebrations.

Americanization could inflict extreme psychic pain upon the new arrivals and their children—Norman Podhoretz called it a "brutal bargain"—but it built a nation out of extraordinarily unlikely elements. Wilson even suggests that the Progressives' Americanization campaign, on top of previous waves of moral reform directed at the young men who had flocked to the cities from towns and villages after the Civil War, made the early apparent success of the New Deal possible: because the American population had been conditioned for generations to revere hard work and personal independence, the temptations to dependency offered by the nation's new social programs were for many years by and large scorned. Wilson believed that the task of Americanization and moral reform could be performed again—if, and it was a big if, America could summon up the necessary cultural self-confidence.

Here were the core ideas of the zestiest conservative faction of the 1990s: character and morality. American society was being subverted from within by moral decay, and the task of conservatives was to resist. Indeed, in the minds of the conservatives who took Wilson's lead—the sort of conservatives who can conveniently be called moralistic conservatives—it was cultural self-confidence, and not big government, that divided right from left. In the wake of the failure of the Reagan gambit, more or less everyone on the Right now accepted at least pretty big government. Instead, argued Professor Lawrence Mead of New York University, one of the leading younger moralists, conservatism now primarily "means using government more vigorously against crime, welfarism, and the failure of ghetto children to learn in school. Liberalism still means bigger government, but it also connotes resistance to enforcement and a greater tolerance for disorder, dependency, and ethnic pluralism. The two sides now differ more sharply on questions of social authority than they do about the scale of government."[4] Moralistic conservatives are ready to deploy social authority to instill bourgeois values in the black urban poor, to assimilate Third World immigrants, and, a little more diffidently, to correct the faults of the American middle class. The state, Irving Kristol argued, must take "a degree of responsibility for helping to shape the preferences that the people exercise in a free market—to 'elevate' them, if you will."[5]

Nobody was more eager to press the up button on that elevator than Bill Bennett. Tall, bulky but not fat, unashamedly rumpled, an ex-smoker always on the verge of regressing, Bennett is sharp-tongued, literate, and fearless. Despite his years in academia, he expresses himself in a pungent urbanese, "yeah" his permanent substitute for "yes." Bennett had caught the eye of Irving Kristol, who put forward his name in 1981 for the chairmanship of the National Endowment of the Humanities.

To get the job, Bennett had to beat out the late M. E. Bradford of the University of Dallas. Bradford was a more distinguished scholar than Bennett, albeit a neglected one, and his ties with the conservative movement went back much further. Too far, in the end, for his own good: he had been an organizer for George Wallace in 1972. Worse, he had condemned Lincoln in writing as a man whose sweeping rhetoric foreshadowed the totalitarianism of Hitler and Stalin. Bradford badly wanted the humanities job, and lobbied for it personally, but the idea of putting forward a nominee of whom the *Washington Post* could report "President Reagan today sent to the Republican-controlled Senate the nomination of a man who likens Lincoln to Hitler" seemed more than necessarily harebrained. So Bennett it was.

Kristol, whom Bennett installed on the NEH board, tells how Bennett baffled his left-leaning staff with the "Hittite solution" to academic trendiness in grantmaking. "Much of what they were doing was absolutely awful. But, for example, one of the things they were doing was spending something like $600,000 a year on a Hittite dictionary and it would take years to get it done." The new NEH board told the staff, "'Make it a million and tell them to take as long as they want.' A Hittite dictionary is a very good thing to have. It does no harm to anybody. That's the way to spend the money."[6] When the disastrous Terrell Bell was finally dinged as secretary of education, Bennett was the conservatives' candidate for the job. It is hard to decide whether Secretary Bennett was among the most or the least successful of President Reagan's cabinet appointees. No other secretary deserves more credit for transforming the public's opinion of his area of jurisdiction. It was Bennett who publicized the (somewhat contradictory) conservative educational ideas of national standards and parental choice. These ideas were unheard of beyond a narrow coterie of devotees in 1984; today they are part of the basic parlance of every reform-minded governor in the United States. At the same time, few cabinet secretaries can have made as little personal difference to the daily operation of their bureaucracy. Even Bennett's admirers concede, as the Heritage Foundation did in 1989, that "Bennett accomplished little to make reforms part of the legislative framework."[7]

Bennett could blame this disappointment on an almost uniquely hostile Congress. The committees to which he reported are subservient to the point of humiliation to the teachers' unions; those unions, in turn, are fervently committed to turning out the dumbest possible high school graduates at the greatest possible cost. But Bennett cannot escape responsibility himself. To a degree remarkable even for a politician, he conflated words and actions. "Government," he has written, "through law, discourse, and example, can legitimize and delegitimize certain acts. In a free society, where the people decide, leaders must understand that few things they do matter more than speaking about the right things in the right way."[8] But a speech about the family is not the same as cutting off the subsidies that promote the disintegration of families. Perhaps it was once true, in a more trusting and deferential society, that a politician could preach sermons and expect them to carry weight. But now? And isn't it weird that conservatives, who have worked so hard to destroy the public's faith in the wisdom and goodness of government, could now talk about government exhorting people to virtue? Who could keep a straight face if President Clinton delivered an address about the sanctity of the family? Could Bill Bennett?

If it is true that America's problems are predominantly cultural, and if, as Bennett liked to insist, "cultural problems require cultural solutions," then what is politics for? People who want to improve their country would then be well advised to write novels or enter the priesthood, not run for Congress or staff the executive branch. In practice, though, Bennett took a more vigorous view of the potentialities of government, particularly at his next job, director of the Office of National Drug Control Policy in the Bush administration, generalissimo of the war on drugs.

Even leaving aside oddities like Customs Commissioner William von Raab's request for the authority to shoot down as a drug smuggler any aircraft that entered American airspace without identifying itself, the war on drugs became the justification for a startling new battery of legal penalties and a frightening degree of surveillance of Americans' financial transactions. In the name of winning the war on drugs, the Treasury ordered in 1989 all domestic banks to record all transfers of dollars outside the country, and ordered all foreign banks that dealt in dollars to report all cash transactions in excess of $10,000—even if all parties to the transaction were citizens of foreign countries. This data was compiled at a new Financial Crimes Enforcement Center in Arlington, along with information from the Internal Revenue Service, the Federal Reserve, and other agencies, providing the Treasury with a complete picture of all the cash transactions of every holder of dollars in the world. The Constitution decrees that forfeiture of property may not be used as a punishment for high treason; but during the drug war it became a routine penalty for drug use. When police dogs sniffed cocaine on three one-dollar bills in the till of a Chaldean merchant in Detroit—meaning, so far as anyone could prove, nothing more sinister than that the merchant had sold a bottle of beer to a drug user, police confiscated all the cash on his premises: $4,381. Federal marshalls spotted twelve marijuana plants on the farm of Robert Machin, a Harvard dropout living in Vermont, and decided, without additional evidence, that he was a trafficker. Forfeiture proceedings were instituted, and Machin and his family would have been ejected from their home but for an uproar in the state legislature.

The war on drugs did not limit itself to protecting society from the depredations of addicts, but actually attempted to cure or treat them. Bennett submitted a $1.5 billion request for drug treatment money in his 1991 budget, an increase of 68 percent from the level of two years before. "My reputation was not that of a big spender," Bennett says in his postgovernment memoir, *The De-valuing of America*. Still, he told George Bush that drugs were "'one issue, Mr. President, where I, a conservative Republican, feel comfortable in advocating a strong federal role.'"[9]

Since leaving government in 1990, Bennett has found himself at loose ends. He rejected the job of chairman of the Republican National Committee, a position from which he might have been able to help save the Republicans from the 1992 debacle. He turned down the North Carolina Republicans when they asked him to challenge incumbent senator Terry Sanford; the man who said yes, Lauch Faircloth, got Sanford's job. But Bennett does not care overmuch for the detail of politics. He perceives his own role as that of a preacher rather than a legislator. Unlike the other leading Republicans, who go on the lecture circuit to raise money, Bennett seems actively to enjoy delivering speeches. His latest book is not about politics at all: it is an anthology of moralistic stories and poems for children, *The Book of Virtues*. Rather than liberate the innate virtues of the common man with libertarian public policy, Bennett thinks that conservative politicians and any future conservative government must exhort them to improve their standard of conduct. This more authoritative conservatism summoned conservatives to more causes than the war on drugs alone.

> We have done this to ourselves. I mean, there's bad stuff emanating from Hollywood, from intellectuals and from books, and from movies and from TV, but people have bought into it, which is the problem. You can rail against the cultural elite all you like, which I do, and I think they have a lot to answer for. But it's a free country. People don't have to listen to it if they don't want to. People do listen to it. . . . I think that . . . we cannot as conservatives fall into the same trap the liberals fall into, which is to say to the American people, you too are victims: it's not your fault; this was done to you. Things were put forward and argued and suggested, but people bought into them. Teachers bought into values clarification, and so did parents; people bought into the notion that you don't have to spend quantity time with your kids, just quality time. People let their kids watch too much TV. People don't check homework. . . . The

political imperative is to not only criticize the cultural elite, the liberal elite, but to say to the American people, "Cut it out."[10]

The fear of saying "cut it out" was to blame for so many of America's social problems. If disorderly, often crazy, often dangerous vagrants thronged the most elegant streets of America's cities in the 1980s, the blame—moralist conservatives argued—belonged to a society that had lost the self-confidence to proscribe intolerable behavior. Some of the homeless were maniacs who ought to have been locked up in mental institutions. Others were addicts, who ought to be in jail or compulsory rehabilitation programs. Others still were professional beggars who should be swept off the streets. Liberals might fool Jack Kemp into regarding homelessness as a consequence of poverty; might even stampede him into backing the McKinney bill that put an additional $600 million of federal money into the hands of state public housing bureaucracies to house the homeless, but moralist conservatives were far more likely to agree with the opinion of former *Public Interest* editor Thomas Main that "homelessness is a much smaller problem, in terms of the number of people affected by it, than is commonly supposed, but it is also much more intractable" and that "dealing with [it] requires a willingness to assert authority . . . as much as it requires an expenditure of resources."[11]

Authority had to be exerted over the nonhomeless poor too. If the poor remained poor, despite the magnificent economic opportunities that abound in American society, their own misconduct must (it logically followed) be largely to blame. And if the realities of modern government meant that society was obliged to support the poor, then society had a right to admonish and correct their misconduct. Bill Bennett tentatively suggested how that might be done.

The most serious problems plaguing the black underclass have to do with a breakdown of the family. Too many

young black children are being raised without the presence
of good men in their lives. How do we begin to reverse this
fact? By crafting economic and social policies that support
the two-parent family; fashioning public policies that reward
right behavior and penalize wrong behavior; using all the
means at our disposal—in our public, private, and social
spheres, through law and moral suasion—to condemn irre-
sponsible acts (for example, fathering children and not supporting them); putting young men in the presence of positive male role models; and insisting that people in
responsible positions affirm the right things (honoring commitments, individual responsibility, hard work, community
norms, and virtue, to name a few).[12]

Bennett's call for new policies to support morality was answered
by James Q. Wilson, who drafted a four-point program to stiffen
the character of the underclass along the lines Bennett advocated: (1) issue vouchers to mothers of "at-risk" children that
would enable them to enroll their children in boarding schools;
(2) put underclass young men to work in a military-supervised
job training program modeled on the New Deal Civilian Con-
servation Corps; (3) prosecute gangs under the laws against
criminal conspiracy; and (4) enforce random drug testing for
probationers and parolees.[13]

Wilson's program may sound drastic, but to the moralists
the pathologies of urban blacks had become the paramount
example of a social problem that did not respond to incentives.
Who could doubt that there was plenty of incentive to escape
poverty? The states had permitted inflation to nibble away at
the value of welfare payments since the mid-1970s. Who could
believe that there was any lack of opportunity for those prepared to work to escape it? America had created 18 million new
jobs in the 1980s. And who could fail to notice that millions of
new immigrants were successfully emerging from poverty all
the time? During the Reagan years, work had been available for
anyone who wanted it.

> In New York City, the poverty rate actually rose, to nearly a quarter of the population . . . despite forceful economic growth. Milwaukee has rebounded from deindustrialization, increasing employment by 83,000 jobs since 1979, yet unemployment and welfare have actually risen in some ghetto areas; black men stand idle on street corners saying they cannot find work, while all around them other people hustle to their jobs. The most remarkable case may be Atlantic City, New Jersey, where billions of dollars have been invested in new hotels and resorts since casino gambling became legal in 1976. In that time, 41,000 new jobs have been created— more than the entire city's population. The city should have become affluent, yet it has collapsed from within. . . . Half the remaining population is on welfare.[14]

The author of those words, former Reagan administration official Lawrence Mead, was startled by the comment of one welfare mother as quoted by the *San Francisco Chronicle:* "'I've had a few small-time jobs, but I quit them because I couldn't even make ends meet. . . .' Why does one quit work when one cannot make ends meet? It is not a reaction that struggling middle-class Americans are likely to understand."[15] "The causes of poverty," Mead decided, "must be sought among the causes of nonwork." And those, Bennett-inspired conservatives came to believe, were primarily moral. Mead, one of the architects of the 1988 workfare plan introduced by President Reagan, believed that the underclass needed to be compelled to work. Poverty, he demonstrated, is very unusual among people who work regularly. While female-headed families suffered a shocking 32 percent poverty rate in 1989, only 7.1 percent of such families were poor when the mother worked full-time for a full year.[16] It is nonwork, not low wages, that overwhelmingly causes poverty. And nonwork occurs not because opportunities are lacking—they are plentiful—but "because work is not enforced."[17] "There is an emerging consensus," George Will perceived in early 1992, "that government has an interest in, and a right to attempt, behavior modification among those who are sunk in dependence on public assistance."[18] Thus the state of Wisconsin docks parental welfare checks for every day children skip school. New Jersey has abolished the practice of bumping up welfare payments for every additional child born into a dependent family, and has used the money saved to reward welfare mothers who return to school or college. At the federal level, however, Will's "emerging consensus" has been less effective. The first drafts of President Clinton's welfare reform plan took elaborate pains to avoid implying anything unflattering about the work habits of the very poor, and the few conservative attempts made to modify the behavior of the poor have been twisted beyond recognition by liberal legislators. President Reagan's Family Support Act of 1988, originally written to mandate workfare, was transformed into a cornucopia of new benefits for the poor; the work required became make-work labor in local public-sector jobs subsidized by the federal government. And, since money has been short and the subsidies lacking, the whole law has been rendered moot until it is, in Washington argot, "fully funded." But if Will is right about the emerging consensus on poverty policy, then new and far tougher policies can be expected eventually to shoot down the slipway from the conservatives' intellectual navy yards.

The new models will differ strikingly from the old. An example of old-fashioned conservative thinking about character was the brilliant article by Charles Murray in the *Wall Street Journal* in October 1993, drawing attention to the fact that the illegitimacy rate among whites had nearly reached the 25 percent level that had prompted Daniel Patrick Moynihan to declare the black family in crisis in 1965. Murray warned that the violence, drug abuse, and ignorance that today characterize black America will quickly reach terrifying proportions among whites as well, and for the same reason: fatherlessness. What to do? Murray recommended abolishing all government benefits for single mothers (except perhaps for medical coverage of children). "The pressure on relatives and communities to pay for the folly of their children will make an illegitimate birth the socially horrific act it used to be, and getting a girl pregnant something that boys do at the risk of facing a shotgun. Stigma and shotgun marriages may or may not be good for those on the receiving end, but their deterrent effect on others is wonderful—and indispensable."[19] This may sound like strong stuff, but from the point of view of the new moralistic conservatism it suffers from two incapacitating flaws. First, it requires conservatives once again to embark on the hopeless struggle to get rid of a federal program (actually a slew of federal programs) that will be defended unto death by powerful constituencies that control large voting blocs in Congress and that influence noisy voices in the media. A future conservative president, or today's conservative governors and congressmen may inwardly agree with Murray that welfare programs are destroying society and must end. They may amend and alter those programs or experiment with replacing them. But no conservative politician yet dares to advocate cutting them off entirely, and scarcely any conservative intellectual or policy wallah is seriously urging them to do so. Second, Murray—whose personal politics are egalitarian, localist, and optimistic—bases his recommendations upon assumptions that will strike other conservatives as excessively hopeful. Even if it were true that it was the availability of welfare that brought the problems of illegitimacy and dependency into being, it does not automatically follow that repealing welfare will bring them to an end—not, at least, very promptly. This particular social transformation may work in one direction only. Once welfare has brought a class of dependent mothers and violent sons into existence, the abolition of welfare may well serve merely to push them deeper into violence and squalor.

For these reasons, conservatives who follow Bennett, Wilson, Kristol, and Mead dismiss the possibility of eliminating welfare and ponder instead greater interventions into the lives of the poorest of the poor. That's what Chester Finn, deputy first to Bennett and then to Lamar Alexander at the Department of Education, advocates. "I believe we are going to have to be prepared more frequently to remove children from their homes and send them into other settings. . . . Parents do not always know best, and their interest is not always foremost."[20] Mead likewise observed that "the dependent poor appear to react more strongly to requirements to work than to opportunities. Public authority has more effect on them than incentives"[21] largely because of the habits of deference and dependence acquired during slavery. Mead concedes that more optimistic conservatives would be horrified at the prospect that, in words he quotes from Charles Murray, "a substantial portion of our population . . . will in effect be treated as wards of the state." But, he asks, "confronted by a dependent class that defeats itself, what can government do but restore order and hope that, over time, it rubs off?"[22]

All conservatives worried about the underclass, but for moralists the underclass took on an especially sinister significance. They saw it as the distillate of all the vices bubbling through American culture as a whole. Are the black poor having illegitimate babies? So is the white middle class—and for the same reason: culturally propagated immorality. "Why this explosion [of illegitimacy]?" asked Irving Kristol. "The obvious explanation is that girls today are far more 'sexually active' (what one used to call promiscuous) than was formerly the case. Why this increase in sexual activity? Well, the popular culture surely encourages it. You can't expect modesty (to say nothing of chastity) from girls who worship Madonna."[23] Cultural evil moved downward from the top of society, like mud tossed into a pail of water. "During the sixties and seventies, the new culture of the Haves, in its quest for personal liberation, withdrew respect from the behavior and attitudes that have traditionally boosted people up the economic ladder— deferral of gratification, sobriety, thrift, dogged industry, and so on through the whole catalogue of antique-sounding bourgeois virtues," claimed Myron Magnet, a fellow at the Manhattan Institute.[24] "The poor didn't just autonomously decide, let's do away with traditional family roles," says Bill Kristol. "They did have certain signals to this effect from the well-to-do, from cultural leaders. If you have a healthy society and economy, the poor will be okay; but if you have an unhealthy economy or a corrupt society, the poor will get hurt worst because they are the weakest."[25]

The poor you have always with you. What perplexed the moralists was American society's sudden inabiliy to cope with the poor—or with drugs or lust or any of the thousand and one weaknesses to which human beings have always been susceptible. In a curious way, moralist conservatives agree with their liberal opposite numbers that the poor are victims. As moralist conservatives see it, in a highly mobile society, the people at the bottom are unlikely to possess very much either in the way of intelligence or of moral firmness. They are easily swayed and misled. If the society is wholesome, then the instructions broadcast to the people at the bottom will be wholesome too. If the elite is corrupt—if for its own weird reasons it idealizes lower-class criminality and irresponsibility—then the instructions sent down the social chain of command will likewise be corrupting. Moralist conservatives eschew sentimentality about the poor: in the absence of restraint and guidance, the poor can be expected to be idle, sexually casual, and violent, and so indeed they are. That's not what puzzles moralists. What puzzles them—what enrages them—is that the elite of society, either because it is gripped by liberal guilt or because it actively identifies with an "adversary culture," cannot bring itself to set and enforce decent standards of conduct.

It is because of the importance they attach to the social chain of command that moralist conservatives care so intensely about education. True, Americans of all political descriptions have always stocked vast, probably excessive, faith in education. Thomas Jefferson hoped that the day would come when politics would simply cease to exist and be replaced by education. But education is a particularly urgent matter for conservatives. Disbelieving in innate human goodness, they believe that virtue must be learned. And suspecting that things are always getting worse, they see in education a chance for the superior generations vanishing from the stage to delay a little bit the inevitable deterioration in the generations now arriving. For conservatives, then, the decay of the standards of American schooling was a deadly serious national problem—maybe the most serious of all national problems. The bellicose language of the 1983 "Nation at Risk" report was no mere publicity stunt:

> If an unfriendly foreign power had attempted to impose on America the mediocre educational performance that exists today, we might well have viewed it as an act of war. As it stands, we have allowed this to happen to ourselves. . . . We have, in effect, been committing an act of unthinking, unilateral educational disarmament.[26]

Teachers and school administrators were producing dumb young people not just out of incompetence and sloth, but because they were actively subverting the traditional beliefs of American society. Kristol noted twenty years ago that "the avant-garde, anti-bourgeois, elite culture— . . . the 'adversary' culture'—of our bourgeois society has been gradually incorporated into our conventional school curriculum and, with the spread of mass higher education, has begun to shape the popular culture of our urbanized masses."[26] Through the 1980s, alarming news about the ideological content of the schools galvanized conservatives. There was the scandal of peace education, the abuse of Holocaust education, multiculturalism in Oregon, and Afrocentrism in New York State. The National Education Association, the nation's biggest teacher's union, was the striking arm of the American Left.

There was going to have to be radical reform. And it was going to have to come from the top. "Many conservatives," wrote Chester Finn,

> have a charming but antiquated devotion to "local control" of schools that bears scant relationship to contemporary

reality. . . . In the general case, we must recognize that local control is indistinguishable from maintenance of the status quo under the thumb of the educational establishment. As for curriculum, standards, and pedagogy, while it is possible for a perspicacious (and well-to-do) family to locate itself in a neighborhood that boasts schools superior to those down the road, and while such defensive strategy is fine for those able to pursue it, more local control is not going to produce many more such schools: If it could, it already would have. Although we may someday regret handing more of the big decisions to the states [from local school boards] (and to such national groupings as the assembled governors), if we want revolutionary changes in American education we have to overhaul its power structure and ingrained practices.[28]

And while, by the time he wrote this, Finn had come to favor a large measure of parental choice in education, the "we" who were going to do the overhauling were to be found in state capitals and, especially, in Washington, D.C.

Let's reject those old bugaboos that a "national curriculum" is a prescription for catastrophe and national exams are a plot to turn us into a land of dutiful robots. Let's instead open our eyes to the fact that we're living amid a catastrophe that might be ameliorated by embracing a national curriculum and an examination system to accompany it.[29]

You don't have to agree with the demented remark of *Chronicles* editor Thomas Fleming that Finn advocates "total education for the total state" to acknowledge that Finn's hopes for a revolutionary change in American education would grant the central political authorities unprecedented control over the character formation of the American public. "My view is that about two-thirds of the high school curriculum, perhaps 80 percent of the middle school program, and virtually all of the content of primary education should be the same for everybody."[30] Parents are to be trusted to choose the school whose teaching methods they like best, but there is to be scarcely any choice at all—at least within the public system—about what is to be taught. And there is to be no flunking Finn's national exam, no abstention, no dropping out.

> Once we have identified the core skills and knowledge that we expect our young people to acquire before entering adult society, we must oblige them to engage in some sort of systematic study until they actually reach that standard, however long it may take.
>
> Of course, we'll need a process for waiving or modifying that requirement in individual cases. Education is not punishment. . . .[Nor do I] suggest that everyone must sit under the roof of a conventional school building until they meet the exit standard. . . . Instruction can occur on the shop floor, in the lab and library, even on television, not only from lectures and books. . . .The important point is that every young person would be obliged to engage in some program of systematic study until he or she can meet the core learning standard for entry into adult society. . . .
>
> Perhaps the best way to enforce this standard is to confer valuable benefits and privileges on people who meet it, and to withhold them from those who do not. Work permits, good jobs, and college admission are the most obvious, but there is ample scope here for imagination in devising carrots and sticks. Driver's licenses could be deferred. So could eligibility for professional athletic teams. The minimum wage paid to those who earn their certificates might be a dollar an hour higher.[31]

From the point of view of educational theory, Finn may be absolutely bang-on. But from the point of view of conservative ideology, we have arrived at a new destination, where the federal government is fully *parens patriae,* charged with responsibility for, among so many other things, the intellectual development of every resident. If the destination is odd, however, the route toward it is not completely unexplored. Barry Goldwater's dictum—coined in the heat of the debate over civil rights—that "social and cultural change, however desirable, should not be effected by the engines of national power"[32] was by no means conservatism's last word on the subject of behavior modification. At least four distinct elements in the American conservative movement pushed conservatives toward accepting government's responsibility for the character of the people: the "traditionalist" conservatism of the 1950s; populism; the residual liberalism of certain recent adherents to conservatism; and the teachings of the German-Jewish philosopher Leo Strauss.

In their 1954 book, *McCarthy and His Critics,* William F. Buckley and his brother-in-law L. Brent Bozell argued that the McCarthy phenomenon—whatever McCarthy's own personal villainies—demonstrated that America was "rallying around an orthodoxy whose characteristic is that it excludes communism."[33] This was both laudable and inevitable, for "not only is it characteristic of society to create institutions and to defend them with sanctions. Societies must do so—or else they cease to exist. The members of a society must share certain values if it is to cohere, and cohere it must if it is to survive. In order to assert and perpetuate those values, it must do constant battle against competing values."[34] Freedom of speech was a venerable American tradition, said Buckley and Bozell's Yale mentor Willmoore Kendall, but so was riding troublemakers out of town on a rail. By temperament, Buckley happened to be a strong individualist (he would later endorse, for example, the legalization of narcotics), but he set sharp limits upon the philosophical claims of individualism. This way of thinking came to be called, in the internal conservative arguments of the 1950s and 1960s, "traditionalism." According to archtraditionalist Russell Kirk, while the "good society is marked by a high degree of order, justice, and freedom," it is order that "has primacy: for justice cannot be enforced until a tolerable civil order is attained, nor can freedom be anything better than violence until order gives us laws."[35] The nineteenth-century jurist James Fitzjames Stephen, a writer much admired by Kirk, summed up the traditionalist

case in his critique of John Stuart Mill. "Complete moral tolerance is possible only when men have become completely indifferent to each other—that is to say, when society is at an
end."[36]

Conservatives have also inherited a predisposition to use
state power from a second strain in their intellectual inheritance, populism. It intensely irritated liberals that the New
Right organizers of the 1970s delighted in describing themselves as "populists." The original Populists had, after all, advocated economic radicalism—although a radicalism very different
from the social work ethos of George McGovern and the other
prairie leftists for whom liberals wanted to reserve the populist
label. But if George Wallace and Richard Viguerie and Terry
Dolan of the National Conservative Political Action Committee
did not advocate government ownership of railways and utili-
ties, they each in their different ways tapped the same vein of
feeling as Tom Watson and William Jennings Bryan a century
before: the grievances of people who identify themselves as
ordinary; who regard themselves as producers of wealth and
feel exploited by a powerful class of parasites; who sense that
their religious and moral convictions are being mocked by a
remote elite, that their economic status is eroding, and that the
central political authorities have no sympathy for them. Like the
old Populists, the new were prepared to use the state to protect
the economic interests of their followers. Viguerie was a
staunch, often demagogic, defender of Social Security and farm
price supports, as well as a protectionist. Wallace was a statist
through and through. And even the Reaganites of NCPAC preserved a discreet silence on the subject of Medicare and student
loans.

Conservatism's antistatist bite was weakened, third, by the
influence of liberal ideas. The conservatives of the 1950s and
1960s had been a pretty odd bunch of characters. As such, they
were able to hold tight to ideas radically different from those of
the rest of the American intellectual world. Richard Weaver, a
highly influential conservative of those days, could quote

approvingly from nineteenth-century polemics denouncing the Republic as flawed from birth: "'The new Republic of '87, being founded on presumptuous confidence in man, was doomed to fail, or to undergo sad changes and transformations. . . . Woe betide all the proud politics of self-idolizing man.'"[37] This was not an attitude calculated to appeal to very many twentieth-century Americans. And, as ever larger numbers of twentieth-century Americans flocked rightward in the 1970s, they brought their less eccentric ways of thinking with them. A "crucial element of modern consciousness," observe the sociologists Peter and Brigitte Berger in explaining how their conservatism differed from that of thinkers like Weaver, "is a generally pragmatic attitude, a vision of the world as 'makable' and, consequently, a 'tinkering' approach to most if not all problems."[38] The conservative movement of the 1980s would accept social tinkering for the same reason that its leading figures put their children in day care and listened to rock music: as a movement grows huge, it numbers more and more conventional people among its adherents. And conventional Americans send their wives to work, love rock music, and believe that coercive collective action, namely government, is the appropriate way to deal with most social problems.

Finally, and perhaps most important, the way to a conservative appreciation of the value and potential of state power was opened by the teachings of the late Leo Strauss. Strauss, a Jewish refugee from Hitler's Germany, was a brilliant philosopher and a magnetic teacher. Directly or indirectly, through his students Allan Bloom, Walter Berns, Harvey Mansfield, and Harry Jaffa, Strauss transformed contemporary conservative political thought. Strauss's ideas are complex, but one of his insights is especially relevant for understanding conservatives' post-1980 zest for activist government: American society is not nearly so sturdy as it looks. Although it is often suggested that the American Republic is what you get when you emancipate human nature, Strauss believed that the United States, like all regimes, rests upon the control of and betterment of raw human nature.

And if the United States should ever decide to stop controlling and bettering human nature—if it should declare itself indifferent to the character of its people—well, the nation would deteriorate rapidly into something very, very nasty.

Thus, the essential message of Allan Bloom's best-selling *The Closing of the American Mind:* the American regime is in danger because America's intellectual elite no longer attempts to refine the 2 million young people in the universities, and, beyond them, the nation at large.

> From the earliest beginnings of liberal thought there was a tendency in the direction of indiscriminate freedom. Hobbes and Locke, and the American Founders following them, intended to palliate extreme beliefs, particularly religious beliefs, which lead to civil strife. The members of sects had to obey the laws and be loyal to the Constitution; if they did so, others had to leave them alone, however distasteful their beliefs might be. In order to make this arrangement work, there was a conscious, if covert, effort to weaken religious beliefs. . . .
>
> It was possible to expand the space exempt from legitimate social and political regulation only by contracting the claims to moral and political knowledge. The insatiable appetite for freedom to live as one pleases thrives on this aspect of modern democratic thought. In the end, it begins to appear that full freedom can be attained only when there is no such knowledge at all. . . . There are no absolutes; freedom is absolute. Of course the result is that, on the one hand, the argument justifying freedom disappears and, on the other, all beliefs begin to have the attenuated character that was initially supposed to be limited to religious belief.[39]

Bloom is expressing, periphrastically, a core Straussian doctrine: liberal theory cannot be relied on to support a liberal regime. Without a stiffening admixture of premodern thinking—religion for the masses, Greek-style civic virtue for the elite—the self-interestedness of modern life will devour all human relationships, "flattening the soul" and incapacitating Americans for self-government. Bloom approvingly parsed Rousseau: "individual self-interest is not sufficient to establish a common good, he insists, but without [a common good], political life is impossible, and men will be morally contemptible. . . . A people will not automatically result from individual men's enlightenment about their self-interest. A political deed is necessary. The legislator must 'so to speak change human nature, transform each individual. . . .'"⁴⁰

Transforming individuals is not a job that stops at the water's edge. We live in a world full of self-indulgent and self-destructive peoples, and after the collapse of communism, many of the same conservatives who pondered the reform of the domestic poor turned their minds to the reform of poor nations abroad as well.

Conservatives had got into the habit during the 1980s of positing democracy (and not, for example, free enterprise) as the ideological alternative to communism. Many of them called for a foreign policy explicitly dedicated not merely to resisting communism but to spreading democracy—not only to Central and Eastern Europe, but to backward lands where nothing like it had ever existed.⁴¹ This crusading ideal made its way into President Reagan's important address to the British House of Commons in 1982 and supplied the rationale for the creation of the National Endowment for Democracy—a program beloved by conservatives for its high-flown purpose and its dizzy checkwriting. But once the ideological utility of democratism came to an end, conservative foreign policy thinking had to contend with a harsh truth: far from teeming with peoples ready and eager to govern themselves, the earth was on the contrary teeming with nations less capable of self-rule than the most pessimistic conservative supposed the American underclass to be. In an article published shortly after President Bush's Christmastime decision to order 28,000 U.S. troops into Somalia, the British historian Paul Johnson followed this truth to a dramatic conclusion:

[The belief that] all peoples are ready for independence
... has been proved illusory, at incalculable cost in human
misery. Many so-called independent and sovereign states
cannot function, and their peoples suffer accordingly. These
include not merely recent creations, like Somaliland, but
longer-established ones like Haiti . . . and Liberia. . . .

Up to now, the United Nations has never once been
able to tackle an African emergency successfully because it
treats symptoms, not causes, often indeed the wrong symptoms. What we shall see, I believe, will be the Security
Council, using one or more advanced powers as its agents,
moving into the business of government, taking countries
into its trusteeship for varying periods, and becoming itself
an architect and exemplar of honest, efficient administration. . . . In short, the Security Council and its agents will
become the last, most altruistic and positive of the imperial
powers.[42]

The intervention in Somalia was only a half-step in the
direction Johnson beckoned toward. "We do not plan to dictate
political outcomes," said President Bush as the troops landed.
"We respect your sovereignty." But preventing greedy tribal
warlords from stealing Western food aid quickly panned out to
be a bigger job than advertised. The warlords, at first merely
surly, soon turned violent, and while the United Nations forces
were free to leave whenever they liked, Western governments
knew that Somali babies would resume dying in the thousands
the moment they did. The predictable failure inherent in the
decision to respect Somali sovereignty prompted the *Wall Street
Journal* to wonder, "Who wants to volunteer to be the first
Governor of Somalia?" The editorial bore the title "Bring Back
Lord Kitchener," and while the editorialist stipulated that "we
are not—repeat not—pining for the return of unfettered 19th
century colonialism," he did compare the old ways favorably to
the new. "Whatever shortcomings history has imposed on
Kitchener, a sense of purpose wasn't one of them."[43]

Abroad, as at home, what distinguished moralistic conservatism from liberalism was not what it wanted to do—both agreed that the nonpoor were obliged to uplift the poor—but the tone with which it wanted to do it. The Right was self-confident; the Left, self-abasing. Abroad, as at home, however, while the talk may be tough, the newest conservative project exudes a hubris that ought to make even the most bountiful Eleanor Roosevelt–type liberal blink.

While optimist conservatism appeals to the congressional wing of the conservative movement, moralist conservatism predominates among conservatism's writers and intellectuals. Optimistic conservatism appeals to politicians because it promises to make everyone happy; moralist conservatism appeals to clever people who value ideas and ideals in politics. Neither optimist nor moralist conservatism, however, is very likely to appeal to the conservative rank and file: the millions who vote in Republican primaries and listen to Rush Limbaugh. They're going to want something a little . . . stronger. And this being America, whatever people want, there's someone to give it to them.

CHAPTER 6

Nationalists: Whose Country Is It Anyway?

"Today we call for a new patriotism, where Americans begin to put the needs of Americans first, for a new nationalism where in every negotiation, be it arms control or trade, the American side seeks advantage or victory for the United States." With these words, columnist, television personality, and former presidential speechwriter Patrick J. Buchanan announced his candidacy for president in a New Hampshire hotel conference room. He had prefigured his slogan in an article the previous year for the *National Interest:* "America First—and Second, and Third." You had to applaud the audacity of it. Who but Buchanan would launch a political campaign on the slogan "America First," fifty years almost to the very day since the Japanese Imperial Navy had sunk American isolationism in the waters of Pearl Harbor?

America First! What old quarrels that slogan dredges up, for the country but especially for the American Right. The epic of American conservatism since 1945 had been the story of William Buckley and his *National Review* purging the Right of the naivety, xenophobia, and general stupidity of America First.

And now here was America First again, reinjected into American politics by a man who understood every nuance of the phrase.

America First was Buchanan's gambit, his bid to mobilize conservatives now that the old call to slash the federal government no longer resounded successfully. With it he hoped to attract America's nationalist hard core, people who felt aggrieved and abused not so much by foreigners as by alien elements within their own country—to unite conservatism and populism together in an ideology that could impose itself on the country more effectively than Reagan's business-oriented conservatism had ever succeeded in doing. It was not Buchanan's gambit alone, of course. Over the five years since he had quit his White House staff job in 1987, an intellectual coterie had assembled around Buchanan, made up of writers and activists who had broken off from the main mass of conservatism over the course of the 1980s, disgusted with President Reagan's weak-willed acceptance of a Martin Luther King holiday and sanctions against South Africa, with President Bush's knuckling under to the 1991 civil rights laws and his upping legal immigration levels by 200,000 a year. They complained that their conservative movement—the conservative movement of Robert Alfonso Taft and Barry Goldwater—had been hijacked. "Before true conservatives can ever take back their country," Buchanan had written in May 1991, "they are first going to have to take back their movement." From whom? From "the neoconservatives . . . the ex-liberals, socialists and Trotskyists who signed on in the name of anti-communism and now control our foundations and set the limits of permissible dissent." As one of the conservatives who would later back the Buchanan campaign lamented, "We have simply been crowded out by overwhelming numbers. The offensives of radicalism have driven vast herds of liberals across the borders into our territories. These refugees speak in our name, but the language they speak is the same one they always spoke."[1]

It was the fault of these neoconservatives, Buchanan and

his allies decided, that the Reagan years had been so disappointing. In a 1988 lecture, Russell Kirk quoted a letter that showed, he said, how hot the bitterness burned: "I believe," wrote his correspondent, "that the chief enemy of American conservatism has not been the Marxists, nor even the socialist liberals in the Democratic Party, but the Neo-conservatives, who have sabotaged the movement from within and exploited it for their own selfish purposes."[2]

So it was time to light out for the territories again, to split with the neocons, to form a conservative movement dedicated not to moral reform, not to economic prosperity, but to the preservation of the American nation. Buchanan was running, quipped Robert Bartley, not against George Bush but against Irving Kristol. Buchanan would likely have agreed. The 37 percent of New Hampshire Republicans who gave their ballots to Buchanan in February 1992 might simply have been punishing their president for three years of economic listlessness. But whatever the spirit with which the voting levers were pulled, the vote total's effect was to convince Buchanan and his allies that their nationalist conservatism was not marginal, not futile, but potentially a potent, even dominant, force in American public life. It was a potent force already: after his presidential bid, and with William Buckley in semiretirement, Buchanan can vie with Robert Bartley and Rush Limbaugh for the title of most influential conservative in the country. He can very reasonably plan for a conservatism finally free of neoconservative "limits of permissible dissent," of a conservatism finally free to express its real convictions. At that prospect, Buchanan and his allies claim to feel a sweeping rush of relief; the relief, one of them wrote, of "breathing clear air again."

It must be said that Buchanan and his friends fling about the term "neoconservative" in a remarkably casual way, rather like the schoolboy in the Philip Roth story who comes home with a black eye and tells his mother that he got in a fight with "the Catholics"—using, Roth says, "Catholic" in the broad sense, to include Protestants. When the term was coined in the

1970s, a neoconservative was a former liberal who had moved rightward in dismay at the Left's unwillingness to stand up to the Soviets abroad and to antidemocratic radicals at home. It was a biographical as much as an ideological description. By using "neoconservative" fuzzily, however, Buchanan was able to do what so many innovators before him have done: dress up his novelty as a return to a preexisting state of affairs. Buchanan said that he was returning to the principles of Taft and the conservatives of the 1940s and 1950s, the "paleoconservatism" of the "Old Right": rolling back the New Deal at home, disentangling America from military alliances abroad. But that simply is not so. The politics Buchanan has been arguing for since 1987—the politics he campaigned for in 1992—bears only a passing resemblance to the conservative politics of the past. For all his attacks on President Bush's spendthrift administration, in New Hampshire candidate Buchanan could bring himself to name only three specific civilian budget cuts. He would repeal half the 1990 congressional pay raise (for a saving of $6 million), eliminate the National Endowment for the Arts (1992 budget: $165 million), and end all foreign aid programs (1992 budget, under the broadest definition of "foreign aid": $13 billion). In the 1992 fiscal year, the U.S. government spent nearly $1.5 trillion, an amount equal to the entire gross domestic product of united Germany. From that vast ocean of money, fed by roaring rivers of unnecessary and destructive spending, greasy with floating blobs of waste, Buchanan could bring himself to blot up rather less than 1 percent. There were, naturally, to be vast sums saved by bringing the troops home from Europe and Korea. There were also going to be equally vast sums spent to keep the United States "permanent mistress of the seas, first in air power, first in space," and to complete the strategic defense initiative. More than this he did not say. Careful analysis of the budget was never a hallmark of the Buchanan campaign, and so it is impossible to know what effect, if any, his defense plans would have had. In any case, it did not matter. The Right, wrote Buchanan's friend and idea-man, *Washington Times* columnist Samuel Francis, should no longer "dwell on limiting the size of government but rather on the issue of who and what controls government."[3]

Like the moralistic conservatives, Buchanan and his friends had lost Reagan and Goldwater's happy faith in the virtue of America. But while the moralist conservatives concluded that the possessors of wholesome values should use the state apparatus to resist the corrupting influence of the adversary culture above, Buchanan perceived that the threat to good order came from below. And rather than compulsory reform of the turbulence below him, he preferred separation from the alien culture and containment of it.

> Last month, during a week at CNN in New York, I rode nightly up Eighth Avenue in a cab; it was like passing through another world. We are two countries; and many Americans in the first country are getting weary of subsidizing and explaining away the deepening failure of the second, and want only to get clear of it.

Two nations. Not two cultures; not two worldviews; two nations—European America and Third World America. One was Buchanan's America; the other was a constant menace to it. Moralist conservatives believed that the danger to American culture came from the top down; Buchanan and his pals feared that it came from the bottom up. The children of the wealthy laboriously mimic the accents and clothing of the slums. The toddlers of Minneapolis bop to the rhythms of the ghetto as broadcast by "Sesame Street." Englewood Cliffs drives into Washington Heights to buy its crack.

A generation ago, that part of Buchanan's message— expressed even more bluntly than Buchanan would dare— would have been an uncontroversial one among conservatives. *National Review* had at first sympathized with the Southern resistance to desegregation, going so far as to defend segregation in a now-notorious 1957 editorial: "the South . . . perceives important qualitative differences between its culture and the Negroes', and intends to assert its own. *National Review* believes that the South's premises are correct. . . . It is more important for any community, anywhere in the world, to affirm and live by civilized standards, than to bow to the demands of the numerical majority."[4]

Nor did the Right use to be bashful about asserting the propriety of Christianity predominating in America. When President Eisenhower personally dedicated a Muslim mosque in Washington, D.C., *National Review* complained that he had "responded beyond the call of duty to the First Amendment. . . . The President has the constitutional duty to see to it that everyone be free to worship as he pleases, but hardly to go about declaring alien religions 'just as welcome as could be any center of worship of any religion.'"[5] Still, since the early 1960s American conservatives have distinguished themselves by an adamant color-blindness. Barry Goldwater voted against the 1964 Civil Rights Act not because he was a bigot but because, in the words of the late M. E. Bradford, he refused to accept that "the traditions of restricted Federal authority produced and nurtured over two hundred years of American history must give way because [of] the grievances and misfortunes of one segment of the population."[6] Ronald Reagan was hated fiercely by American blacks, but any injuries he did them were the incidental results of what he and his administration were deeply convinced was race neutrality. By the end of the 1980s, however, many conservatives found that they simply could not continue to look past race and ethnicity.

The American complexion visibly darkened in the 1980s. The white proportion of the population dropped from 83 percent in 1980 to just over 80 percent in 1990. (When Buchanan was born in 1938, the country was 90 percent white.) Even more rapid demographic change is coming. While blacks account for 12 percent of the population as a whole, and Hispanics for 9 percent, 15 percent of all children younger than five are black and 13 percent are Hispanic. With greater demographic heft came greater visibility and cultural power. British history slowly seeped out of the curricula of the nation's high schools to be replaced by happy talk about African culture. Spanish-language signs proliferated in California, Florida, and Texas. George Washington and Abraham Lincoln lost their individual holidays; Martin Luther King gained one. The political furor over sanctions against South Africa announced that American blacks would now demand that American foreign policy accommodate their particular ethnic feelings as it had accommodated those of the Irish, Jews, and Greeks before them. Lawyers came to court wearing kente cloths; the parks of New York, Chicago, and Washington suddenly boomed to the beat of rap music.

Most conservatives at least professed to be unalarmed about this gradual transformation of the country. They claimed that America was a nation founded upon a "proposition"; anyone who assented to the American proposition could become an American. The editorialists at the *Wall Street Journal* effusively welcomed the new arrivals. Bill Bennett claimed that the new immigrants made better citizens than many of the Anglos whose families had lived here for 200 years, and that the blame for any difficulties posed by immigration fell upon the weak-willed elite that failed to insist upon prompt assimilation. To Buchanan and his friends, this universalism was so much sentimental flim-flam. American civilization was the product of a particular people. To preserve that civilization, it was necessary to preserve the people that had created it. The Declaration of Independence and the Constitution had not created America; the Declaration and the Constitution were created by Americans. Bolivar wrote constitutions every bit as noble as that composed in Philadelphia; it was the Anglo-American character that made the Philadelphia constitution a success and the Caracas constitution a failure. History had demonstrated that non–British Isles immigrants from Europe had made good enough citizens, but why run the awful risk of cultural suicide a second time? And, through the 1990s, this argument won converts, most notably George Will, who had championed immigration for twenty years. "America," Will wrote in July 1993, "is more than an arena for wealth creation. It is a culture."[7]

The risk of cultural suicide vastly outweighed the dreary problems of fiscal policy that had absorbed the energies of the Republican Party for the past twelve years. "The issues that began to matter in this past election," Francis wrote after the 1992 election,

> economic digestion by foreign powers, the danger not only of crime but of outright anarchy, cultural disintegration under the impact of massive immigration and militantly antiwhite and anti-Western multiculturalist movements— have to do with whether the American nation, as a political unity and a cultural identity, will live or die.[8]

Those were the stakes as Buchanan saw them too. What clinched his decision to enter the 1992 race was not George Bush's 1990 agreement to raise the top rate of income tax in exchange for some restrictions on federal expenditure, much as Buchanan disliked the budget deal. The clincher, Buchanan told his confidants, was the president's signing of the 1991 civil rights act. With Euro-American and Third World American interests starkly pitted against each other, the president had preferred Third World America. Buchanan decided that the time was ready for mutiny.

Patrick J. Buchanan was an unlikely mutineer. All his life he had hewed to the straight path. The fourth of eight children of a father "whose trinity of political heroes consisted of Douglas MacArthur, General Franco, and the junior senator from Wisconsin they called Tail Gunner Joe," Buchanan's verbal pungency had won him an editorial writer's job at the *St. Louis Globe-Democrat* by the age of twenty-three. He quit that job in 1965 to take a gamble on the apparently defunct career of Richard Nixon. For nine years, he loyally served as a speechwriter and adviser to Nixon, whose offenses against conservative principles from the SALT arms control treaty to wage and price controls considerably exceeded and outnumbered George Bush's. The book Buchanan wrote when he emerged from the White House in 1974, *Conservative Votes, Liberal Victories*, is a decoction of 50 percent Buckley and 50 percent Bartley, with Irving Kristol politely thanked in the acknowledgments. In his first ten years as a syndicated columnist, Buchanan sounded much like every other conservative in Washington—snazzier and funnier than most but, in substance, the same.

If Buchanan is an unlikely insurgent, he's an even unlikelier politician. Fans of his fluent counterpunching on television may find this hard to believe, but Buchanan is simply a rotten campaigner. He shuffled through the diners and coffeehouses of New Hampshire, mumbling and looking embarrassed. His voice is inaudible more than fifteen feet away; he is tall, but so thin that he appears alarmingly elongated, with narrow shoulders, long arms, and small, delicate hands. Back at the restaurant of the Sheraton Wayfarer near Manchester, the best hotel in the state, he would joke and chaff with his fellow journalists from Washington, but he seldom smiled when talking to a voter.

Unlike Ronald Reagan's rebellion against the milk-and-water Jerry Ford in 1976, Buchanan's insurgency won only qualified support from the conservative press. Just days before Buchanan declared his candidacy, William Buckley published a long essay on anti-Semitism in *National Review* that said of Buchanan, "I find it impossible to defend Pat Buchanan against the charge that what he did and said during the period under examination amounted to anti-Semitism." In a sympathetic primary-season interview, Allan Ryskind, the editor of the venerable conservative weekly *Human Events*, chided Buchanan for cluttering his message with what Ryskind dismissed as a lot of irrelevant junk about protectionism and ethnicity. *Commentary* and the *American Spectator* condemned him as sinister; the *Wall Street Journal* treated him as a joke. But the irrelevancies that so annoyed Buckley and Ryskind and that so offended *Commen-*

tary and the *American Spectator* were intensely relevant to Buchanan—vastly more relevant than the economic issues that preoccupied mainline conservatives. Ronald Reagan loved economic factoids; tell him a good story of bureaucratic meddlesomeness, and he'd repeat it in every speech he gave for the rest of his life. Not Buchanan. For him, he said, the phrase "voodoo economics" was redundant. "Tribe and race"—those were the causes that moved men. His conservatism was a nationalist conservatism above all—a conservatism that attached far more importance to cultural and security issues than to maximizing growth and efficiency. Buchanan was slow to absorb all the implications of his nationalism. In his 1988 memoir, he still thought that "among the great American achievements of the twentieth century is free Asia, democratic and capitalist." "To squander that in an absurd 'trade war' because we cannot compete with Korean cars or Japanese computer chips would be an act of almost terminal stupidity for the West."[9] He also confessed that he had inwardly believed, at the time they took place, that the civil rights movement's civil disobedience campaigns were justified by natural law, even though he would later write editorials for the *Globe-Democrat* attacking them. But his thinking was jogged along by a new set of friends: the writers who published in *Chronicles* magazine.

Chronicles—originally *Chronicles of Culture*—was founded in 1976 by Leopold Tyrmand, an irritable Polish émigré with the usual émigré conviction that America was going to hell in a handcart. Tyrmand managed to convince the president of the Rockford Institute in Rockford, Illinois—one of the oldest, if least effective, of conservative think tanks—that he should be given a magazine with which to say so. Tyrmand died in 1985, and his job was taken over by his deputy, Thomas Fleming. Fleming is a strange man: a bearded leftover from the 1960s, an unsuccessful poet, briefly a teacher of Classics at a small South Carolina college, who drifted into journalism and found himself in Rockford. But he quickly proved to be a nervy editor. The 1980s were prosperous years for conservative journalists, but not for conservative journalism. Editors lost their best writers to administration jobs, talent was spread thin as new periodical after new periodical opened, and the natural savagery of journalists was thwarted by their responsibility to defend their allies in the administration. As Reaganite opinions lost their power to shock, conservative journalism lost its verve.

Fleming never lost his power to shock, and his magazine trembled with the energy of the early *National Review*. Over his tenure as editor, circulation quadrupled to a peak of nearly 15,000 at the onset of the 1990 recession. (It has slipped since.) The energy must have been infectious, for it was not very long before Buchanan's columns and speeches were repeating ideas and phrases from the magazine, and particularly from the columns of Samuel Francis. Francis is a huge man with a bright red face, who puffs cigarettes below anachronistic black horn-rims. A Ph.D. from the University of North Carolina, he was brought to Washington by the late Senator John East of North Carolina. From East's staff, he jumped to an editorial page job on the *Washington Times*. His bitterness against neoconservatives was aggravated when he was passed over for the top job on the *Times*'s editorial page in favor of Tod Lindberg, a much younger man who happened to have roomed with Norman Podhoretz's son at the University of Chicago—a coincidence that Francis and his friends imbued with sinister significance. It was Francis whom Buchanan chose to fill his syndicated column when he took leave to run for the Republican nomination.

Fleming and Francis's connections with genteeler sorts of conservatism had been smashed in spectacular fashion—so spectacular, in fact, that it landed on the front page of the *New York Times*. In 1989, a spat erupted between the Rockford Institute—*Chronicles*'s sponsor—and Richard John Neuhaus, a Lutheran cleric who had run Rockford's New York–based Center on Religion and Society since 1984. Neuhaus had been dismayed by *Chronicles*'s turn toward nationalism, and in particular its March 1989 "Nation of Immigrants" issue, which had editorially concluded that the loss of ethnic homogeneity caused by immigration was "quite as serious as even the most frightened alarmists have suggested." Neuhaus complained in a private letter to the president of the Rockford Institute that "with respect to immigration policy, race and ethnicity, 'the most frightened alarmists' are sundry white citizens' councils and nativist protective groups, plus not a few in the Margaret Sanger tradition of racial eugenics." In case the lead editorial had failed to make its meaning clear, that same issue had run not one but two short pieces hailing the flamboyantly anti-Semitic writer Gore Vidal as "an authentic champion of a peculiarly American conservatism, a conservatism vastly nobler than that of the typewriter hawks and blow-dried Republicans of Washington, D.C." Neuhaus had complained about the March issue to his friend Michael Joyce, the chief money-man at the Bradley Foundation, the behemoth that had been donating some $280,000 a year to Neuhaus's institute. Neuhaus's former associates at Rockford—terrified that he would declare independence and take Bradley's money with him—arrived one May morning to shut the office up, seize its equipment, and hurl his files onto Madison Avenue. The plan was not very smart: the Rockford people looked like vindictive fools, Neuhaus did start an independent institute, and the Bradley money did follow him.

For Fleming and Francis, the breach with Neuhaus cut the last remaining tether to conservatism's respectables. But by then they were happily working out a new philosophy—and a new set of alliances—that separated them from those respectables permanently. That new philosophy put the defense of the white American middle class at the center of its concerns.

The defense of the white middle class, however, required a clear and explicit rejection of the old doctrine of strictly limited government. "A Middle-American nationalism," Francis wrote in June 1992,

> must expect to redefine legal rules, political procedures, fiscal and budgetary mechanisms, and national policy generally

in the interests of Middle Americans, and it must do so with
no illusions about rejecting, decentralizing or dismantling
the national state and the power it affords. Middle American
interests are dependent on the national state.

Thus, campaigning in New Hampshire, Pat Buchanan
attacked President Bush for failing to extend federal unemployment insurance benefits quickly enough to New Hamp-
shirites in need. Since the 1930s, the federal government had
provided workers who lost their jobs with twenty-six weeks
of unemployment benefits. During hard times, Congress
generally extends those benefits, and so it did in November
1991. By the time of the New Hampshire primary, however,
a worker who had lost his job in February 1991 was facing
the exhaustion of his benefits. Congress voted on February 5
to extend benefits for thirteen more weeks. Buchanan had
opposed these extensions throughout his career. Quite suddenly, he switched sides. "You can't go into those unemployment offices, see those guys about to lose their homes
without saying, 'Well, we ought to go ahead with 12 [sic]
more weeks of unemployment benefits.'"[10]

Sympathy for the economic plight of blue-collar workers in
New Hampshire was not just bleeding-heart sentimentalism: it
propelled Buchanan toward accepting an active federal responsibility for promoting industry—and protecting it from foreign
competition. Buchanan's standard stump speech told an anecdote about a visit to a lumber mill on the Canadian border.
Shaking hands with the workers, the candidate found himself
face to face with a burly giant of a man. The man stood silent
for a moment, staring at the floor, and then looked up to say
only, "Save our jobs." As a story, it is as kitschy as Steinbeck at
his most gooey, but it led to a serious point:

> I see Mr. Bush, and excuse me, some of my conservative
> friends, by their willingness to allow the ruthless destruction
> of so many of the industries vital to our defenses, as

engaged in the unilateral disarmament of our country. I can't understand it. On the grounds of national interest, I favor policies that won't let certain defense-related industries go under.[11]

Buchanan there is speaking with his more free enterprise–minded friends at *Human Events,* and so he is still paying obeisance to the "national security" argument for trade protection. On the campaign trail, though, the circle of protection widened well beyond defense industries.

Do we want to keep the textile manufacturing base in the United States? Do we want to keep GM and Chrysler and Ford? Do we want to keep Boeing and McDonnell-Douglas? . . . We have got to address the fact that the Asian countries and European countries are practising a form of protectionism and adversarial trade. They are capturing markets by undercutting and dumping and by targeted trade, and they have been doing this to make their countries No. 1.[12]

No longer are democratic Japan and Korea proud American accomplishments; now they are leading threats to America on a planet where the relations between nations are inherently hierarchical and adversarial. "The rising economic power of Japan has filed a claim to displace the United States as [the] dominant power of the 21st century. . . . The 20th century was the American Century, but they intend to make the 21st . . . the Century of Asia."[13] With reporters he liked, Buchanan went further yet. The *Economist* stringer who followed Buchanan to Mississippi reported that

Mr. Buchanan has greater ideas still for the nationalist state than merely dishing out credits to any industry (oil and gas, aerospace, textiles, ship-building) that suffers from foreign competition. For instance, he privately admits he is tempted by the idea of paying for those credits—and much more—

by throwing up a wall of tariffs around the American economy.[14]

As Buchanan's protectionism became more and more explicit, free-trade conservatives attempted to read him out of the party. Bill Bennett flew to Manchester before the primary to warn that Buchanan "cannot be allowed to hijack conservatism." But Buchanan's views—although certainly a minority opinion—did not lack supporters on the Right. There is, as always, a cynical explanation of why this should be so: the influence of billionaire textile magnate Roger Milliken. Milliken has generously bankrolled conservatives and conservative causes—especially if they agree that his operations should not have to face excessive competition from abroad. But cynical explanations do not quite explain everything. Buchanan understood that many conservatives saw trade not as an economic issue, but as an issue of sovereignty and group loyalty. Protectionism is a way for conservatives to show solidarity with their fellow-Americans, especially blue-collar fellow-Americans, without explicitly endorsing the redistribution of wealth.

Which is why so many would-be populists of the Right have been drawn to the protectionist cause. Barry Goldwater had been one of just eight senators to vote against the 1962 law that gave President Kennedy the authority to engage in the Kennedy round of General Agreement on Tariffs and Trade negotiations. Pat Robertson campaigned as a protectionist in 1988. So did George Wallace, in both 1968 and 1972. Richard Viguerie, the direct-mail whiz who in his heyday had his stethoscope pressed as close to the chest of the American conservative as anyone, argued as long ago as 1983 that "the official trade policy of the United States should be 'fair trade'—that is, no imports produced with slave labor, no imports from foreign plants built by the U.S. taxpayer and no imports from countries which don't allow our products into their country."[15]

Reagan's first secretary of the interior, James Watt, was credited with being the most right-wing member of the cabinet.

He too was convinced that the United States was a victim of foreign predators who trampled on trade rules. He urged that

> a "market access fee" be assessed to each country seeking to sell its manufactured goods in America. . . . We would not charge countries exporting non-manufactured goods such as bananas or coffee beans. But countries exporting manufactured products, such as automobiles, would be hit. The fees generated could be channeled into Social Security or unemployment benefits.[16]

And in November 1991, just before the beginning of campaigning in New Hampshire, a group of conservative activists called a press conference in Washington to announce their repudiation of free trade. Among them was Paul Weyrich, president of the Free Congress Foundation, the stablest of the new right-wing organizations that had come to life in the late 1970s, and one of the founders of the Heritage Foundation. "We are here," Weyrich said, "to warn the Republican Party that they had better take this issue seriously."

Weyrich was not just blowing hot air. While the congressional Republican Party overwhelmingly endorsed the North American Free Trade Agreement, the endorsement was not quite unanimous. North Carolina Senator Jesse Helms voted against NAFTA as did his protégé Senator Lauch Faircloth. And many of the Republicans who voted in favor of the treaty were swung not by the ambiguous pact's free-trade aspects but by its protectionist subthemes. Suggestively, the manager of the Republican pro-NAFTA forces in the House of Representatives, Newt Gingrich, is by no means a believer in free trade. In conversation, he praises Henry Cabot Lodge and the protectionist Republicans of the 1920s, and warns that in the absence of trade controls, world industrial wages will be determined by the pay scale of South China.[17]

Protectionism has infected conservatives and Republicans beyond the precincts of Congress too. With no apparent reluc-

tance, Ronald Reagan imposed "voluntary" import controls on
Japanese cars in 1981 and negotiated a semiconductor deal with
Japan in 1985 that raised the price of computer chips, both
domestic and foreign, in the United States, and guaranteed the
United States a 20 percent share of the Japanese market. Altogether, between 1981 and 1989 the proportion of imported goods
subject to some sort of trade restriction nearly doubled. Informal
harassment, made possible by more permissive rules on anti-
dumping lawsuits, multiplied. President Reagan appointed an
avowed protectionist, Alfred Eckes, to the chairmanship of the
International Trade Commission (America's trade court). In a
1991 anthology of conservative protectionist writing, *America
Asleep*, Eckes cited the long protectionist history of the Republican
Party and concluded that "in place of a quixotic pursuit of abstract
ideals, it is time for Republicans to take a hard-nosed approach
compatible with American interests and ideals. Surely the Party's
patriarchs, from Lincoln to Teddy Roosevelt, are more experi-
enced and eminent teachers than some abstract, academic scrib-
bler from Scotland."[18] That's Adam Smith he's talking about.

Even so radical a free-market economist as Paul Craig
Roberts was persuaded that textile protectionism was compatible with conservative economics. In a January 1991 column in
the *Washington Times*, Roberts complained that

> lost jobs are the first casualties of the United States' con-
> frontation with Iraq in the Persian Gulf. To secure Turkey's
> support in the coalition against Iraq, President Bush sub-
> stantially increased Turkey's quota to export apparel, fabric
> and yarn to the United States.
>
> In effect, we paid for Turkey's support by sacrificing
> American textile jobs. . . . This loss of jobs and shareholders'
> wealth is probably worth thinking about before the U.S.
> government callously discards any more U.S. apparel jobs in
> pursuit of diplomatic goals.[19]

In fact, it was Hong Kong apparel jobs that were callously
discarded; Turkey's quota increase was compensated for by

quota reductions for East Asian exporters. But even if Roberts's facts had been right, why should a free marketeer care? Roberts's answer, like that of a growing number of other Republicans, was that conservatives should be free marketeers only to the water's edge. Beyond that, they should recognize, in the words of William Hawkins, who runs a small conservative think tank in Tennessee largely funded by textile money, that the "globe is divided into competing nation-states showing considerable political, cultural and ideological diversity. . . . Economics cannot differ fundamentally from the broader political environment which defines how the world is organized."[20]

Free enterprise up to the twelve-mile buoys, close government control beyond them—only a country as big and rich as the United States could entertain that delusion. As every country that has dabbled in protectionism, including the United States, has learned, in practice a protectionist government finds itself drawn into the minutest questions of business life. Shall soft drinks be sweetened with corn syrup or sugar? Shall American computer makers be allowed to buy superior Japanese flat screens? Which investments shall foreigners be permitted to make? Most conservative protectionists simply refuse to think about the consequences of their America First principles. The writers at *Chronicles* plunged straight ahead.

> The quality of the American population, its education, its economy and technology, and its social discipline are all, in one sense "assets" by which the national well-being and security of the country may be measured. They are therefore proper objects of public concern, and while that does not mean that the federal government should manage the population, it does mean that the concept of "America First" implies a nationalist ethic that transcends the preferences and interests of the individual or the interest group and may often require government action.[21]

The necessary connection between nationalism and statism was well understood by the ideological movement that most closely resembles nationalist conservatism, the National Efficiency campaign in Edwardian Britain. National Efficiency's most vigorous pamphleteer, Leopold Maxse, was the editor of an idiosyncratic magazine of the same name as that which William Buckley would found fifth years later, *National Review*. Maxse warned that the Kaiser's Germany was overtaking Britain by means of a four-point program of national power: protective tariffs, military conscription, social welfare programs designed to toughen the physiques of the boys who would be conscripted, and universal technical education to improve their minds. Maxse urged Britain to follow Germany's example.

Like Maxse, American nationalists are haunted by an awareness of decline. Buchanan reminisced in his memoirs about the journalist Stuart Alsop, who died in the belief that "America's greatness lay behind her. He had been privileged, he said, to live through the glory years, but a day was coming for America he really did not care to see. To me, he, too, was right."[22] Extensive social welfare programs—other than Social Security of course—are not listed on the American nationalists' agenda. But enhancing the quality of the American population is. And their favored mechanism for achieving that enhancement of the population is the one place where the nationalist position is vastly popular among the conservative rank and file: cutting off immigration, especially nonwhite immigration. Ten years ago, Richard Viguerie noticed how his direct-mail audience twitched at the subject of immigration, and during the controversy over the guerilla war in Central America Patrick Buchanan often argued that the threat of millions of Hispanic refugee immigrants pouring over the border would win the sympathies of wavering audiences for the Nicaraguan contras.

The conservative and Republican leadership has tended to favor relatively open immigration in recent years for both practical and idealistic reasons. Business needs labor. Educated immigrants from Europe, the Indian subcontinent, and the Far East have brought the country skills it otherwise would have lacked, while Latin America and the Caribbean have sent workers eager to work hard for low wages in domestic service, the hotel and restaurant industries, textiles, and agriculture. To libertarian-minded conservatives, the free movement of people is the natural corollary to the free movement of goods and capital. Immigration advocacy has offered Republicans an opportunity to prove themselves color-blind. To conservatives who care about cities, the influx of Koreans, Mexicans, and Barbadians is about the only good news American urban neighborhoods have had in forty years. And to Jewish, Irish, Italian, and other conservatives from immigrant backgrounds, the celebration of immigration seemed to honor the accomplishments and sacrifices of their own forebears. In 1989, with President Bush backing legislation to raise the ceiling on legal immigration from 500,000 to 700,000 arrivals a year, it might even have seemed that immigration exclusion would be picked up as a cause by the Democratic Left, many of whose important constituencies—organized labor, environmentalists, blacks—dislike immigration as wholeheartedly as the most mossbacked Republican nativist.

Since the onset of the 1990 recession and the terrorist attack by a conspiracy of Arab immigrants upon the World Trade Center in New York, however, a slow but noticeable movement has been felt on the Right. Conservatives have begun to complain about immigrant criminality: Buchanan claimed that illegals were responsible for half the crime in San Diego. Nearly one-third of the first 6,000 people arrested after the Los Angeles riots were illegal aliens; half the criminals arrested in New York's tough Washington Heights precinct were illegal immigrants.[23]

Meanwhile, hard-pressed Californians have suffered tax increase after tax increase to pay for social services increasingly driven by the demands of impoverished Mexican and Central American immigrants. These costs might have been swallowed, if unhappily, as the price of absorbing people who would go on to pull their own weight in society. But evidence is mounting that a rising proportion of the recent immigrants never will.

Economist George Borjas, in a book increasingly widely cited among conservatives, found that immigrants' skills and incomes have dropped sharply since 1965, when the United States shifted to a family-reunification immigration policy from one based on national origins. "Immigrants who arrived in the 1950s have about 25 percent higher lifetime earnings than immigrants who arrived in the late 1970s."[24] Not only are immigrants faring less well than they used to: they are working less and taking welfare more. By 1980, one-quarter of all immigrant households from the Dominican Republic and 12.7 percent of all households from Mexico had at least one family member on welfare, as compared to 8 percent for the native-born.[25] A 1985 study of Haitians in Miami found that close to one-third were receiving welfare.[26]

In his speeches, Buchanan stressed that the United States must slow immigration not just because the newcomers were working out less well than previous generations of immigrants, but because the failure to exert political control over the population was in itself a failure of sovereignty. "Our own country is undergoing the greatest invasion in its history, a migration of millions of illegal aliens yearly from Mexico. . . . A nation that cannot control its own borders can scarcely call itself a nation any longer."[27]

Not all immigration, of course, was equally problematic. As Peter Brimelow and Laurence Harrison argued in two quite different major articles that appeared within just a few weeks of each other in the National Review and the National Interest, some immigrants were much more problematic than others. "The heavy flow of unskilled immigrants," warned Harrison, "has braked labor productivity, technological advance and per capita income and has contributed to the drop in the real income of nonsupervisory workers." Brimelow observed that

> cultural traits, such as attitudes to work and education, are
> intrinsically related to economic success. Germans, Japanese,
> and Jews are successful wherever they are in the world.

> Conversely . . . national origin, a proxy for culture, is an excellent predictor of economic failure, as measured by the propensity to go on welfare. . . . There can be absolutely no question that the cultural characteristics of current immigrant groups will have consequences for the U.S.—in this case economic consequences—far into the future.[28]

Characteristically, Sam Francis took these thoughts to the furthest possible logical extreme—and then a little further still.

> Immigration from countries and cultures that are incompatible with and indigestible to the Euro-American cultural core of the United States should be generally prohibited, current border controls should be rigorously enforced, illegal aliens already here should be rounded up and deported, and employers who hire them should be prosecuted and punished.[29]

Unlike most of the nationalists, Francis worried about the effects of white-skinned immigration too. Francis fretted in print about how the music of Tin Pan Alley, often Jewish or black in origin, had replaced the ballads of the Scots-Irish as America's distinctive musical form in the nineteenth century. Like French trade negotiaters and generations of unremembered Canadian culture bureaucrats, Francis believed that the American soul lived in constant danger of submersion from abroad: "As for immigrants from less backward countries, we should balance considerations of whatever gains they might bring to our economy with at least equal consideration of their long-term impact on our cultural identity (including our economic and scientific culture)."[30]

Concern for the cultural homogeneity of the United States can lead to some surprising political conclusions. It caused Buchanan, for instance, to favor independence for Puerto Rico, gloomily predicting that otherwise "we could well have created a Northern Ireland in the Caribbean, and scheduled our own *intifada* for the new century." At the same time, he glanced

covetously at Canada, or at least at Canada's western and
eastern provinces, where the old English, Irish, and Eastern
European stocks continue to dominate demographically.

> Since the maritimes have much in common with us, in trade
> patterns, language, culture, why should they not join the
> U.S., with whom they share a common border?. . .
>   There is nothing wrong with Americans dreaming of a
> nation which, by the year 2000, encompasses the maritime
> and Western provinces of Canada, the Yukon and North-
> west Territories, all the way to the Pole, and contains the
> world's largest island, Greenland, purchased from Denmark,
> giving the Republic a land mass rivalling that of the
> U.S.S.R.[31.]

Far more than Hispanic immigration, however, it is the
existing, native-born black population—and the demands of its
elite that the United States reorganize itself to be a multicultural
society, as African as it is European—that worries nationalist
conservatives. The alarm felt concerning black cultural power
explains the sudden explosion of vilification against Martin
Luther King that has spread itself across the pages of the
nationalists' publications a quarter of a century after the civil
rights leader's murder. It was *Chronicles* that worked hardest to
obtain the news that the editors of the King papers at Boston
University had discovered extensive plagiarism in his academic
work, although the story was ultimately broken in the *Wall
Street Journal*. And it was in *Chronicles* that King's plagiarism
was most triumphantly and repeatedly discussed. Among the
most relentless of the King-haters published in the pages of
Chronicles was Llewellyn Rockwell, president of the Ludwig von
Mises Institute in Auburn, Alabama. Why did he hate King so
much?

> King, one, stole virtually every word he "wrote," from high
> school to his last sermon; two, rejected the central claims of
> Christianity in graduate school and never returned to them;

three, had a sex life worthy of Magic Johnson; four, advocated racial redistributionism; five, called himself a Marxist
in private; and six, coordinated his schedule, finances,
speeches, publications, and strategy with members of the
American Communist Party.[32]

It profoundly offended the *Chronicles* crowd that there existed
conservatives—like William Bennett—who regarded "if not
Malcolm X, then at least Martin Luther King, Jr., . . . as an
exemplar of American values on the same level as Washington
and Jefferson."[33] Pat Buchanan cried "God bless Arizona"
when that state alone refused to adopt the King holiday.

While the Rockfordites professed to be disgusted by King's
sexual conduct—"King bedded other men's wives, other wives'
men, underaged girls, and young boys. [My] guess is that even
holes in the ground had to watch out"[34]—in reality, it was the
substance of King's work that horrified them. "'Forced integration. . . is to racial harmony what a shotgun wedding is to
romance.' And King was holding the shotgun."[35] In the name
of integration, Buchanan had complained in 1975, laws were
being enforced that "put blacks in the same preferred racial
position as whites enjoyed decades ago."[36] Explaining his bitter
hostility to the Supreme Court nomination of Clarence
Thomas, whom he considered to be nothing better than an
affirmative action hire, Rockwell wrote, "Thomas calls the segregation of the Old South, where he grew up, 'totalitarian.' But
that's liberal nonsense. Whatever its faults, and it certainly had
them, that system was far more localized, decent, and humane
than the really totalitarian social engineering now wrecking the
country."[37]

Above all, however, King symbolized those "limits on permissible dissent" that Buchanan had found so constricting. In a
January 1992 talk, Tom Fleming bitterly complained that the
American Left wanted to demonize America's past. "That's
why we're forced to bend the knee tomorrow [the King holiday]
to *Mr.* Martin Luther King. . . . We're supposed to hate Washington, Jefferson, our ancestors, ourselves." Thus, "the first

piece of business on our agenda is the restoration of debate and free expression."[38] And so it was. In a January 1992 speech to a conference of nationalist conservatives, Professor Murray Rothbard—whose extreme libertarianism and isolationism had taken him from the Taft Right in 1950 to the pro-Hanoi New Left by 1975—told the sad story of how that free expression had been lost. "One after another," Rothbard lamented as his audience cheered and laughed and stamped its feet,.

> Buckley and *National Review* purged and excommunicated all the radicals, all the non-respectables. Consider the roll-call: isolationists (such as John T. Flynn), anti-Zionists, libertarians, Ayn Randians, the John Birch society, and all those who had continued, like the early *National Review*, to dare to oppose Martin Luther King and the civil rights revolution even after Buckley had changed and decided to embrace it.[39]

At this point, we're heading off to the booby hatch. But before dismissing the mouthings of the nationalist Right altogether, ponder this sobering fact: it is not just the oddball Right that sneers at King. The black nationalist Left does so too, more consistently and fiercely. It is not just the nationalist Right that rejects the possibility that blacks and Spanish-speaking immigrants will assimilate to Anglo-American culture and conform to the code of behavior expected by Anglo-Americans; if the American intellectual elite, Right and Left, subscribes to any orthodoxy today, that's it. Conservatives absorb the ideas and assumptions of the dominant culture too; they cannot help it. Buchanan, Fleming, Francis, Rockwell, Rothbard, and their circle believe what Donna Shalala and David Dinkins and Henry Louis Gates believe: that America really is—or is becoming—a mosaic; that it is—or is coming to be—characterized by a "diversity" that cannot be reduced to a common Americanism of recognizably English origin. Nationalist conservatives accept the truth of everything that America's most advanced liberals propound. They just don't like it. But wasn't that the very reaction to be expected? If left-wing politics has become identity politics—the assertion of raw ethnic and racial grievances and interests—was it not inevitable that right-wing politics would follow? "Someone's value are going to prevail," Buchanan wrote. "Why not ours? Whose country is it anyway?"[40] Is not the real surprise that this nationalist reaction has come so late, and that it is still so weak? And doesn't it seem likely that it is going to grow a lot stronger? America, Fleming predicts, will soon be "a nation no longer stratified by class but by race as well. Europeans and Orientals will compete, as groups, for the top positions, while the other groups will nurse their resentments on the weekly welfare checks they receive from the other half."[41] Stripped of its pejorative language, isn't that exactly what the designers of President Clinton's cabinet think?

And if these nationalist conservatives relish the possibility that America's internal racial discontents will lead to inter-ethnic violence, they are not original in that either. Leftists and black nationalists have enjoyed terrifying liberal-minded Americans with that possibility since 1965. Buchanan and Co. resemble James Baldwin and other prophets of the "fire next time" in welcoming violence; they differ only in favoring one side rather than the other. After the Adams-Morgan riot in 1991, Buchanan had mocked Washington Mayor Sharon Pratt Dixon's attempts to mollify that Hispanic neighborhood's supposed grievances. "Rioters do not need to hear a lot of bullhocky about 'communicating' and 'dialogue.' They need to hear through a police bullhorn the three little words that say it all: 'Lock and load!'"[42] And after the L.A. riots, Samuel Francis suggested that the entire country had been on the verge of race war.

> Americans will never know how close the rest of the country actually came to mutating into one huge Los Angeles during those four days, but it may have been a lot closer than they realize. Racial "disturbances" were reported in no less than 12 other cities around the country. In Las Vegas, actual riots

continued for some days afterwards. Omaha reported at least 11 racially motivated assaults on whites by blacks. In Madison, Wisconsin, the windshields of parked police cars were smashed, and Baltimore, Pittsburgh, Tampa, Birmingham, and other cities also had trouble. In the Washington area, there were several reported black racial assaults on, insults to, and harassments of whites, and other cities and areas no doubt had their own small tales that never made the news at all, as well as innumerable episodes that no one even mentioned. To alert observers . . . it seemed as though the whole national edifice might crumble into cinders.[43]

To avert catastrophe, it would be necessary to rethink the principles of American democracy. Some of the more pessimistic nationalists had abandoned hope that democratic excesses could ever be curbed. "Why appeal to the need for a leavening of aristocracy and constitutionalism in the life of a democracy," asked Clyde Wilson, editor of the John C. Calhoun papers. "That question was settled at Appomattox, a century and a quarter ago, in favor of aggressive and self-congratulatory democracy." But other nationalists believed that America might come to see some restriction on democracy as necessary to preserve American civilization and hold underclass savagery at bay. That's certainly what Pat Buchanan hoped. Having read a newspaper story about Ecorse, Michigan, a small town that had put itself in the hands of a receiver, Buchanan wondered why this sort of one-man rule might not deliver New York from its fiscal troubles too.

Of IBM, the Marine Corps, the Redskins, and the D.C. Government, only leaders of the last are chosen by democratic procedure. Yet who would choose the last as the superior institution? Anyone who grew up in D.C., when there was no right to vote, and no city government, can empathize with the Congolese peasants who begged the Belgian diplomat to ask the king if he would be willing to take them back.

The cure for the ills of democracy, said Al Smith, is more democracy. The Happy Warrior had it wrong. If the people are corrupt, the more democracy, the worse the government.[44]

A year and a half later, and he was suggesting one-man rule for Washington, D.C. "Some months ago, the editorial writers up at the Wall Street Journal were waxing enthusiastic about a 'MacArthur Regency' in Baghdad. Right kind of regime—they just had the wrong capital. Where is the American Caesar when we really need him?"[45]

Was this not perhaps the underlying meaning of the Oliver North episode? Few conservatives paid much attention to the intricacies of the Boland Amendment's legal validity. They saw a fearless Marine standing up to a corrupt packet of legislators and telling them to go to hell. Elected or not, Buchanan wrote, Congress possessed less legitimacy than North:

> It is said that what these men did was cover up a conspiracy to violate the Constitution of the United States, and lie about it to Congress. Which is one way of putting it.
>
> Another is to say that Congress, by approving military aid to the Contras who went out to risk their lives, then chopping off that aid, was guilty of a criminal betrayal. That when Ollie North sought to save his abandoned comrades, he acted with greater honor and decency than those who passed the Boland Amendment. That the CIA men who discovered Ollie's diversion, and did not report it, were loyal to a cause that was just. They too believed stopping the Soviet Empire in Central America was vital to the security of the country they had taken an oath to defend. Why did they dissemble to Congress? Perhaps because they came to believe Congress was on the other side.[46]

Buchanan is often compared to Father Coughlin, but he more closely resembles the nineteenth-century authoritarian Charles Maurras, who contended that France was divided into two countries, the "*pays légal*" of liberalism, parliamentary chat, and constitutions, and the "*pays réel*," the real France—military, royalist, and Catholic. As for Ollie North, he is the favorite to represent the Republicans in the 1994 Virginia senatorial election, to the party's shame.

The nationalists' skepticism about democracy was fueled by the excessive rhetoric about Third World democracy in which many conservatives indulged in the 1980s. At its height, democratism could venture pretty deeply into utopianism, as in a 1989 book by Gregory A. Fossedal, a former *Wall Street Journal* editorialist, which claimed that "either America will help secure the rights of man for all, everywhere, or America itself as a free and democratic state, will perish."[47] The book was illustrated by maps that showed democracy advancing through history, with, for instance, China colored in undemocratic black under the Manchu emperors in 1875 but happily semidemocratic gray in the midst of its vicious civil war in 1935; Alaska groaning in semidemocracy in 1935 but brilliantly democratic white in 1988. Fossedal was extreme, but not atypical. Democracy was the juiciest boondoggle of the Reagan years. Happy young Republicans and Democrats enjoyed free trips to tropical islands to attend conferences sponsored by the National Endowment for Democracy. Former socialist activist and Jeane Kirkpatrick aide Carl Gershman was given a big government stipend to publish a quarterly *Journal of Democracy,* to which Reaganite writers sent manuscripts rejected by *Commentary* and the *New Republic.*

This large and lucrative enterprise was dubbed "global democracy" by disgusted nationalists—who, not very incidentally, were never very successful at enjoying its spoils. For the most part, the nationalist attack upon democratism was just a dumbed-down rehash of the realist-versus-idealist argument that has diverted generations of students of American foreign policy. But when war broke out in the Persian Gulf in the summer of 1990, nationalism suddenly took on new and substantial meaning. After a brief flurry of indecision, President Bush despatched troops to Saudi Arabia and mobilized for the war that would eject Iraq eight months later, at a cost of at least

100,000 Iraqi lives and barely 100 Americans. It might have seemed that here, for the first time since 1945, was a war a foreign-policy realist could love. Nobody entertained any illusions about the moral bona fides of the client for whom America was fighting: the most avid hawks conceded that the Kuwaitis were nasty pieces of work. The war was fought over two of the most hard-edged of foreign policy interests: control over the oil fields of the Persian Gulf and the preservation of the developed world's monopoly of nuclear weapons. While President Bush's occasional reference to a "new world order" was certainly immodest, it was soon clear to everyone but Pat Robertson—who heard it as a reference to the coming reign of the Antichrist—that the phrase was almost entirely void of content.

All of which explains why the preponderance of the American Right favored the war. That's the dog-bites-man story. The news was that, for the first time since Inchon, a nontrivial minority of American conservatives had found a war they opposed. They saw in the war the final evidence for Russell Kirk's 1988 crack that "not seldom it has seemed as if some eminent Neoconservatives mistook Tel Aviv for the capital of the United States." The Iraq war, they decided, was a Jewish war. When George Bush accused Saddam Hussein of being a "second Hitler," he might well have remembered how few conservatives had wanted to fight the first one.

Every charge with which the postwar foreign-policy Right would bait the Left—sentimentalism about totalitarian foreign powers, the naïve projection of American legalism upon an unruly world, an underestimation of the effectiveness of armed force, and a ridiculous overestimation of the effectiveness of economic sanctions—the Right stood guilty of in 1940 and 1941. In the summer of 1940, as German troops occupied Paris, Robert Taft warned that it would be just as dangerous to overestimate as to underestimate the gravity of the situation. In March 1941 Taft was still insisting that "war is even worse than a German victory." In July 1941, as German tanks raced to Moscow and Hitler's military brutally seized the Balkans,

Greece, and Crete, the America First publication "Did You Know?" was assuring its readers that the United States could live with total Nazi domination of the European continent. "Nazi Europe will have to import. . . . The bargaining advantage will rest with the Western hemisphere countries."[48]

The reckless folly of America First was wildly popular on the anti–New Deal Right. By Pearl Harbor, the organization counted some 800,000 dues-paying members.[49] While left-wing isolationists, such as the socialist Norman Thomas, the union leader John L. Lewis, and the historian Charles Beard, acted in concert with America First, its principal sponsors were names that would be familiar on the Right into the 1980s. The largest single donor, William Regnery, was the father of Henry Regnery, who would found the publishing company that produced most of the important conservative books of the 1950s and 1960s. (The younger Regnery, who had been a student in Nazi Germany in the 1930s, showed a curious partiality throughout his long career for anti-interventionist, anti-British, and anti-Israeli books.) Another large backer was H. Smith Richardson of the Vicks Chemical Co., whose family foundation would be an important source of funding for conservative causes throughout the 1980s. Russell Kirk actually voted for Norman Thomas in 1944 in gratitude for his opposition to the war.

America Firsters were by no means pacifists. Relatively few of them were actively pro-Nazi. Many more were reflexively anti-British and determinedly anticommunist. They subscribed to Charles Lindbergh's statement—made just after the Germans invaded the Soviet Union—that "I would a hundred times rather see my country ally herself with England, or even with Germany with all her faults, than with the cruelty, the godlessness, and the barbarism that exists in Soviet Russia." They feared, as America First's statement of principles proclaimed, that "our intervention would only destroy democracy, not save it." Wartime enlargements of the power of the state had been reversed after the Civil War and the First World War. But in the new political world of the New Deal, any additions to federal and presidential power were likely to prove permanent. The historian Harry Elmer Barnes told an America First meeting in Buffalo in January 1941 that Lend-Lease would give President Roosevelt more power than Hitler had had in 1935.

After the war, conservatives preferred to forget about America First. The most painstaking history of the conservative movement in America, George Nash's, opens in 1945. Most conservative after-dinner speakers like to begin in 1955, with the founding of the impeccably interventionist *National Review*. (That allows them to sidestep Taft's refusal to endorse NATO and the career of Joe McCarthy too.) But just as the collapse of communism released ancient hatreds throughout Eastern Europe, it uncorked them in America. To Patrick Buchanan, the Gulf War offered the sublime opportunity to reenact the Great Debate of 1940–41. In the role of Britain—slyly manipulating U.S. politics to maneuver American boys into fighting its wars—was Israel. Playing the part of the striped-pants boys around Colonel Stimson were the Jewish neoconservatives of New York and Washington. City College stood in for Groton as the training-ground for internationalists who owed their loyalties to a foreign power. Buchanan himself would revive the boffo box-office performance of Charles A. Lindbergh.

Lindbergh had predicted that the United States could not win a war against Nazi Germany; Buchanan used similar defeatism as an argument against war with Iraq. His notorious television remark that "there are only two groups that are beating the drums for war in the Middle East—the Israeli Defense Ministry and its amen corner in the United States" almost uncannily paralleled Lindbergh's notorious September 1941 warning that "the three most important groups who have been pressing this country toward war are the British, the Jewish and the Roosevelt administration." Just as Lindbergh warned in that same Des Moines speech that American Jews should "be opposing [war] in every possible way, for they will be among the first to feel its consequences," because "toleration is a virtue that depends on peace," Buchanan ominously ticked off the names of Jewish advocates of war: Kissinger and Krauthammer, Rosenthal and Perle. And as Lindbergh had claimed that Jews were a "danger" to the United States because of "their large ownership and influence in our motion pictures, our press, our radio, and our government," so Buchanan decried the excessive influence within the conservative movement of the hated neocons.

For Buchanan, at least, "America First" certainly did not mean doctrinaire isolationism, or even doctrinaire Realpolitik. A year after his passionate animosity against war in the Gulf, Buchanan himself was "pounding the drums" for a war in Yugoslavia. As Serbs and Croats massacred each other, Buchanan urged President Bush to send the Sixth Fleet to relieve Dubrovnik, to bombard the Serbs from the air and force Serbia to recognize Croatia within the extensive borders drawn by Marshall Tito. As to how to reconcile this bellicosity with his earlier restraint, how to identify some greater American interest in Croatia than there had been in Kuwait, Buchanan could only argue,

> Croatia is not some faraway desert emirate. It is a "piece of the continent, a part of the main," a Western republic that belonged to the Hapsburg empire and was for centuries the first line of defense of Christian Europe. For their ceaseless resistance to the Ottoman Turks, Croatia was proclaimed by Pope Leo X to be the "Antemurale Christiantatis," the bulwark of Christianity.[50]

Now that's solid strategic thinking.

The experience—new to almost all conservatives—of having opposed a war, and particularly a war that was hugely popular with their fellow-citizens, induced in nationalist conservatives a surge of radical alienation from their country. "What a country we have become," keened Tom Fleming in December 1991, "with our patriotic songs and yellow ribbons commemorating something like a genocidal slaughter of a primitive people." The January 1992 meeting of the nationalist John Randolph club in an plasticated neoclassical hotel smack in the fields of suburban

Virginia—"the estates-general of a Buchanan presidency," as one of the speakers smirked—frequently sounded like a New Left gripefest. "We have suffered through fifty years of a militarized society," complained Rockford Institute president Alan Carlson. "The U.S. government has probably killed more people outside its own borders than any other. Or am I overlooking something?" cheerfully asked soon-to-be-fired *National Review* editor Joe Sobran. To most conservatives, the victory in the Gulf was the vindication of a decade and a half spent teaching Americans not to be afraid to use their power in the national interest. The victory was made possible not just by a decade-long rearmament program, but also by a decade-long reeducation program. At this apogee of success, though, many veterans of in the conservative movement felt gnawingly unsatisfied. "I always feared the domestic Left more than Moscow," M. E. Bradford said at the January meeting. "I fear it even more now, since sometimes it calls itself conservatism. And the danger is perhaps greater now that Communism is out of the way." What Bradford meant by "the Left" is what all the nationalist conservatives have come to hate most: those Americans who believe that the essence of American life is universally accessible; that American ideals can be exported abroad and that foreigners who come to America can be made American.

A little pamphlet by Catholic University of America professor Claes Ryn (who is, ironically, himself foreign-born—but fortunately in Nordic Sweden), "The New Jacobinism," argues the point elliptically but unmistakably. Just as the Jacobins of the French Revolution wanted to remake the world to force it to conform to their republican ideology, so the new Jacobins want to impose another panacea—a nonce-ideology that, for many of them, had replaced their youthful Marxism, "democratic capitalism." Against this new Jacobinism, nationalist conservatives must reassert the truth of particularity: the particularity not just of Africans and Russians and Germans, but of Americans too. "The central task of an authentic conservatism . . . is the survival and enhancement of a particular people and its

institutionalized cultural expressions," wrote Sam Francis.[51]
This kind of rhetoric raises the possibility that the quilts, hand-
crafted pottery, and folk-singing that have made the Left so dismal for a generation are about to spread to the Right. "All the
products of one period resemble one another," Marcel Proust
observed, noting the similarity between the work of a flowery
poet of the 1840s and the design of stock certificates from the
same decade. There is indeed a spirit of the age. Nationalist
conservatism simply imports left-wing identity politics into a
new context. If the rights of blacks, gays, and Hispanics were to
be asserted, why not those of middle-aged Irish Catholics or
white Southerners? If the interests of blacks and whites, women
and men, Anglos and Hispanics really were so radically different, if even their epistemology was different—as the fashionable
new "critical race theorists" argued in the law schools and the
humanities departments—who but the sappiest white, man, or
Anglo would take the black, woman, or Hispanic's side of the
argument? The nationalists may take their descent, as they say,
from the oldest strain of American conservatism. At the same
time, however, they are truly multiculturalism's children.

CHAPTER 7

The Pseudo-Menace
of the Religious Right

In the months after the Houston convention, the papers were suddenly full of complaints from Republicans who claimed they had enlisted in the Reagan Revolution to resist the Soviets or roll back taxes, but who now felt conscripted into new wars over sexual morality or the American identity. Like defeated Republican candidate Bobbie Kilberg, they complained that the party had come under the control of a "religious . . . far right" possessed of a "single-minded purpose that mainstream Republicans often lack."[1] Like William Safire they yearned for a conservative politics that would defend the individual equally "against the intrusions of big government" and "majoritarian morality."[2] This complaining and this yearning delighted the nonconservative press, which gleefully predicted that the Republican Party would soon be torn into pieces by the conflict between libertarian conservatives and the Religious Right.

This prediction is, not to be too subtle about it, completely wrong, and for two reasons. Conservatism is divided, yes, but not between libertarians and fundamentalists. First, there is no Religious Right, not, at least, as the term is commonly used.

Second, while disliking both big government and majoritarian morality may make emotional sense to many people, it is an emotional attitude that is intellectually contradictory and therefore difficult to translate into public policy. Politicians who claim to oppose both will consistently find themselves obliged to choose one or the other. For this reason, the "don't tread on me" libertarianism espoused by Safire seldom wields much influence. For proof of this proposition, look at the career of the man who has most conscientiously tried to practice what might be called "individualist" conservatism.

William F. Weld was a Boston district attorney of aristocratic background, all too neatly symbolized by the ornate Beaux-Arts boathouse his family gave Harvard in 1902. A Weld had been one of the wealthiest men in seventeenth-century Massachusetts; an abolitionist Weld had nearly been lynched in the 1830s; another had served as governor of Massachusetts in the 1880s. Unlike many descendents of Boston's Brahmins, Weld had remained a Republican, accepting a position in the Ed Meese's Justice Department. He resigned in 1987, to protest Meese's allegedly lax ethical standards, and three years later declared himself a candidate for governor. The ensuing race was by far the most interesting of the 1990 electoral cycle. Weld promised to deregulate Massachusetts' labyrinthine controls on business, to cut the state income tax, to introduce an investment tax credit, and to eliminate the state's 6 percent capital gains tax. He called himself a "filthy supply-sider," and strongly backed both the death penalty and the Second Amendment's guarantee of the right to keep and bear arms. At the same time and without apology, Weld pledged himself to support legal abortion and gay rights. Weld's opponent, Boston University president John Silber, was a loud, blunt man, a passionate old New Dealer who believed that strong, authoritative government could solve almost any social problem. He opposed Weld's tax cut—and also gay rights, abortion, women in the workforce, and the mollycoddling of minority groups. In the aftermath of the Weld-Silber contest, which Weld won by an adequate three-percentage-point margin, conservative pundits briefly found themselves confronting a new and puzzling phenomenon. If it came to a choice, which *did* they care more about, taxes or abortion?

This dilemma vexed them throughout Weld's first year in office. At a time when state governments everywhere else were raising taxes to cope with the national recession, Weld cut his budget instead. Not "cut" in the Washington sense—spending less than you had been planning to—but cut in the sense that prevails outside Washington, actually spending less than had been spent the year before. Conservatives had to applaud Weld's fiscal discipline—and had to overcome their puzzlement that this same fiscal disciplinarian was sponsoring the nation's most radical laws to protect homosexuals from harassment. Some Wall Street Republicans even began to see in Weld an attractive modern alternative to Jack Kemp (who clung to a pro-life position unpopular among the party's big donors) as the party's nominee in 1996.

But Weld's new libertarian synthesis did not last. After the fiscal stringency of his first year, the governor gave up the fight. Weld's next three budgets requested total spending increases of nearly 17 percent. His fiscal 1994 preelection budget alone contained an 8.5 percent spending increase, to fund—among other worthless and improper projects—loans to startup companies judged uncreditworthy by private-sector bankers and subsidies to firms that exported their products abroad. Spending for fiscal 1994 was scheduled to reach $15.3 billion, or $300 million more than Pennsylvania would need to govern twice as many people.[3] The income tax cut and the capital gains cut were by then long shelved. Weld now described himself, only half jokingly, as "not only a Keynesian, but a leveler." Along the way, he jettisoned his anti–gun control views too. As his 1994 reelection campaign drew close, Weld looked not so much like something new, but like that most antique of all Boston political artifacts: the patrician liberal Republican in the style of Elliott Richardson, Governor Frank Sargent, and senators Leverett

Saltonstall and the younger Henry Cabot Lodge.

Much of the change in Weld could be explained away by the Republican losses in the 1992 midterm elections in Massachusetts and by the unexpected length and severity of the post-1989 recession in the state. But Weld was responding, too, to the fundamental contradiction within his own beliefs. It is not so easy to put together a politics that defends the individual against both big government and majoritarian morality. Political thinkers have been at work on this job since John Stuart Mill, who warned that a conformist society can practice a "tyranny more formidable than many kinds of political oppression, since, though not usually upheld by such extreme penalties, it leaves fewer means of escape, penetrating much more deeply into the details of life, and enslaving the soul itself."[4] And, almost without exception, they have found the dilemma unsolvable, as in fact Mill himself did—he ended his days a socialist.

To understand why this should be so, consider a not unrealistic situation involving just a few of America's civil rights laws. Suppose a young couple in a conservative town believes that marriage is a hypocritical institution and determines to live together without it. They attempt to rent an apartment together—and no landlady will accept them. The young man is fired from his job; the girl is told to her face by her boss that she is a slut. When he hears about their immoral way of life, the owner of their favorite restaurant refuses to seat them any longer. Eventually the two have a son. When the boy applies to the local private college, he is denied a scholarship because of his illegitimacy. None of these manifestations of moral outrage involves any action at all by any branch of government. Every one of them would have been legal—and quite likely to happen—in the United States forty years ago. Every one of them would be illegal today. The Federal Fair Housing Law of 1968 and most state fair housing laws forbid landlords to reject tenants because of their marital status. The employment provisions of the 1964 federal Civil Rights Act, and of nearly all state civil rights acts, would bar the young man's employer from dismissing him; the girl's boss has almost certainly committed an act of sexual harassment. If a single paper napkin in the joint crossed a state line, the restaurant is engaged in interstate commerce and is therefore subject to the public accommodation rules of the 1964 Civil Rights Act. And if the son's school accepts a single federal dollar for any of its activities—or if any of the students attending the school is receiving a federal student loan—it is subject to the education title of the act, which outlaws discrimination against the children of unmarried parents.

In other words, our young couple has been granted extraordinary protection against majoritarian morality—but only because the behavior and opinions of everyone around them have been subjected to the power of big government to an extent that would have amazed Americans half a century ago. Virtually everything now described as discrimination was once seen as an expression of a fundamental right: the landlady, the restaurant, and the man's employer were exercising their rights of contract; the girl's employer was exercising his right of free speech; and the college was exercising its right of freedom of assocation and (if a church school) freedom of religion. To liberate the young couple from the tyranny of the majority's morality, the government had to abridge the ancient common law rights of everyone else in the community. This is not intrinsically a bad thing—we also used to have a common law right to dump as much garbage in the ocean as we wanted—but even if it is a good thing, it represents an enormous expansion of the coercive power of the state. Had they lived under a regime of minimal government, our young couple would have been well advised to swallow their principles and find a justice of the peace.

Of course, it is not always true that protection from moral majorities and protection from big government conflict with each other. There are cases—the AM radio disk jockey whose smutty talk offends the community into which he broadcasts— where minimal government would make life easier for the dissenting or deviant individual.[5] Howard Stern would prosper in the libertarian utopia as much as the puritanical townspeople who won't do business with the unmarried couple. But the AM disk jockey is the exception: on most occasions in contemporary American life where individuals seek defense against the disapprobation of their neighbors, the dissenters' right to do as they please requires the state to use its power to curb the majority's freedom to condemn, to shun, and to exclude—in other words, the majority's rights to speak, to associate, to contract, and to dispose of its property. A hard-working governor may well be too busy to sort out the implications of the contradiction between antimajoritarianism and minimal government, but it controls his actions and thinking nonetheless, as indeed it has affected Weld's. For his bill to protect homosexual students from insults and hostility to be effective, it must introduce an altogether unprecedented degree of state supervision of the conduct of heterosexual students into Massachusetts' high schools. Weld's hopes of assisting homosexual couples to adopt children will require the law to override the rules and customs of the private-sector child welfare organizations that now administer adoption. Isaiah Berlin warned in his famous essay on negative and positive liberty that justice could sometimes require liberty to be constricted for the sake of equality. As an undogmatic man of social democratic inclination, Berlin was unbothered by such constrictions. What did bother him, however, were the semantic tricks by which abridgments of liberty were portrayed as their exact opposites. Renaming equality as freedom debased the idea and value of freedom—a danger, Berlin felt, to which contemporary social democracies were peculiarly susceptible. In similar fashion, laws designed to protect unpopular minorities from majoritarian morality may be defended in the name of toleration and equality, but it is dishonest to pretend that they are liberty-enhancing. Such laws use state power, and use it in megatonnages scarcely ever before seen in the history of American governance. It is the logic of the situation, and not the alleged power of the Religious Right, that dooms to ineffectiveness conservatives and Republicans who want to mix free-market economics with social permissiveness.

Naturally, that sort of Republican doesn't see things in quite this way. Permissive Republicans believe that they are locked in a deadly struggle with a fanatical fundamentalist minority. Every time a permissive Republican loses a primary contest, the newspapers echo with caterwauling that the country has taken a giant step backward toward the Spanish Inquisition. After Bobbie Kilberg lost her bid for the Republican nomination as lieutenant-governor of Virginia in the summer of 1993, she broke party solidarity to publish a vehement letter in the *Washington Post*. Kilberg—a feminist activist who had served as a White House aide during the Bush administration—was defeated by a Christian fundamentalist and lawyer named Michael Farris at a political convention touted as the largest in American history: more than 13,000 voting delegates attended. Her defeat, Kilberg warned, was not merely the rejection of a too-left candidate associated with a failed administration; no, it was an ominous signal that the Virginia Republican Party was in danger of falling under the sway of a dangerous band of fanatics. Kilberg's noisy complaints convinced the state's Republican leadership that Farris was a menace; the senior Republican in the state, Senator John Warner, flatly refused to endorse him.

What was it about Farris that was so alarming? Before his run for the lieutenant-governorship, Farris had made a name for himself representing parents who objected, for religious reasons, to books on school reading lists. In one instance, his clients wanted *Macbeth* removed because the witches on the heath smacked to them of occultism. When ridiculed for this, Farris pointed out that *Macbeth* filled a prominent place on the reading list he and his wife had devised for the home-schooling of their own children, and that he was only defending his clients' right to have their children instructed as they believed proper. That just made matters worse. What kind of a nut teaches his kids at home? Kilberg supporters asked. Later in the campaign, Farris let slip his opinion that the world would be a better place if young people married earlier in life and dated less before marriage. That was another gaffe: what kind of nut doubts that wide and varied sexual experience before marriage is a good thing?

The Kilberg fusillade against Farris did enough damage to lose him his race even as the Republican nominee for governor, George Allen, won crushingly. But the fusillade was not aimed at Farris alone. Farris genuinely was what Kilberg said he was—someone motivated by sectarian religious views—but the platform of the Farris campaign was made up of orthodox conservative planks, school choice above all. Even Farris's gaffes were thoughts that as mainstream a conservative as Bill Bennett might have articulated. It was not Farris's eccentric biography that Kilberg was condemning as outside the Republican "mainstream," although the eccentricity of the biography helped to make the charge stick: it was the entire conservative social message.

You can see this even more clearly in the accusations lodged by a far more distinguished Republican than Kilberg, California representative Tom Campbell, after his primary defeat in 1992. Until that defeat, Campbell had raced through a career of legendary success: magna cum laude at the Harvard Law School, a Ph.D. in economics from Chicago, a Supreme Court clerkship, appointment to the faculty of Stanford Law School, and election to the House of Representatives—from libertarian Republican Ed Zschau's old Silicon Valley district—on his first try at age thirty-seven. Slim, gray-haired, and extraordinarily precise in his speech, Campbell was often called "the most intelligent man in the House of Representatives," which, he modestly joked, was as complimentary as being described as the tallest building in Topeka. After only four years in the House, Campbell had positioned himself to repeat Zschau's run at the U.S. Senate as a new-style conservative: enthusiastically committed to free-market economics, but also sympathetic to abortion and gay rights, environmentalism, and expansive civil rights enforcement. When Campbell lost to an anti–gay rights, antienvironmentalist, anti–even-one-dollar-in-defense-cuts talk-show host named Bruce Herschensohn, it was the first recorded failure of his career. Understandably he was sore about it, and he grew even more sore after Herschensohn lost the general election to a shrill parody of a San Francisco Democrat, Representative Barbara Boxer, a candidate whom Campbell might conceivably have beaten. It was to save the Republican Party from Herschensohn and his ilk that Campbell announced in mid-December 1992 the formation of a "Republican Majority Coalition." The name of Campbell's group paid homage to the Committee for a Democratic Majority that had galvanized hawkish Democrats against the McGovernite wing of the party in the 1970s and early 1980s. Campbell likewise deputized himself to rescue Republicans from their enemy within, and he persuaded Henry Kissinger, senators Nancy Kassebaum of Kansas and Arlen Specter of Pennsylvania, as well as former New Hampshire senator Warren Rudman, to sign his manifesto. The manifesto demanded that "issues such as abortion, mandatory school prayer, sexual orientation, the teaching of creationism and other similar questions recently inserted into the political context should instead be left to the consciences of individuals." It added, "We reject litmus tests, intolerance, bigotry, anti-semitism and extremism. . . . We believe economic and fiscal conservatism [alone] should be the defining principles of the Republican Party."

Campbell could hardly seriously suggest that the man who bested him in the primary—an assimilated Jewish bachelor who liked a drink, had won an Academy Award in 1969, and who lost the race in large part because he was accused of visiting a strip joint—was a fundamentalist kook. Farris may have been sectarian; Herschensohn was just a conservative. In the eyes of Campbell, Rudman, and the rest, however, even that was too provocative. Not just the pro-life position on abortion, but the whole gamut of conservative social policy was to be lumped together with litmus tests, intolerance, bigotry, anti-Semitism, and extremism. Which really is rather overwrought. Commentators sympathetic to Campbell-style Republicanism—like the *National*

Interest editor who explained shortly after the November election that "Bush lost because he ran as the candidate of the radical right against two centrists"[6]—might imagine that the Republican Party of 1993 had somehow become more extreme than the Republican Party of 1983. But that's not credible. George Bush, that sad John P. Marquand figure, a cat's paw of the "Radical Right"? Really?

In truth, terms like the "Religious Right" or "the Radical Right" function far more as oratorical devices than as categories of political analysis. When a performance artist who takes off her clothes onstage and smears her naked body with chocolate loses a government grant; when a lesbian mother loses a custody fight; when a school board provokes a parents' rebellion against graphic sexual instruction of their children; it is hardly surprising that they will be reluctant to admit that very large numbers of Americans find their conduct deviant or bizarre. They will naturally want instead to brand their detractors as deviant and bizarre.

Aside from this use to inflame angry feelings, it is hard to know what the term "Religious Right" is supposed to mean. If it means right-wingers whose political ideas follow from their religious faith, well, that definition fits William F. Buckley and Midge Decter as neatly as it does Michael Farris, Pat Robertson, or Jerry Falwell. If it refers to those conservatives who take non-liberal positions on the index of prohibited issues proclaimed by the Republican Majority Coalition—abortion, prayer, homosexuality, and the teaching of creationism—then the Religious Right encompasses the editorial boards of the *Wall Street Journal* and *Commentary,* and most of the staff of most of the highest-tone conservative think tanks. So that's not a very useful definition either.

Only if the term is meant to distinguish those sections of the conservative movement who live in the fundamentalist subculture—who attend fundamentalist churches, send their children to private Christian schools, and separate themselves from the secular world as far as they can—does it mean very much:

but those people are so few in number and so politically weak as to cause one to wonder how they could possibly have generated so much fuss.

While enormous numbers of Americans, upward of 50 million, describe themselves as "evangelical" or "born again," those terms are so capacious as to be useless. The number of white Southern Baptists, Pentecostals, and charismatics, who together form the potential political base of a Religious Right is not large: perhaps 15 million people spread over some thirty states. There are twice as many black Americans. Of course, even smaller groups than the fundamentalists can wield great political power. To do so, however, they must either be geographically concentrated, like the Mormons of Utah, or focused on a single issue that nobody else much cares about, like Cuban-Americans, or else they must be able to muster financial and intellectual power disproportionate to their number, like Jews. A dispersed, poor, relatively uneducated group with unpopular opinions on the most bitterly contested controversies of the day is not going to win very many fights, and is hardly in a position to start them. Look at the dismal failure of Pat Robertson's 1988 campaign for the Republican presidential nomination. The televangelist sent a delicious frisson of terror up the spines of the political press when, by mastering that state's convoluted rules, he managed to send the biggest block of delegates to the Michigan state convention in January 1988 and then proceeded to finish second in the Iowa caucuses. But before anyone could finish typing up a worried manifesto, the Robertson campaign imploded. In the first contest where any significant number of the Republican rank and file was able to vote, the New Hampshire primary in February, Robertson ranked fourth, barely ahead of Pete du Pont, who ran on a daring promise to abolish Social Security. Of the three candidates still in the game for the primary in evangelical South Carolina, Robertson placed third—despite the precaution of adding protectionism to his sermons in a futile effort to pick up textile workers' votes. Two weeks later came Super Tuesday and the utter obliteration of the Robertson presidential quest. Since then, fundamentalist political activism has taken the form of Gary Bauer's Family Research Council, a nonelectoral group that carefully dovetails its strategy with those of secular conservative organizations, and Ralph Reed's Christian Coalition, which similarly functions as a subordinate unit within the larger conservative movement.

Look too at Tom Campbell's list of issues "recently inserted into the political context": abortion, school prayer, sexual orientation, and the teaching of creationism. Who inserted them? For upwards of thirty years, beginning with the 1962 Supreme Court decision banning school prayer, through Jimmy Carter's campaign to deny tax-deductible status to religious schools whose enrollments did not match the racial composition of the surrounding area, and up to the National Endowment for the Arts' grants to artists who made blasphemous use of Christian themes, the political authorities have poked and insulted religious people in the name of one liberal cause or another. When the authorities encountered resistance—feeble and localized as it generally has been—liberal-minded people have found it all too easy to think, in the words of the old French proverb, "*Cet animal est très mechant; quand on l'attaque, il se defend.*"*

It is often observed that it is human nature to dislike those whom we have injured; perhaps that's why America's secularizing elites so readily imagine a vast theocratic menace out there, poised and waiting to spring should the Supreme Court slumber for even a moment.

Faith is unquestionably a force in American political life. Religious people do vote and think differently from nonreligious people. The Bush campaign's own surveys showed that the best predictor of whether voters who had supported him in 1988 would support him again in 1992 was not income or region, but church attendance. And of course there are towns and counties in the United States where fundamentalist voters can muster a

---

*"What a wicked animal; when attacked, he defends himself."

local plurality and delete books from the school curriculum. Still, the important organs of conservative ideology remain unblinkingly secular. Yes, *National Review*'s sensibility retains its Catholic tinge, and *Commentary* is published out of the offices of the American Jewish Committee, but they both pose their arguments in purely secular terms, as do the *Wall Street Journal* editorial page, *Human Events*, the *American Spectator*, the *Public Interest*, *Modern Age*, the *National Interest*, and even *Chronicles*. Within the Republican Party, the influence of fundamentalist clerics, negligible to begin with, is further on the wane. The party's pro-life commitment did not make an appearance until page twenty-two of the 1992 platform; it was prominently displayed on page thirteen in 1980. The appeal to "family values" at the Houston convention was likewise secular: if anything, it was the last gasp of the conservatives' antistatist impulse of the late 1970s and early 1980s. Having failed to convince Americans to reject intrusive government for the sake of economic liberty, the Houston Republicans tried to mobilize them to oppose intrusive government for the sake of the integrity of the family. "This is the ultimate agenda of contemporary socialism under all its masks," says page four of the 1992 Republican platform. "To liberate youth from traditional family values by replacing family functions with bureaucratic social services. That is why today's liberal Democrats are hostile toward any institution government cannot control, like private childcare or religious schools." Accordingly, and with isolated exceptions, Houston's specific proposals for promoting family values reprise old Republican favorites, especially tax relief. There is very little in the platform that smacks of sectarian tyranny, and quite a lot that reads like a desperate attempt by *Washington Post*–reading sophisticates to disguise an essentially stand-pat program as a plan for furious activity. The clue that gives everything away is the platform's scattered, forced invocations of God. People who genuinely believe in God talk about Him either less or more. The platform tosses off references to God the way a high-school teacher who wants to seem with-it uses ghetto slang, in the same desperate and doomed effort to establish rapport with an alien audience.

Indeed, at a conservative conclave in January 1991, Irving Kristol argued that neither the conservative movement nor the Republican Party is nearly interested enough in religion.

> Too many of our conservative intellectuals—I would say all conservative intellectuals—are too secular in their mind sets, whether they're secular or not in their daily habits, as most are, but they're too secular in their mind sets. There is just no way in which we are going to be able to answer the kinds of questions that are being thrust upon us by the Newest Left . . . without having a solid grounding in a religious tradition which authorizes our answers and which proposes other models of human relations and other ways of looking at human beings and their place in the world.[7]

One of the other guests, Terry Teachout, an editorialist for the *New York Daily News,* asked Kristol whether "intellectuals who lack religious faith can effectively advocate it for others." Kristol's reply was a nervous "yes."

Good thing, because the conservative movement is secular to its toes. Even those conservatives, like Kristol and Pat Buchanan, who believe that excessive secularism is a genuine problem, believe it for secular reasons. They expect that a more devout America would be a better-behaved America. Churchgoers occupy the same place in the conservative intellectual's imagination that the proletariat once did in the imagination of the revolutionary intellectual: a mass that will muscle the intellectual's theories into power. But like the proletariat, American churchgoers will almost certainly disappoint the intellectuals who trust in them.

Kristol has long argued that the next century will be more religious than this one has been. Even if the prediction proves true, conservatives should not get comfortable too quickly. While the religion making the most rapid conquest of America's upper classes, environmentalism, does resemble the tough religions of the past—demanding ascetism and mortification of the flesh—the religions of America's lower classes are blemished by the same hedonistic self-indulgence that disturbs conservatives about American politics generally. Are Americans drifting away from bourgeois individualism, with its emphasis on self-mastery, to expressive individualism and its cult of self-gratification? Do they insist too much upon their rights and heed too little their responsibilities? All of these faults can be laid at the door of religious America every bit as much as secular America. Spend any time listening to the sermons of Pentecostals and Baptists, and it strikes you that they think of God very much in the same way that Great Society liberals thought of government: a distant benevolent agency that showers goodies upon all those who ask, without demanding anything very much in return—except for the occasional campaign contribution. Secular conservatives, who value religion for its positive social effects, habitually confuse the unyielding Calvinist faith that shaped the country's heroic early character with the God-will-make-you-rich/God-will-make-you-thin/God-will-improve-your-sex-life religion that fills American television sets and suburban churches today. American spiritual life does not stand apart from, as a refuge from and a witness against, the excesses of American culture. It fully participates in that culture, receives its ideas from that culture, and is decisively shaped by that culture. In their faith as in their politics, Americans are keenly aware of what they want the authorities to do for them and strikingly indifferent to their obligations to the authorities. If fundamentalist America is too poor and weak to bear out secularist fears, it shares too many of the sins of secular America to sustain conservative hopes. Fundamentalists will go on giving conservative Republicans their votes, but it is not from them that the conservative movement of the future will draw its ideas.

CHAPTER 8

1996

"Look, we all know what's going to happen in '96," says the Republican operative in his cheerless office in one of those colonnaded buildings that sprang up in Washington at the end of the 1980s boom. "We're going to nominate Kemp. He's got by far the best organization, and the guy with the best organization always wins. Then Clinton will punch his lights out." The operative savors his phrase and goes on.

> I mean, what's Jack going to say? The economy will be bopping along at 3 percent. Who's going to listen when he promises to cut the capital gains rate and goose growth to 3¼? And selling apartments to welfare mothers at half-price? They're going to love that in Dayton. Barring recession—and assuming that Clinton is not impeached for adultery—Kemp has no message. Anyway, the big news for me isn't '96, it's '94. I think we can win a majority in the House of Representatives before the century's out—especially if the Democrats hold the White House. And since there's a lot more that we want to prevent than we want to do, Congress is the best place for us to be.

If that operative is right, the Republican Party is treading the same sad path the Democrats trod after 1980. Having gone down to defeat in 1980 with a candidate the liberal wing of the party had never liked, the Democrats pooh-poohed the significance of their defeat and proceeded to nominate the most unreconstructed New Dealer in their party in 1984. Likewise, the Republicans seem now to be determined to nominate the most cheerful supply-sider in theirs, and on the same theory: if the voters reject ham and eggs, it is because they want double ham and double eggs. As P. J. O'Rourke said in his speech to the very first big conservative powwow after the election—the *American Spectator* twenty-fifth anniversary dinner in early December 1992—"We didn't lose this election. Some people we know lost this election. Some people whose politics we can sort of tolerate lost this election. But we didn't lose this election." Hence Walter Mondale; hence Jack Kemp.

Fortunately for the party's electoral prospects, there's good reason to doubt that the double-ham-and-eggs theory will prevail. Yes, Kemp is adored within the party, but he was adored in 1988 too. That did not prevent him from fizzling out in New Hampshire. Perhaps his New Hampshire political machinery hums more efficiently now than it did then; and of course next time he will not face an incumbent vice president. But there is still plenty that can go wrong. Political machinery is not after all machinery. It is human, and therefore fickle, always liable to be swayed by a fresh face. If Kemp is the Republican Walter Mondale, the party does not lack for Gary Harts: politicians who can plausibly claim to represent something new—governors like Pete Wilson of California and Carol Campbell of South Carolina, Tommy Thompson of Wisconsin, and John Engler of Michigan; senators like Phil Gramm and even Bob Dole; former Bush administration figures like Dan Quayle (no kidding) and Richard Cheney; and private citizens like Pat Buchanan and Ross Perot. With the exception of Perot and perhaps Wilson, all of them could be described as "conservatives," but none of them is a sunny tax-cutting Reaganite. Except for Campbell and Gramm, all of them have so far interested themselves far more in social than in fiscal issues. And all of them, without exception, have rejected optimistic themes for moralist and nationalist ones.

In this progress-minded country, it is always pejorative to be associated with the past rather than the future. To say that Kemp is out of date is, in most people's ears, to say that he is somehow not as good as the candidates who are up to date. But that's just a prejudice. Walter Mondale's anachronistic romance with big labor was a lot more attractive than Gary Hart's zealous techno-liberalism. Kemp's naive enthusiasm makes a poignant and attractive contrast to the grim realism of the rest of the Republican Party and conservative movement. Attractive or not, however, what is obsolete is obsolete. Nothing in politics, the famous British historian F. S. Oliver remarked, is sadder than the "man of sterling character whose genius is so antipathetic to the particular emergency in which he finds himself as to stupefy his thoughts and paralyze his actions. He drifts to disaster, grappling blindfolded with forces which are beyond his comprehension, failing without really fighting. And yet had the difficulties been of some different order, they might have been much greater than they were, and he would have surmounted them victoriously."[1] That is exactly Kemp's plight. He wants to refight the 1980 campaign, or better still, 1960's. He wants to get the country moving again. But the country is moving, and very fast. The question is, is it moving in the right direction?

One of the first important Republicans to adapt himself to the new doubtful conservative politics was, curiously, Governor Pete Wilson of California. As mayor of San Diego and then as a U.S. senator, Wilson carefully cultivated a reputation for moderation. Conservatives in the California party have never liked or trusted him. He is, among other offenses, pro-choice on abortion. And he in turn scorns members of the right-wing Orange County faction of the California party as "cavemen." But it is conservatives to whom he owes power, and, since his departure from Washington in 1990, he has twice turned to conservative nationalist themes to salvage his career at moments of danger. Trailing San Francisco mayor Dianne Feinstein in the 1990 gubernatorial race, he seized upon the issue of racial quotas. Feinstein had promised to appoint women and blacks to her administration in strict proportion to their share of California's population. For a California Democrat, this was hardly a loopy idea: State Assemblyman Tom Hayden actually persuaded the Democratic legislature to pass a law requiring universities not only to accept but to graduate minority students in proportion to state population. But as property prices tumbled and the aerospace industry dismissed workers by the thousands, the mood of California's shrinking white majority hardened. According to journalist Peter Brown, who describes the race in his book *Minority Party*,[2] Wilson's tough television ads blasting Feinstein's quota pledge destroyed her lead in the polls and won him the election. In office, Wilson reverted to his temporizing Bushite ways, coping with the recession by raising taxes to close a budget gap. At the end of his first year in office, his approval ratings had badly slipped. He needed a new issue— and deftly found it. The reason he had raised taxes in 1991, Wilson began to argue, was that out-of-control spending forced him to. And why was spending racing out of control? Because of illegal immigration from Mexico and Central America.

"According to current, but unofficial estimates of the U.S. Census Bureau," said the governor in the statement he issued announcing his new crusade, "there are 4 million illegal immigrants in this country. California is the home to 52%, or more than 2 million."

The federal government has established a system that provides incentives to undocumented immigrants to violate U.S. immigration laws. As a result of federal mandates, states are required to provide health care and education services to illegal immigrants and their children. Further, the federal government confers citizenship to children born to parents residing illegally in the state, guaranteeing them education, welfare and health care. The federal government has failed to fully reimburse states for costs associated with its immigration policies.[3]

By Wilson's estimate, illegal immigration added more than $1.7 billion to the state budget in 1993–94, including nearly $500 million in Medicare costs, $350 million for jailing felons who turned out to be illegal immigrants, and $236 million in welfare costs. Educating the children of illegal immigrants cost the state and localities more than $1.1 billion in 1993–94. All those costs had ballooned in just a very few years: in the worst case, the cost of Medicare for illegals had multiplied fifteen times since 1988–89.

Californians seem to be convinced by Wilson's argument. Over the second half of 1993, Wilson sponsored twenty-two laws aimed at controlling the costs imposed by illegal immigration. As Wilson identified himself with anti-immigrant themes, the number of Californians rating his performance "good" or "fair" rebounded smartly, to 61 percent, his best level in a year and a half. While the 1991 tax increase, the lingering recession, and his past reputation as a wishy-washy moderate have together damaged Wilson too badly to give him very much of a chance at the presidency in 1996, he has road-tested a powerful local—and maybe more than local—issue for anyone who cares to pick it up.

Governor Thompson of Wisconsin has road-tested another. A tax-cutter in the 1980s—he reduced the state's capital gains and inheritance taxes—in his second term his conservatism has focused instead on the reform of the character of his state's poor. The rest of the country thinks of Wisconsin as the land of cheese and Annie Hall's parents, but the old breweries and heavy industry of Milwaukee attracted their share of the great black northward migration: 250,000 blacks now live in Wisconsin, one-quarter of them on one of the most generous welfare programs in the nation, courtesy of Wisconsin's German and Scandinavian social democratic traditions. When Thompson took office, Wisconsin offered a three-person welfare family the fifth most generous allotment in the nation, more generous even than New York City's. Since then, Thompson has not only cut welfare payments by some $25 per family per month; he has also attempted to use welfare to elicit better behavior from the poor. So his "learnfare" program cuts the stipends of welfare recipients whose children miss school, and his "bridefare" initiative raises the incomes of married welfare women over the unmarried. Fathers of children on welfare are required to pay child support. If they do not have jobs, the state gives them one—without pay. Now Thompson is proposing an even more ambitious plan. He has notified Washington of his intention to quit the national Aid to Families with Dependent Children program in 1998. Freed from federal strictures, Wisconsin will experiment in two yet-to-be-selected counties with a strict "two years and out" program.

All this has made Thompson a political celebrity. Interviewing him is not easy. After weeks of waiting for an appointment to be scheduled, I gave up my plans to see him in Madison. In the end, he called me on his car phone as he drove from Madison to Milwaukee, his voice fading in and out as he passed from one cell zone to another. Thompson could not be less interested in political theory. All he knows, he says in his gruff way, is that people are collecting too dang much money for not working. He wants to see everybody on the job, and he's prepared to make the jobs himself if need be. When asked why he prefers his way—the stick—to Jack Kemp's—the carrot—he seems genuinely puzzled. He's never thought of it that way before. All he knows, he says again, is that when you cut people off welfare, they're really off welfare.

Thompson has survived politically—even thrived—as he pursues his radical behavior modification goals in part because the 1990 recession largely bypassed his state. Even more important is a tacit deal with dissidents among the state's black elected officials, such as Polly Williams, the assemblywoman who sponsored Wisconsin's pilot educational choice program. Thompson's black allies had previously been considered radicals. Williams came to favor vouchers because she wants blacks to be educated in all-black schools. She was linked politically to city councilman Michael McGee, who bombastically threatened the state with civil war if hundreds of millions of dollars in "reparations" to Wisconsin blacks were not forthcoming by 1995. But the apparent paradox is illusory: black television host Tony Brown observes that it is the black Right that has the most in common with white liberals and the black Left that is the natural ally of the white Right. The black Right, Brown says, believes in integration. It wants to attend white schools, live in white suburbs, and work in white corporations. It believes in using the political institutions of the white majority— principally the courts, but also government in general—to extract benefits from whites for blacks. The nationalist black Left rejects those aspirations. It does not believe that integration is possible or even desirable. It wants to create independent black institutions—black schools, black suburbs, and black corporations. It has little faith in white political institutions, or in white goodwill more generally. Let blacks enrich themselves and then whites will have to treat them with respect, however little fraternity the two races may ever actually feel.

If the Republicans want a moralistic conservative who begins with a bigger clatch of electoral votes than Thompson does, they might turn to Michigan's John Engler. In his first two years in office, Engler faced a recession-induced budget deficit. Engler balanced the state's finances with cuts in the welfare budget. He scrapped Michigan's general assistance program, an unusually lavish program for which even able-bodied men were eligible. In a burst of countervailing Kempism, he then raised the maximum dollar amount of assets welfare recipients could own before losing their eligibility. In fine moralist style, Engler used the money to finance the state's costly education system: Michigan spends more than $6,000 per year per student, 20 percent more than the national average. Education spending has risen by 8 percent a year since Engler took office in January 1991—an increase that Engler called for and still supports.[4] Engler practices a centralizing reformism of the Bennett-Finn variety: while he evangelizes for school choice, he has committed himself to funding schools not by local property taxes but by a rise in the state sales tax, shifting the balance of power in educational matters, as Chester Finn calls for, from localities to the statehouse. Engler's execution of this maneuver has antagonized some Republican legislators from wealthier districts, as has his advocacy of school choice. The news that the governor favors a program that might enable black students from Detroit to enroll in high schools in Birmingham or Grosse Pointe has unaccountably failed to enthrall voters in those towns.

The reformist conservatism of governors Thompson and Engler represents the institutionalization of conservatism as a theory of government. In his funny book about the Bush administration, John Podhoretz observes that Ronald Reagan was entirely uninterested in good government. "For that reason he was not tagged with the blame for scandals that occurred on his watch. They somehow only proved Reagan right; they were proof of his contention that the system was out of control."[5] But state and local government seldom welcomes revolutionaries. In the Northern states in particular, where the Democratic Party is indelibly associated with corrupt urban political machines, Republican politicians who aspire to longevity in office must convince suburban voters of their stolid competence. That's what Engler and Thompson have set out to do, and to a very considerable extent they have succeeded. It might even be said that Engler and Thompson—and a third governor, equally competent but less highly rated in the presidential sweepstakes, Carroll Campbell of South Carolina—share more in common with the reform Republicans of the late nineteenth and early twentieth centuries than with the crusaders of the Goldwater campaign and the early Reagan administration; Campbell in some ways the most of all. Despite raising teachers' salaries and the funding of extensive schemes to reduce the state's high infant mortality rates, since winning election in 1986 Campbell has managed to cut income taxes and balance the state's budget. Like that of the Progressives before World War I, Campbell's free-market faith is flexible: he attracted the

BMW North American factory to his state with $130 million in subsidies—less than homely Alabama had to pay to attract Mercedes-Benz, but a shocking sum all the same. He has cheerfully deployed subsidies, built roads, and trained specialized workers for private industry at public expense, all in order to drag into modernity what had been among the most backward states in the country (South Carolina was the last state to grant the vote to all white men and was disgraced by some of the nation's dirtiest elections well into the 1960s). He even looks modern—handsome in exactly the same way that every other handsome Republican is handsome; handsome in a way that makes it impossible to remember what he looks like the moment after he leaves the room.

If reformist conservatism is the future, it is peculiar that the Republican who has done the most to publicize moralistic politics will not share in its success: former vice president Dan Quayle. Reporters and other wiseacres have a tough time taking Quayle seriously, but it remains historical record that Quayle delivered the most memorable political speech of 1992, the Murphy Brown speech, on the cultural issue of fatherlessness. His convention speech zeroed in on culture as the great issue dividing Republicans from Democrats: "Americans try to raise their children to understand right and wrong, only to be told that every so-called lifestyle alternative is morally acceptable. That is wrong. The gap between us and our opponents is a cultural divide. It is not just a difference between being conservative and liberal; it is a difference between fighting for what's right and refusing to see what's wrong."[6] Quayle has retired to Indiana, where he heads his own mini-organization within the free-market Hudson Institute. While casting a primary ballot for Quayle might seem to many Republicans a witty way of spiting the media, his former supporters no longer feel any special obligation to defend him now that he has ceased to be the highest-ranking orthodox conservative in Washington; even Bill Kristol, who defended Quayle so ardently that you couldn't help wondering whether it was possible that he really meant it, has severed his links with his former boss.

If Kemp does blow up in the primaries or before, the likeliest Republican alternative to him in 1996 will be President Bush's defense secretary, Richard Cheney. Cheney, who formed a committee at the end of 1993 to explore his presidential prospects, is the most popular Republican on the lecture circuit after Kemp. So far, retaining that popularity has been easy. Cheney does not release texts of his speeches to the media, does not grant interviews, and avoids discussions of controversial issues like abortion (he is pro-life, but close-mouthed). We do know his congressional voting record, which was frugal—in his memoirs, David Stockman says that Cheney was one of a handful of Republican representatives never to ask for anything in return for his votes in favor of the Reagan budgets. Cheney's wife, Lynne Cheney, was a staunchly conservative director of the National Endowment for the Humanities. Cheney's one published speech since the formation of his presidential committee took a tough line against the Clinton health care plan. "It's my view that the so-called crisis in health care has been constructed to justify the radical restructuring of one-seventh of our national economy and a vast expansion in the role and power of the federal government."[7] Yet Cheney also endorsed Bobbie Kilberg over Michael Farris in the Virginia Republican primary that was seen by moderate Republicans as a titanic struggle between the "Religious Right" and the forces of enlightenment. Cheney unreservedly backed assistant secretary of defense Pete Williams when it was doubted that a man rumored to be homosexual himself could properly explain the military's ban on homosexuals in military service. And Cheney's own personal ties were with President Ford, whom he served as chief of staff and whom he still visits regularly, rather than with the man who cost Ford his job, Ronald Reagan.

Still, conservatives who have spent time with Cheney have been dazzled by him, particularly Stuart Spencer, Ronald Reagan's veteran campaign manager. *Human Events* reports

that Spencer has told his present employer, Governor Campbell, that he will be unavailable to manage a Campbell campaign in 1996 if Cheney runs. With his twisted lip, Cheney
looks tough, and in speech his gravelly voice sounds tough. So
do his words. Cheney has set himself to convincing Americans
that for a great imperial power like the United States, foreign
affairs must always rank as a high, even supreme, national pri-
ority—which means, first, convincing nationalist conservatives
of it.

> We have turned inward as a nation and signed on to the
> proposition that the only truly important matters on the
> public policy agenda are domestic issues. . . .[And] we
> Republicans bear part of the responsibility for this state of
> affairs.
>
> We are the ones who acquiesced last fall in the
> Democrats' assertion that the 1992 campaign for the
> Presidency should only address domestic issues. We bought
> off on the notion that the public didn't want to hear about
> foreign policy and national security issues. . . .
>
> But our first failing was in allowing ourselves and the
> American people to be lulled into a false sense of security—
> into believing that all is right with the world and that the
> end of the Cold War as we've known it for the last 40 years
> meant that it was safe to devote all our time and attention to
> domestic pursuits.[8]

The only hint Cheney offered of the details of his foreign
policy views, beyond the general statement that foreign policy is
very important, was a stirring defense of the importance of a
strong Ukraine: an interesting remark that prefigures what may
soon become one of the lasting ideological rifts of the
post–Cold War foreign policy—the split between those who
sympathize with Russia and those who prefer independent
Ukraine. Since the Gulf War, prominent people have arrived at
their foreign policy views—for intervention in Bosnia or against,
for intervention in Somalia or against, for intervention in Haiti

or against, for more assistance to Central European democracies or against—in a relatively ad hoc way, based on what seem
to them to be the merits of particular situations. There was no a
priori way to predict that Anthony Lewis and Norman
Podhoretz would support intervention in Bosnia and that
Robert Bartley and Henry Kissinger would oppose it, as one
once could have predicted who would support the invasion of
Grenada and who would not. Russia versus Ukraine, however,
is predictable in the way that Grenada was: essentially people
who want the United States not to involve itself overmuch in
European affairs from now on—Pat Buchanan, Warren
Christopher, the Arms Control Assocation, the editors of
Foreign Policy—favor Russia, because Russia will not need
American help. People who want to remain involved on the old
continent—such as Cheney and Kissinger—favor Ukraine,
because Ukraine will need American help. This is not to suggest that these arguments do not have a rational basis, or
indeed that one set of arguments might not be stronger than the
other; only that this is an ideological conflict, like that over
Middle East policy, in which the commitment comes first and
the rational arguments, no matter how forceful, arrive only
later. Cheney's speech declared him to be outside the nationalist, isolationist camp. It will be interesting to see whether other
conservatives follow him; especially interesting since the government of Ukraine has retained so much more of its
Communist oppressiveness than the government of Russia.

In his speech deploring Republicans' apathy toward foreign
policy, Cheney did not take time to complain of their apathy to
size-of-government issues. But that apathy is just as noticeable,
and among its proofs are the fading presidential prospects of
Texas Senator Phil Gramm, the Republican presidential aspi-
rant most eager to take an ax to the domestic functions of government. Gramm has about the slimmest chance of any of
these politicians in 1996. Gramm's anti-spending record is by
no means perfect: he endorses the subsidy to mohair wool—
condemned by the *National Journal*'s Jonathan Rauch as the

most ridiculous spending program for its size in the entire budget—because mohair sheep are a Texas product. He indefatigably lobbied on behalf of the now-canceled $10 billion supercollider project and Sematech, the horrific federal subsidy for the manufacture of semiconductors, both of which also happen to be located in Texas. Antitax Republicans bitterly recall Gramm's vote for and advocacy of President Bush's 1990 tax increase—an increase cobbled together in order to avoid the sequestration of funds provided for under Senator Gramm's own Gramm-Rudman antideficit act. For all his sins, though, Gramm remains the most articulate and impassioned promarket voice in the Senate. No senator of comparable intellectual power has as strong a voting record for less government, not even Jesse Helms. Senator Gramm was the first prominent Republican to declare unequivocal opposition to the Clinton health plan, or any health plan that would enlarge the coercive powers of the federal government. His Gramm-Rudman Act of 1985 bespoke a willingness to shut down the entire federal apparatus rather than let it grow beyond the public's willingness to pay for it in direct taxes. As a member of the House of Representatives, Gramm was the author of the two Gramm-Latta laws that enacted David Stockman's budget cuts. If there were such a thing as a Hero of Capitalist Labor medal, Gramm has abundantly earned it.

Detractors say that Gramm is mean. Even the usually gentle authors of the *Almanac of American Politics* concede, "There is a note of anger to him—a sharp edge of hostility to those whose view of America is quite different. In this friendly country, angry candidates—Patrick Buchanan, Jerry Brown are 1992's examples—do not wear well."[9] American politics does reward the anemic quality of niceness, or at least the appearance of it, and that quality fierce old Gramm lacks. But conservatism has not been entirely well served by geniality. It broadcasts wrong messages. Reagan's geniality misled his supporters into underestimating the resolution required of them if the frontiers of the state were to be rolled back. Reagan's manner was contrived to say, "Look, I wouldn't be doing any of this if any truly needy person anywhere in the country would suffer by it." When it later emerged that after all some needy persons had indeed suffered by some Reaganite measure, conservatives were left gasping. The point of the conservative policy revolution in North America and Great Britain in the 1980s was to slow down the coercive redistribution of wealth. The Reaganite version of that policy revolution, unlike the Thatcherite, was covert. Reagan's determination to seem nice hampered his ability to be radical. Reagan's geniality broadcast a dangerous message to his opponents too. It told them he could be beaten, and it taught them how to do it: by presenting him with hard-luck stories.

Any policy change in a nation of 235 million is going to produce losers. Compulsory airbags in cars will crush drivers' hands and wrists in a certain statistically predictable number of accidents. Pure water laws can shut down family farms that cannot afford fancy drainage techniques. Year-round daylight savings time forces rural children to walk to the bus stop in the dark where onrushing motorists may kill them. A Yiddish saying has it that "for instance isn't proof," and the ability to show that tighter eligibility for Social Security disability payments has impoverished Mr. Gonzales in Albuquerque does not prove that tighter eligibility is not, overall, more fair than slack eligibility. But Ronald Reagan was always vulnerable to a story about poor old Mr. Gonzales—which is why he declared so much of the federal budget off limits to budget cutters so early in his administration. Federal spending will keep on growing, and therefore federal taxes will keep on rising, until a president is elected who does not hear every pathetic anecdote as proof that money must be lifted out of the pockets of Mr. Rodriguez to give to Mr. Gonzales. In contemporary American parlance, reluctance to take from Rodriguez to give to Gonzales is "mean"; which is why conservatives need to find themselves the meanest guy they can.

Unfortunately, with the exception of Gramm—and a scattering of other unblinking congressional Republicans, particularly the indomitably flinty Representative Richard Armey, also of Texas—conservatives display less of such "meanness" with every passing year. Redistributionism has formed and shaped our collective sense of justice so entirely that even the most defiant nonconformist, on honest self-examination, must confess to it. Here's one telltale sign. Think of the subtitle of William Bennett's 1992 book, *The De-valuing of America: The Struggle for Our Children and Our Culture.* What is the locution "our children" doing in Bennett's mouth? The phrase contains the thought that one's obligations to all the other children in the country are similar in nature to one's obligations to one's own; that a purely political bond—that between citizens of one nation—can resemble in some meaningful way the biological bond between parent and child. For people who are always trying to extend the reach of the political, this is an attractive claim to make. It comes naturally to Mario Cuomo, because Cuomo understands its radical implications. "They are not my children, perhaps. Perhaps they are not your children. But Jesse [Jackson] is right; they are our children and we should love them."[10] Why is Bennett going along? Simply because "our children" is a phrase that has been injected into the language, a phrase that politicians sprinkle on their speeches as if it were parsley. For someone who is constantly called upon to speak in public, it would require an extraordinary mental effort not to use the phrase. Even Pat Buchanan, who revels in the epithet "pit bull of the Right," is not exempt from the redistributionist mentality, from the bedrock assumption that government is responsible for protecting us all. Imagine what Robert Taft would have said to that New Hampshire man who asked him to "save our jobs." He would have explained, in his pedantic way, that government cannot save any particular job, should not save any particular job.

If conservatives are indeed due for a longer spell out of power than they realize, as even unfriendly observers of the Clinton White House seem to think, they are going to be called on to rethink profoundly their philosophy of government. On present evidence, they seem determined to rethink it along moralist and nationalist lines, scaling down their once vehement antigovernment message to a "yes, but" skepticism about the too-rapid expansion of government. The historically minded might even wonder whether they are not groping their way back toward the political formula that has won more presidential elections than any other: active government intervention in the economy to promote welfare and assist private business, conservative moral reform at home, and the assertion of American nationality. That was the governing formula of the Republican Party in its great age of success, 1896 to 1932—tariffs, Prohibition, the exclusion or Americanization of immigrants—and of the Democratic Party in its heyday too, from the end of the radical New Deal in 1938 to the splintering of the party after 1968: subsidies and tax preferences for business; subsidies to home ownership and college education to improve the character of the people; and the forced transformation of the South into a normal part of America. It is the formula on which both Ulysses S. Grant and Harry S Truman campaigned. At the end of 1993, it looks very much like the philosophy of government President Clinton is bumbling his way toward: clapping controls on the cost of health care to large businesses; workfare and national service; a crackdown on illegal immigration. And it is the formula with which Ross Perot beguiled one-third of the Republican vote: the promise that government will be "run like a business"; that lobbyists and corrupt pols will be run out of the capital; and that Americans will be protected against the sucking of their livelihoods and wealth southward to Mexico.

The activist government/conservative moral reform/nationalism formula successfully speaks to American anxieties that the country's great prosperity may prove fleeting, that moral standards are crumbling, that this huge continental nation is too variegated to survive. America is a nervous country, and more nervous now than it has been in a very long time. In Canada, the American habit of flying the flag everywhere is thought to prove how secure Americans are in their national identity. On the contrary, nations secure in their identity—France or Japan, for example—never make a cult of the flag. That sort of ostentatious patriotism is the behavior of newly assembled nations that fear that the bonds that hold them together are weak and must be reinforced, like Germany and Italy a hundred years ago, like India or Nigeria today.

But while a new politics of economic activism plus conservative moral reform plus nationalism beckons to conservatives weary of the losing struggle against big government and eager to come to grips with the country's social decay, the summons is a treacherous one. The politics of Kemp, Bennett, and Buchanan cannot deliver on their promises, because they accept as immutable the very force creating the social conditions they decry.

Twenty years ago, an economist named Sam Peltzman noticed that drivers who wore seatbelts, while suffering far fewer accidents than drivers who did not, inflicted far more. The safer the driver personally felt, the more carelessly he drove. The welfare state functions as a political safety belt, reducing the riskiness of all of our lives; and just as with real safety belts, there are what Peltzman called "feedback effects" from our newfound sense of personal security. Some of these effects are undoubtedly good. Unemployment insurance, by easing fears of job loss, does seem to relax workers' apprehensions about technological change. Other effects, however, are not good.

Consider the example of what ranks in conservative thinking as the most corrupted institution in American society: the university. Suppose that there were no student loans and very little of any other sort of state aid to higher education; imagine that every student (save those who could win a scholarship from the university itself) were paying the full cost of his or her own tuition and that the university had no sources of income other than tuition, alumni gifts, endowment income, and grants from governments and corporations for specific research projects. In such a world, the universities would not look at all like the schools that now enrage conservative critics of American higher education. The less motivated students, or those students seeking only, as one conservative academic puts it, to prove the negative point that they are not so idle and incompetent as to fail to get a B.A., would drop away. The students who remained, paying $1,000 or more per course, would become more discriminating consumers. Some demand for film studies, black studies, gay studies, and courses on the novels of Louis L'Amour would of course linger on—but in a cash-on-the-barrelhead university, the demand for such courses would be much reduced, and so, pretty quickly, would be the supply. Fewer faculty would be able to teach those courses; faculty who could teach nothing else would have to find new lines of work, and ambitious young scholars would write dissertations that identified them as willing to teach and capable of teaching the subjects that the customers were going to demand. How and why Jacques Derrida, Michel Foucault, and Franz Fanon came to loom so huge in American higher education is a big and vexing question. At least part of the answer is that American universities teach what they do for the same reason Polish factories used to turn out pairs of boots with two left feet: because an absence of consumer sovereignty enables them to get away with it. The factories make what pleases them; and because the consumers are paying with soft currency, they take whatever it pleases the factories to make. With greater sacrifices demanded of the families of those who sought higher education, the proportion of Americans going on to university would shrink. That would in turn mean that state governments could no longer count on higher education to remedy the deficiencies of high school education. America turns out students the way General Motors used to turn out cars: slovenly and stupid assembly workers bang the doors on any old way they feel like, counting on a highly paid team of fixers at the end of the line to redo and repair their bungled work. If the refinishers were to go out of business, the high schools would have to be run like a Toyota line instead: the job would have to be done right the first time. It is sometimes thought to be a paradox that America has by far the most elaborate system of higher education in the industrialized world and among the very worst systems of primary and secondary education. In fact, the two complement each other like fresh fruit and yogurt. If the yogurt weren't sour, you wouldn't need to mix fruit into it; if the high schools were better, Americans could close many of their universities.

Nobody can promise that the end of state aid to universities would chasten them immediately. Organizations like the Ford and Rockefeller Foundations could still channel billions to the university's most destructive personalities and functions. It would take a generation, perhaps more, for the pranksters and sophists in the academy to retire. But I think we can say confidently that if large-scale state aid to higher education had never been tried, the universities would be more wholesome places today; that if massive aid ended tomorrow they would tend over time to become more wholesome; and that so long as universities remain free of any need to earn a living by charging students the full cost of each and every course of study, they will continue to act as they act now. It is conceivable, as moralist conservatives would argue, that the providers of subsidy, if enlightened by conservative ideology, could press the universities to reform. William Bennett tried to do just that at the National Endowment for the Humanities. The effort reminds me of Yuri Andropov's hope of salvaging the Soviet economy by sending out policemen to force everyone to work harder and drink less: there will never be enough police to keep an eye on every resentful worker.

The same feedback effect drives the crisis of family breakdown. You can never reform welfare in a way that simultaneously encourages people to work and that provides them with a decent livelihood if they don't. I'm not suggesting—not very confidently anyway—that abolishing AFDC now would undo the harm the program has done. It is quite possible that you don't exit this trap by the same route by which you entered. But if welfare had never been enlarged in the mid-1960s, if a sixteen-year-old who got pregnant in 1993 had the same five unpleasant options she did in 1963—give up the child, get an abortion, drop out of school and take a job, beg her furious parents for help, or somehow persuade the father to marry her and take a job himself—isn't it probable, as Charles Murray contends, that today's sixteen-year-olds would be as unlikely to give birth out of wedlock as those of 1963 were? Even if Madonna's songs were broadcast twenty-four hours a day on every AM band? Of course it is true that the world in which the teenager of 1993 lives is not as hostile to illegitimacy as the world in which her grandmother lived. Yes, "the culture" has deteriorated. But if the culture that abhorred illegitimacy has vanished, perhaps it is because it is hard for most people to believe for very long in the wrongness of something that the government rewards. Fitzjames Stephen observed 130 years ago that while it is true that most people refrain from stealing because they believe stealing to be wrong, and not because they fear hanging, it is also true that the reason most people believe stealing to be wrong is that thieves are hanged.

It really should not surprise anyone that the welfare state has weakened family structures. That was what social programs were meant to do. The family used to be connected by its members' mutual responsibility for child-rearing, unemployment, sickness, old age, disability, and burial. A woman who gave birth outside of marriage was burdening her mother and father. A man who abandoned his children was abandoning his pension. But while strict mutual responsibility did a fair job of deterring illegitimacy and abandonment, it never succeeded very well at coping with illegitimacy and abandonment when they occurred. The welfare state was intended to replace those old family functions, and thus reduce the economic importance of the family—which, predictably, weakened the family's stability. No, there's no clamor for going back to the old ways. For the old, a check from Social Security is more reliable, more generous, and less intrusive than support from one's children; from the child's point of view, even a 15.3 percent payroll tax is a lot less trouble than having to look after a bedridden old mother in the spare room.

It is certainly more agreeable to slice "duty" out of the lexicon, to visit your aged parents knowing that it is someone else's job to provide for them, to drop one's children off at day care instead of begging a favor from a sister or mother. But it is not very realistic of conservatives to expect that the family can survive in its pre–Social Security form in a Social Security world. Affection is one of the most impermanent and weakest of human ties, but affection is now all that holds families together. Bill Bennett's search for "economic and social policies that support the two-parent family" is going to be disappointed. "Supporting the family" in Washington parlance is code for subsidies and welfare programs—family leave, day care—that is, for more of the forces in modern life that are subverting the family. Family leave and day care strike at the family's core economic logic, the sexual division of labor, depriving the family of the glue of mutual self-interest.

One last welfare state "feedback effect." Henry George compared the act of raising a single tariff to hurling a single banana into a cage of monkeys: all the unlucky monkeys shriek and rage until a banana is thrown to them too. The conservative demand that America's warring ethnic, religious, racial, and even sexual minority groups hush their squealing and complaining and concentrate instead on what unites them as Americans seems to me to be equivalent to attempting to teach the monkeys table manners. So long as society hurls economic and psychic rewards at everyone with a plausible claim to victimhood, people are going to cultivate their grievances against the rest of society. We can ask them to stop feeling aggrieved. But it is probably simpler to quit tossing bananas at them. Why is there a Congressional Black Caucus? For the same reason that there is a high-tech caucus, and a women's caucus, and a textile caucus, and that there will someday soon be a gay and lesbian caucus—because government is dispensing multimillion dollar benefits, and only the organized can hope to capture any of them. Political organization is only worthwhile when the local rules extend the hope of collecting unearned rewards; otherwise individuals would devote the time they spend on organizing to useful work. If campus pressure groups cannot intimidate teachers and administrators into raising grades, then black and Hispanic students who want better grades have no choice but to study. If Americans regarded economic redistribution as unthinkable, blacks and Hispanics who wanted to enrich themselves would have no choice but to work. But if deans and corporations are seen to knuckle under to moral blackmail, agitation and speechmaking become profitable as well as pleasurable. So long as billions of dollars can be extracted by any group that can represent itself as piteous enough—former coal miners, the old, the sick—political entrepreneurs are presented an alluring menu of incentives for playing on their followers' grievances, mobilizing their resentments, intensifying their group identity, and whipping up suspicion of outsiders.

The welfare state underwrites particularism even more explicitly. Social critics of the 1950s bemoaned American conformity. That conformity was, it is now clear, a passing phase: a lingering effect of the military discipline that an unprecedented number of Americans had been subject to for an unprecedented length of time, and of the timidity ingrained in the generation that remembered the Depression. It is also probably true, though, that a market economy tends to suppress non–economically useful differences. If I am bearded, and I notice that my boss and the last four men in my section to win promotion are clean-shaven, I will find myself slowly nudged toward the barbershop. If the owner of the gas station across the road from mine smiles a lot, and I don't, I will find myself forcing a cheerful manner myself, no matter how snarly I may inwardly feel. People who do not have to work for a living, however, can indulge themselves in a hundred little peculiarities of behavior—one reason that the English upper class is so famously odd. Millions of Americans now live as free from the pressure to conform as any English lord, thanks either to the direct receipt of welfare or to civil service employment where promotion is by seniority and firing is unheard of. That fact, as much as any fashion change, explains the sudden flaunting of ethnic difference in manner and dress that so distresses Patrick Buchanan in his native city. Relatively few vice presidents at Procter & Gamble would dare wear a kente cloth or a keffiyeh; nobody who intends to earn very much of a living in the polymer business can hope to get away with not learning English; but city hall employees and welfare mothers can do both.

So the cultural conservatives are simply deluding themselves when they hope for escape from the unpleasant task of resisting every enlargement of the ambit of government action and trying, when opportunity presents itself, to reduce that ambit. However they describe their decision, conservatives who throw in the towel on issues like Social Security and Medicare and welfare in order to direct their full attention to "the culture" are attempting to preserve bourgeois values in a world arranged in such a way as to render those virtues at best unnecessary and at worst active nuisances. The project is not one that is very likely to succeed.

What are the bourgeois virtues anyway? The paramount ones are thrift, diligence, prudence, sobriety, fidelity, and orderliness. Compared to the military, saintly, and romantic virtues— zeal, courage, passion, love of beauty, pride, and indifference to worldly goods—it is not a very poetic list. But they are the virtues that settled America (combined, of course, with a canny eye for the quick buck), and they are the virtues whose ebbing conservatives mourn. The bourgeois virtues developed into an almost national cultural norm because they were essential to survival in a country that was, until the 1930s, simultaneously rich in opportunities and full of terrible dangers from which there was no protection except one's own resources and the help of friends and family. The opportunities remain, but the dangers have dwindled. Why be thrifty any longer when your old age and health care are provided for, no matter how profligately you act in your youth? Why be prudent when the state insures your bank deposits, replaces your flooded-out house, buys all the wheat you can grow, and rescues you when you stray into a foreign battle zone? Why be diligent when half your earnings are taken from you and given to the idle? Why be sober when the taxpayers run clinics to cure you of your drug habit as soon as it no longer amuses you? Why be faithful when there are no consequences at all to leaving your family in search of newer and more exciting pleasures? Why be neat and uncomplaining when squalor and whining are indictments not of you, but of society—and when the whinier and more squalid you are, the more society will pay to eradicate your problems? True, some virtues linger on after they have outlived their usefulness. True too, the bourgeois virtues retain much of their usefulness when combined with talent. If diligence can earn you $150,000 a year as an engineer, you'll be diligent, even if President Clinton helps himself to half the proceeds. If your mental life is interesting to you even when undrugged, those taxpayer-funded clinics will not beckon. But for the less capable, who always outnumber the capable, things look rather different. (As they may do for many of the highly capable too: what modern tycoon feels the need to build churches? What Hollywood mogul hesitates to discard an aging wife?)

If the old American culture and the old American character were rational responses to the riskiness of life, you cannot alleviate that riskiness and expect the old culture and the old character to persist. The children of a self-made man are different from their father: more optimistic, often more generous, more sensitive, and more tolerant, but less careful, less provident, less hardworking, less self-controlled. In the same way, the citizens of a socially insured America will act and think differently from the citizens of self-reliant America. If you prefer the older character, it is wishful thinking to duck out of the struggle to return to the older way of life that brought that character into being. And, despite the failure of the Reagan gambit, it isn't even necessary.

The welfare state that conservatives are so frightened to fight is a desperately unstable institution. Its costs rise without respite, because it tempts people into ever greater helplessness and dependence on it. Despite ever-stricter eligibility rules, federal spending on food stamps, AFDC, and Medicaid rose by nearly 50 percent in the first six Reagan years, because—while each welfare family got less—the total number of welfare families rose. The faster the welfare state's costs rise, the more the economy that supports the welfare state stagnates, in large part because of the disincentives created by the welfare state's high taxes, but also because the welfare state's temptations sap the brutal acquisitive drive that propels economies forward. As the government sectors of the world's two dozen welfare states have swelled, their growth rates have slowed, their unemployment rates have risen, their poor have behaved in increasingly pathological ways, and—of greatest immediate interest—their public accounts have become more and more disordered. Comparatively speaking, the trend has not yet gone very far in the United States—only 14 percent of federal revenues are now spent to pay interest on the federal debt; neighboring Canada pays 35 percent—but the proportion is climbing.

And as it does, terrible resentment will be ignited. If taxpayers now think that they send money to Washington and get little in return, wait until one dollar in six or one dollar in five vanishes right off the top to the federal government's creditors. Nor, as the Canadians have demonstrated, can you solve the problem by raising taxes, for a country whose debt is compounding rapidly has already passed the point at which further taxes raise more revenues than they lose by slowing the economy or driving transactions underground. Pressed by taxes, angered by the declining quality of public services, feeling cheated by government and not knowing why, American voters sink deeper and deeper into the mistrustful mood that characterized the electorate in 1992, when almost one voter in five cast a ballot for the most sinister demagogue to seek the presidency since Huey Long was cut down in 1935. In Canada, where taxpayers get 65 cents in services for every dollar they pay in taxes, the English think that the French are scooping up the missing 35 cents and the French think that the English are intercepting it. In the United States, whites will blame blacks and immigrants, and blacks will blame whites and immigrants.

Some conservatives take comfort in the welfare state's travails. Irving Kristol says that we are living through the "end game" of the welfare state. The editors of the *Wall Street Journal* cite polls in which a clear majority of Americans claim that they would prefer to receive fewer services from government and pay less in tax than receive more and pay more. Newt Gingrich's theory is that within the next half-dozen years the number of people who understand that they are never going to get their money's worth out of Social Security will for the first time outnumber those for whom the system is a net benefit. The baby boomers will realize they're not getting a good deal and will rebel against it. All of this will happen soon and automatically, like the proletarian revolution in Marxist theory, so why stir up trouble prematurely now? The ricketiness of the welfare state does not embolden Gingrich to vote against the dangerous contraption; precisely the opposite, it excuses him from doing much of anything, since the end is preordained.

But nothing is inevitable and very few things are even predictable. If the welfare state is unstable, if its costs must outrun its revenues and if debts accumulate in ways that rile society's constituent groups against one another, yes, then the thing will collapse. But there is no guarantee that the collapse will lead to a more enterprising, self-reliant, and virtuous society. It is as likely that what comes next will be worse. If conservatives believe that Herbert Stein's Iron Law ("if something can't go on forever, it will stop") applies to the future of the redistributive state, then they'd better start acting now to ensure that the political regime that emerges from the welfare state's demise is an improvement upon it, just as the Herbert Crolys and Frances Perkinses and Walter Lippmanns of the 1910s and 1920s labored to convince Americans of the rightness of their preferred regime long before the much-anticipated arrival of the crisis of laissez-faire capitalism.

As the United States finances its commitments to the old with ever-heavier impositions on the young, as it tends the sick with invisible taxes on the healthy, as it hastens the promotion in the labor force of the black and Hispanic by penalizing the white and Oriental, as it supports the poor in ways that abuse the neighborhoods and schools that formerly belonged to the middle class, a lot of free-floating intergroup animosity will be released into the atmosphere. Animosity is always someone's opportunity. In 1992 Patrick Buchanan hoped it would be his. He happened to be wrong, but next time he, or someone like him, may be a little closer to being right. If conservatives like Kristol and Gingrich and others can anticipate this dangerous outcome, then they should be acting now to lead the country safely through it, by doing as the conservatives of the 1950s did—by discarding all consideration of what the public wants to hear, and telling the public what it needs to know to respond intelligently when the crisis does arrive. The radicalism of William F. Buckley, Jr., and the *National Review* was dismissed in those days as impractical by President Eisenhower's "Modern Republicans." But the fence-straddling of the Modern Republicans is now just a memory; Buckley, as much as one man can, changed the country's politics.

That is a course of action that demands perhaps too much of a politician, but it is not unreasonable to expect it of writers and intellectuals. One of the truly deplorable things that happened on the Right in the 1980s was the overidentification of conservative intellectuals with the executive branch of the federal government. With almost every clever conservative under the age of thirty-five aspiring to a job as a speechwriter, as a special assistant to a cabinet secretary, or, best of all, a member of the president's personal staff, the mode of thought of a generation of young writers became partisan to a degree not seen in American letters since—when? The 1930s? They—we— thought about policy and elections so hard that we seldom stopped to think about philosophy. We identified our principles with the interests of an administration and, worse, of particular persons within that administration. We became what the British would call "ministerial"—no matter how remote from government we might be, we thought as members of a government do. We learned to limit our own speculations to what the balance of political forces at that particular moment declared feasible; we wrote articles as if they were memoranda to the president, banning the not immediately practical from our discourse.

And as the distressing social trends of the 1970s—family breakup, illegitimacy, crime, ethnic balkanization, declining educational standards—continued without a break through the 1980s, conservatives turned those same ministerial eyes to them too, devising clever policies to mend the rotting fabric of society. It was often ingenious, but also too often beside the point. It is the post-1933, post-1965 scale and scope of American government that creates the preconditions for the social decay conservatives bemoan. So long as colossal government exists, policy palliatives, no matter how ingenious, can do scant good.

If this were the end of the story, it would be a sad end. But it does not have to be the end. The conservative movement can still redeem and revivify itself; it just has to take a step backward from presidential and congressional politics. The country must be governed, and it must be governed by people who won't spend it into bankruptcy or regulate it into gross wastefulness. Restraining government to the minimum size feasible under present political conditions, and doing what it can to alter those political conditions, is the task of the Republican Party, and it is a fine, worthwhile task. But conservative intellectuals should be at work on something a little more ambitious than the Republican Party's next campaign manifesto. They should be showing the public the necessary connection between the social pathologies it loathes and fears and the social programs it still rather likes—not just the programs for the poor that have created the underclass, appalling though those programs may be, but also the broader programs and laws that have corroded the economic functions of the family, set ethnic groups at one another's throats in pursuit of set-asides and special favors, outlawed the expression of moral outrage at irregular conduct, and diminished the necessity of thrift. Conservatives are not libertarians. They do not believe that maximum personal liberty is a good in and of itself, without regard to its consequences. "The effect of liberty to individuals is, that they may do what they please," wrote Edmund Burke, the hero of American conservatives, "we ought to see what it will please them to do, before we risk congratulations." It is not to maximize liberty as an end in itself that conservatives have advocated minimal government. They have advocated it because they admired a certain type of character—self-reliant, competent, canny, and uncomplaining—and minimal government was the system of government under which the character they admired flourished best.

Contemporary conservatives still value that old American character. William Bennett in his lectures reads admiringly from an account of the Donner party written by a survivor that tells the story in spare, stoic style. He puts the letter down and asks incredulously, "Where did those people go?" But if you believe that early Americans possessed a fortitude that present-day Americans lack, and if you think the loss is an important one, then you have to think hard about why that fortitude disappeared. Merely exhorting Americans to show more fortitude is going to have about as much effect on them as a lecture from the student council president on school spirit. Reorganizing the method by which they select and finance their schools won't do it either, and neither will the line-item veto, or discharge petitions, or entrusting Congress with the power to deny individual NEA grants, or court decisions striking down any and all acts of politically correct tyranny emanating from the offices of America's deans of students—worthwhile though each and every one of those things may be. It is social conditions that form character, as another conservative hero, Alexis de Tocqueville, demonstrated, and if our characters are now less virtuous than formerly, we must identify in what way our social conditions have changed in order to understand why.

Of course there have been hundreds of such changes—never mind since the Donner party's day, just since 1945: the tripling of the average real income; the reduction in manpower need on farms and in factories; suburbanization, freeways, and mass communications; the nation's first military defeat; the eclipse of religion; cheap and accessible birth control—one could fill the page. But the expansion of government is the only one we can do anything about.

All of these changes have had the same effect: the emancipation of the individual appetite from the restrictions imposed on it by limited resources, or religious dread, or community disapproval, or the risk of disease or personal catastrophe. Tom Wolfe has described this emancipation vividly. For years, intellectuals had pitied the helplessness of the common man, but

> once the dreary little bastards started getting money in the 1940's, they did an astonishing thing—they took their money and ran! They did something only aristocrats (and intellectuals and artists) were supposed to do—they discovered and started doting on Me! They've created the greatest age of individualism in American history! All rules are broken! The prophets are out of business! Where the Third Great Awakening will lead—who can presume to say? One only knows that the great religious waves have a momentum all their own. Neither arguments nor policies nor acts of the legislature have been any match for them in the past. And this one has the mightiest, holiest roll of all, the beat that goes ... Me ... Me ... Me ... Me ... [11]

Conservative intellectuals, like all intellectuals, have been both fascinated and repelled by this liberation of appetite. Nationalist conservatives deal with the problems it creates by blaming America's social problems on the appetites of the population groups they dislike, and trusting in the continuing goodness and self-discipline of the right sort of Americans, the "conservatives

of the heart." Optimist conservatives cheerfully say that
appetites have not been liberated enough, that ever fuller consumer choice must be extended to ever larger numbers of people over ever larger areas of life. Moralist conservatives, influenced by the Straussian philosophers who regard appetite as the
central organizing principle of modern regimes, worry hardest
over the problems it raises, but all their worrying yields only
gimmicks palpably unequal to the problem the moralists perceive. We cannot rescind the emancipation of appetite; but we
can make its indulgence riskier by cancelling the welfare state's
seductive invitation to misconduct.

Conservatism was never supposed to be a sunny political
ideology. It was always a doctrine for the tough-minded.
Conservatives have never had much use for the utopian or the
visionary:

> You know the type as well as I do. Give the forward-looker
> the direct primary, and he demands the short ballot. Give
> him the initiative and referendum, and he bawls for the
> recall of judges. Give him Christian Science, and he pro-
> ceeds to the swamis and yogis. Give him the Mann Act, and
> he wants laws providing for the castration of fornicators.
> Give him Prohibition, and he launches a new crusade
> against cigarettes, coffee, jazz, and custard pies.[12]

But the Reagan interlude turned our heads. It misled us into
thinking that the American people were with us—not in a
casual, happenstance sense, but deeply, even when conservative
ideology might deny them some benefit out of the Treasury or
upbraid them for something it would give them pleasure to do.
And as we have discovered the uncomfortable truth that they
are not with us, *we* have adapted to *them*. That adaptation
explains the conduct and rhetoric of Kemp, it explains Bennett,
it explains Buchanan, it explains the whole roster of first- and
second-tier conservative presidential candidates. It explains,
finally, the triviality and cynicism that have characterized too
much of conservative politics over the past few years.

Conservatives suffer a very different political problem from liberals these days. Avowed liberals have a difficult time winning power in this country; avowed conservatives do not. You no longer get far in public life by preaching that the poor are poor because someone else is not poor, or that criminals can be rehabilitated, or that American troops should get their orders from the United Nations. There's no liberal Rush Limbaugh. But exercising power—that is a very different business. When conservatism's glittering generalities, "you are overtaxed," turn into legislative specifics, "you must pay more to send your kid to the state university," we run into as much trouble in midsession as the liberals do at election time. Twelve years of twisting and struggling to escape this snare have just entangled us ever more deeply in it, until we have arrived at the unhappy destination this book describes. Is there a way out? Only one: conservative intellectuals should learn to care a little less about the electoral prospects of the Republican Party, indulge less in policy cleverness and ethnic demagoguery, and do what intellectuals of all descriptions are obliged to do: practice honesty, and pay the price.

Notes

Chapter 1. Athwart History

1. Richard M. Weaver, *Ideas Have Consequences* (Chicago: University of Chicago Press, 1948), 2.
2. Whittaker Chambers, *Witness* (Chicago: Henry Regnery, 1952), 9.
3. William Kristol, interview with the author, 15 December 1993.
4. Irving Kristol, "My Cold War," *National Interest* (Spring 1993): 144.
5. Quoted in William J. Bennett, *The De-valuing of America: The Fight for Our Culture and Our Children* (New York: Simon & Schuster, 1992), 258.
6. Ralph Z. Hallow, "Health Care Reform Splits Republicans," *Washington Times*, 15 December 1993, p. A4.

Chapter 2. Houston: "Wall-to-Wall Ugly"

1. Joe Klein, "Little Lies and Big Whoppers," *Newsweek*, 31 August 1992, 36. Thanks to the Media Research Center for this and the three succeeding quotes.
2. Curtis Wilkie, "GOP Compass Direction: The Far Right," *Boston Globe*, 18 August 1992, p. 10.
3. "Playing for the Big Bounce," *Time*, 31 August 1992, 14.
4. Charles Kuralt, live broadcast, CBS, 17 August 1992.
5. D. James Kennedy, address, in *Proceedings of the Thirty-Fifth Republican National Convention*, 345. (Hereafter referred to as *Proceedings*.)
6. Pat Robertson, address, in *Proceedings*, 504.
7. Patrick J. Buchanan, address, in *Proceedings*, 374.
8. Richard Bond, address, in *Proceedings*, 53.
9. Dan Lungren, address, in *Proceedings*, 394.

10. Michael Deland, address, in *Proceedings*, 402.

11. Fred Brown, address, in *Proceedings*, 431.

12. James Watkins, address, in *Proceedings*, 469.

13. William Althaus, address, in *Proceedings*, 410.

14. Craig McFarlane, address, in *Proceedings*, 336.

15. "The Vision Shared: Uniting Our Family, Our Country, Our World," *Proceedings*, 275.

16. James Watkins, address, in *Proceedings*, 469.

17. Mary Fisher, address, in *Proceedings*, 513.

18. "The Vision Shared," *Proceedings*, 270.

19. Ibid., 283.

20. 1957 Report by Planned Parenthood of Connecticut. Cited in Peter Smith, "The History and Future of the Legal Battle over Birth Control," *Cornell Law Quarterly* 49 (1964): 281.

21. George F. Will, interview with the author, 15 December 1993.

22. George Bush, address, in *Proceedings*, 598.

23. Lynn Martin, address, in *Proceedings*, 533.

24. Patrick J. Buchanan, address, in *Proceedings*, 375–76.

25. "Agenda for American Renewal," Bush campaign pamphlet, October 1992.

26. Michael Barone, *Our Country: The Shaping of America from Roosevelt to Reagan* (New York: Free Press, 1990), 669.

27. Newt Gingrich, interview with the author, 30 March 1993.

28. Irving Kristol, "A Conservative Welfare State," *Wall Street Journal*, 14 June 1993, p. A14.

29. James Q. Wilson, "Why Reagan Won and Stockman Lost," *Commentary* (August 1986): 20.

30. Charles Heatherly and Burton Yale Pines, eds., *Mandate for Leadership III* (Washington, D.C.: Heritage Foundation, 1989), 146.

31. Patrick J. Buchanan, "The Coming Resurrection of the GOP," *Wall Street Journal*, 21 January 1993, p. A14.

32. M. I. Finley, *The Ancient Economy* (Berkeley: University of California Press, 1973), 87.

Chapter 3. The Failure of the Reagan Gambit

1. This sounds incredible, but it's true. In 1979, the U.S. government spent $387.1 billion for nondefense purposes. If growth in the nondefense budget had been held to the rate of inflation, it would have

reached approximately $600 billion by 1989. The 1989 defense budget was $303 billion, so total federal expenditures that year would have amounted to $900 billion, as opposed to actual expenditures of $1,144 billion, or 17 percent of 1989 GNP versus 22 percent. The five percentage points of GNP thus saved would have sufficed to eliminate the 1989 deficit (3 percent of GNP) with enough left over to eliminate the corporate income tax (whose revenues equalled 2 percent of GNP) or slash the FICA payroll tax (whose revenues equalled 7 percent of GNP) by one-third.

2. Barry Goldwater, *The Conscience of a Conservative* (Washington, D.C.: Regnery Gateway, 1990), 17.

3. Jack Kemp, *American Renaissance* (New York: Harper & Row, 1979), 10–11.

4. Paul Craig Roberts, *The Supply-side Revolution* (Cambridge: Harvard University Press, 1984), 40.

5. Jude Wanniski, *The Way the World Works*, 3rd. ed. (Morristown, N.J.: Polyconomics, 1989), 205.

6. William Niskanen, *Reaganomics: An Insider's Account of the Policies and the People* (New York: Oxford University Press, 1988), 84. A family at the median income level's marginal tax rate rose from 30.1 to 32 percent. The 1986 tax reform reduced the marginal tax rate of the median-income family by four-tenths of one percentage point.

7. Unpublished study by three Congressional Budget Office staffers, cited in the *New York Times,* 1 October 1992, p. D1. 1980 average effective federal tax rate: 23.3 percent; 1985 rate: 21.7 percent; 1993 rate: 23.2 percent.

8. Reagan also did away with the revenue sharing—direct grants to state governments to use as they saw fit—instituted by President Nixon.

9. Martin Anderson, *Revolution* (New York: Harcourt, Brace, 1988), 243.

10. John McLaughlin, "Reagan's Double Shuffle," *National Review,* 24 February 1984, 23.

11. David Stockman, *The Triumph of Politics* (New York: Harper & Row, 1986), 130.

12. Niskanen, *Reaganomics,* 302–3.

13. Terrell Bell, *The Thirteenth Man* (New York: Free Press, 1988), 2.

14. Ibid., 35.

15. William French Smith, *Law and Justice in the Reagan Administration* (Stanford, Calif.: Hoover Institution, 1991), 79–83.

16. Harry Walters, interview with the author, 6 May 1993.

17. Niskanen, *Reaganomics*, 26–27.

18. Ronald Reagan, *An American Life* (New York: Simon & Schuster, 1990), 316. See entry for January 28, 1982.

19. Stockman, *The Triumph of Politics*, 309.

20. Dinesh D'Souza, "Thinking Ahead Conservatively," *American Spectator* (August 1985): 13.

21. George F. Will, *Statecraft as Soulcraft* (New York: Simon & Schuster, 1983), 128.

22. Lawrence J. White, *The Savings & Loan Debacle* (New York: Oxford University Press, 1991), 7.

23. Ibid., 86.

24. Federal Reserve data, as gathered in *Grant's Interest Rate Observer*, 12 April 1991.

25. Patrick J. Buchanan, Speech at Duke University, 28 April 1992.

26. Roger Kimball, *Tenured Radicals* (New York: Harper & Row, 1990), xi.

27. Kemp, *American Renaissance*, 7.

28. George Gilder, *Wealth and Poverty* (New York: Basic Books, 1981), 14–15.

29. Allan Bloom, *The Closing of the American Mind* (New York: Simon & Schuster, 1987), 74–75.

30. American Family Association pamphlet, Spring 1992.

31. Irving Kristol, *The Democratic Idea in America* (New York: Harper & Row, 1972), 29.

32. These and the following statistics, unless otherwise indicated, are drawn from the 1993 Statistical Abstract of the United States.

33. Midge Decter, "Sex and God in American Politics: What Conservatives Really Think," *Policy Review* (Summer 1984): 23.

34. "Who's Minding the Kids?", a Family Research Council report, 1991.

35. It's an interesting aside to note how uncontroversial the invocation was. It was written by a Reform rabbi, and among the things it thanked God for was the wonder of America's diversity. Religious people are often treated as fanatics, but one has to wonder at the fanaticism of the Weisman family, who took their objection to this religious pablum all the way to the highest court in the land.

36. Patrick J. Buchanan, address, in *Proceedings of the Thirty-Fifth Republican Convention*, 337.

37. "No Guardrails" (editorial), *Wall Street Journal*, 18 March 1993, p. A12.

38. William J. Bennett, *The De-valuing of America: The Fight for Our Culture and Our Children* (New York: Simon & Schuster, 1992), 33.
39. Samuel Francis, "The Education of David Duke," *Chronicles* (February 1992): 8.
40. Christopher Jencks and Donald Peterson, *The Urban Underclass* (Washington, D.C.: Brookings Institution, 1991), 164–65.
41. Ibid., 182–87.
42. Irving Kristol, *Memoirs of a Neoconservative* (New York: Basic Books, 1983), 3–4.
43. Mickey Kaus, *The End of Equality* (New York: New Republic Books, 1992), 107.
44. Committee for the Free World, "A Farewell, a Thank You, and a Prayer," *Contentions* (December 1990).
45. Dinesh D'Souza, *Illiberal Education* (New York: Free Press, 1991), 50.
46. Ibid., 146.
47. Linda Chavez, *Out of the Barrio* (New York: Basic Books, 1991), 161.
48. Ibid., 15.
49. Ibid., 132.
50. R. Emmett Tyrrell, *The Conservative Crackup* (New York: Simon & Schuster, 1992), 204.

Chapter 4. Optimists: Wrong but Wromantic

1. Jack Kemp, Speech at the Heritage Foundation, 6 June 1990.
2. Jack Kemp, address, in *Proceedings of the Thirty-Fifth Republican Convention*, 484.
3. Quoted in Robert Guskind and Carol F. Steinbach, "Sales Resistance," *National Journal*, 6 April 1991, 798.
4. Ibid., 803.
5. George F. Will, interview with the author, 15 December 1993.
6. Jack Kemp, interview with the author, 29 November 1993.
7. James Pinkerton, "Life in Bush Hell," *New Republic*, 14 December 1992, 27.
8. Newt Gingrich, address, in *Proceedings*, 305.
9. Ibid., 478.
10. Evans and Novak, "GOP Heir Apparent," *Washington Post*, 4 November 1992, p. A19.

11. Fredric Smoler, "We Had a Great History and We Turned Aside," *American Heritage* (October 1993): 56.

12. When I interviewed Bill Bennett for this book, he asked at the end, "Aren't you the fellow who predicted that Jack Kemp and I wouldn't get along?"—referring to an article of mine in the *American Spectator* that pointed out the gap between Kemp's optimism and Bennett's pessimism. Yes, I said. He flashed a big grin: "Boy, did you ever get that wrong."

Chapter 5. Moralists: The Threat from Above

1. James Q. Wilson, *On Character* (Washington, D.C.: American Enterprise Institute, 1991), 12.

2. Ibid., 21.

3. James Q. Wilson, "How to Teach Better Values in Inner Cities," *Wall Street Journal,* 18 May 1992, p. A10.

4. Lawrence Mead, *The New Politics of Poverty* (New York: Basic Books, 1992), 2.

5. Irving Kristol, *Reflections of a Neoconservative* (New York: Basic Books, 1983), 76.

6. *Conversations About Culture,* unpublished transcript of the W. H. Brady Conference on Cultural Politics, Chicago, January 1991, p. 90.

7. Charles Heatherly and Burton Yale Pines, eds., *Mandate for Leadership III* (Washington, D.C.: Heritage Foundation, 1989), 181.

8. William J. Bennett, *The De-valuing of America: The Fight for Our Culture and Our Children* (New York: Simon & Schuster, 1992), 37.

9. Ibid., 97.

10. William J. Bennett, interview with the author, 31 March 1993.

11. Thomas Main, "What We Know About the Homeless," *Commentary* (May 1988): 31.

12. Bennett, *The De-valuing of America,* 198.

13. James Q. Wilson, "How to Teach Better Values in Inner Cities."

14. Mead, *The New Politics of Poverty,* 81.

15. Ibid., 83. Quote is from March 28, 1988.

16. Ibid., 51–52.

17. Ibid., 134.

18. George F. Will, "A Sterner Kind of Caring," *Newsweek,* 13 January 1992, 68.

19. Charles Murray, "The Coming White Underclass," *Wall Street Journal,* 29 October 1993, p. A14.

20. Chester Finn, *We Must Take Charge: Our Schools and Our Future* (New York: Free Press, 1991), 277–85.
21. Mead, *The New Politics of Poverty*, 168.
22. Ibid., 184.
23. Irving Kristol, "Family Values—Not a Political Issue," *Wall Street Journal*, 7 December 1992, p. A14.
24. Myron Magnet, *The Dream and the Nightmare: The Sixties' Legacy to the Underclass* (New York: William Morrow, 1993), 19.
25. Bill Kristol, interview with the author, 15 December 1993.
26. "A Nation at Risk" is cited in Finn, *We Must Take Charge*, 11.
27. Irving Kristol, *On the Democratic Idea in America* (New York: Harper & Row, 1972), 17.
28. Finn, *We Must Take Charge*, 233–34.
29. Ibid., 247.
30. Ibid., 254.
31. Ibid., 256–58.
32. Barry Goldwater, *Conscience of a Conservative* (Washington, D.C.: Regnery Gateway, 1990), 31.
33. William F. Buckley and L. Brent Bozell, *McCarthy and His Critics* (Chicago: Henry Regnery, 1954), 311.
34. Ibid., 323.
35. Russell Kirk, *The Roots of American Order*, 3rd. ed. (Washington, D.C.: Regnery Gateway, 1991), 6.
36. James Fitzjames Stephen, *Liberty, Equality, Fraternity* (Chicago: University of Chicago Press, 1991), 149.
37. Albert Taylor Bledsoe, quoted by Richard Weaver, in *The Southern Tradition at Bay* (Washington, D.C.: Regnery Gateway, 1989), 129.
38. Peter Berger and Brigitte Berger, "Our Conservatism and Theirs," *Commentary* (October 1986): 63.
39. Allan Bloom, *The Closing of the American Mind* (New York: Simon & Schuster, 1987), 28.
40. Ibid., 189.
41. See, for example, Gregory A. Fossedal, *The Democratic Imperative: Exporting the American Revolution* (New York: New Republic Books, 1989), and Joshua Muravchik, *Exporting Democracy: Fulfilling America's Destiny* (Washington, D.C.: American Enterprise Institute, 1991).
42. Paul Johnson, "Wanted: A New Imperialism," *National Review*, 14 December 1992, 30–31.
43. Editorial, "Bring Back Lord Kitchener," *Wall Street Journal*, 7 December 1992, p. A14.

Chapter 6. Nationalists: Whose Country Is It Anyway?

1. Clyde Wilson, quoted in Paul Gottfried and Thomas Fleming, *The Conservative Movement* (Boston: Twayne, 1988), 71.

2. Russell Kirk, *The Neoconservatives: An Endangered Species* (Washington, D.C.: Heritage Foundation, 1988), 3.

3. Samuel Francis, "The Education of David Duke," *Chronicles* (February 1992): 9.

4. Editorial, "Why the South Must Prevail," *National Review*, 24 August 1957, 149.

5. "The Week," *National Review,* 13 July 1957, 57.

6. M. E. Bradford, Lecture to Philadelphia Society, 1986, in *Reactionary Imperative* (Peru, Ill.: Sherwood & Sugden, 1990), 97.

7. George F. Will, "Closing the Golden Door," *Washington Post,* 29 July 1993, p. 25.

8. Samuel Francis, "The Survival Issue," *Chronicles* (February 1993): 8.

9. Patrick J. Buchanan, *Right from the Beginning* (Boston: Little, Brown, 1988), 348.

10. Quoted in *New York Times,* 15 February 1992.

11. Allan Ryskind and M. Stanton Evans, "Buchanan on the Issues," *Human Events,* 8 February 1992, 10.

12. Patrick J. Buchanan, Announcement speech, Concord, N.H., 10 December, 1991.

13. Ibid.

14. "Patron Saint of Hopeless Causes," *Economist,* 14 March 1992, 32.

15. Richard Viguerie, *The New Right: We're Ready to Lead* (Falls Church, Va.: Viguerie, 1981), 189.

16. James Watt, *The Courage of a Conservative* (New York: Simon & Schuster: 1985), 147.

17. Of course, in some very abstract sense that is true. If a worker in South China can produce ten stuffed panda bears a day and is paid $1, that does affect the global wage structure all the way up through the girls assembling computer keyboards in Singapore and French wine bottle blowers to the Boeing machinist earning $50,000 a year. But it does not follow that the machinist's wage will fall to $1 a day.

18. Alfred Eckes, "A Republican Trade Policy: Reviving the Grand Old Paradigm," in *America Asleep: The Free Trade Syndrome and the Global Economic Challenge—A Conservative Foreign Economic Policy*

for America, ed. John Creegan (Washington, D.C.: U.S. Business and Industrial Council, 1991), 71–93.

19. Paul Craig Roberts, "Trade-offs for Gulf Support?" *Washington Times,* 18 January 1991, p. F3.

20. William Hawkins, "The Anti-History of Free Trade Ideology," in *America Asleep,* 43–70.

21. Samuel Francis, "Principalities and Powers," *Chronicles* (December 1991): 11.

22. Buchanan, *Right from the Beginning,* 13.

23. William McGowan, "Race and Reporting," *City Journal* (Summer 1993): 51.

24. George Borjas, *Friends and Strangers: The Impact of Immigration on the U.S. Economy* (New York: Basic Books, 1990), 117. Borjas uses present value of projected lifetime earnings to compensate for the fact that earlier immigrants are further advanced in life than more recent arrivals. Comparisons are to the late 1970s because he used data from the 1980 census.

25. Ibid., 153.

26. Cited in Lawrence E. Harrison, *Who Prospers? How Cultural Values Shape Economic and Political Success* (New York: Basic Books, 1992), 156.

27. Patrick J. Buchanan, Speech to Los Angeles World Affairs Council, 19 May 1992.

28. Peter Brimelow, "Time to Rethink Immigration," *National Review,* 22 June 1992, 42.

29. Samuel Francis, "Principalities and Powers," *Chronicles* (December 1991): 11.

30. Ibid.

31. Patrick J. Buchanan, "Manitoba, U.S.A.?" *New York Post,* 14 April 1990, p. 13.

32. Llewellyn Rockwell, "Doing Well, Done Better," *Chronicles* (March 1993): 28.

33. Samuel Francis, "Principalities and Powers," *Chronicles* (February 1993): 9.

34. Sarah Barton, Rockwell-Rothbard Report (January 1991), p. 2.

35. Ibid.

36. Patrick J. Buchanan, *Conservative Votes, Liberal Victories* (New York: Times Books, 1975), 53.

37. Llewellyn Rockwell, "Lamentations of a Recovering Marxist," *Chronicles* (August 1991): 28.

38. Thomas Fleming, "The New Fusionism," *Chronicles* (May 1991): 10–12.
39. Murray Rothbard, Speech to John Randolph Society, 18 January 1992.
40. Buchanan, *Right From the Beginning,* 342.
41. Thomas Fleming, "The Real American Dilemma," *Chronicles* (March 1989): 11.
42. Patrick J. Buchanan, "'Dialogue' is not for Hoodlums," *New York Post,* 11 May 1991, p. 13.
43. Samuel Francis, "Mayday," *Chronicles* (September 1992): 9.
44. Patrick J. Buchanan, "D.C.: A Liberal Wasteland," *New York Post,* 24 January 1990, p. 17.
45. Buchanan, "'Dialogue' is not for Hoodlums."
46. Patrick J. Buchanan, "Here Comes Iranscam—Again!," *New York Post,* 17 July 1991, p. 21.
47. Gregory A. Fossedal, *The Democratic Imperative* (New York: New Republic Books, 1989), 238–39.
48. America First Committee, *Did You Know?* (newsletter), July 1991.
49. Wayne Cole, *America First: The Battle Against Intervention, 1940–41* (Madison: University of Wisconsin Press, 1953), 30.
50. Patrick J. Buchanan, "Heroic Allies Show Their Stripes," *New York Post,* 9 November 1991, p. 15.
51. Samuel Francis, "The Buchanan Revolution, Part 1," *Chronicles* (July 1992): 12.

Chapter 7. The Pseudo-Menace of the Religious Right

1. Bobbie Kilberg, Letter to the Editor, *Washington Post,* 11 July 1993, p. C8.
2. William Safire, "Bush's Gamble," *New York Times Magazine,* 18 October 1993, p. 62.
3. The comparison belongs to Jeff Jacoby, the chief editorial writer for the *Boston Herald.*
4. John Stuart Mill, *On Liberty* (New York: Norton, 1975), 6.
5. Is the same thing true of abortion? That depends on whether you begin by believing that the fetus is a person: if the fetus is a person, then in any society short of utter lawlessness, the government must still punish those who kill it; only if you assume that the fetus isn't human can abortion be thought of as potentially pitting the individ-

ual mother against the state. In other words, this is yet another of those arguments about abortion where the conclusion you come to is identical to the assumption you begin with.

6. Michael Lind, "The Exorcism," *New Republic,* 14 December 1992, 20.

7. Irving Kristol, remarks recorded in *Conversations About Culture,* unpublished transcript of the W. H. Brady Conference on Cultural Politics, Chicago, January 1991, pp. 85–86.

Chapter 8. 1996

1. F. S. Oliver, *The Endless Adventure,* vol. I (London: Macmillan, 1931), 19.

2. Peter Brown, *Minority Party* (Washington, D.C.: Regnery Gateway, 1991).

3. Gov. Pete Wilson, press release, 9 August 1993.

4. Michigan calculates its educational spending differently from most other states, dividing the amount spent by the number of students in class on the first Friday of the school year, rather than dividing by the average number of students in attendance throughout the year. For that reason, the dollar figures used in the state's own documents are somewhat lower than that quoted in the text, or about $5,200 per student in 1994.

5. John Podhoretz, *Hell of a Ride* (New York: Simon & Schuster, 1993), 152.

6. Dan Quayle, *Proceedings of the Thirty-Fifth Republican Convention,* 586.

7. Richard Cheney, Speech to the American Enterprise Institute, 8 December 1993.

8. Ibid.

9. Michael Barone and Grant Ujifusa, *The Almanac of American Politics, 1994* (Washington, D.C.: National Journal, 1993), 1207.

10. Mario Cuomo, *Proceedings of the 1992 Democratic National Convention,* 243.

11. Tom Wolfe, "The Me Decade," in *Purple Decades* (New York: Farrar, Straus, 1982), 292–93.

12. H. L. Mencken, *Prejudices, Third Series* (New York: Knopf, 1977), 218–19.

Index